INTERTEXTUALITY
AND
THE READING
OF MIDRASH

Indiana Studies in Biblical Literature

Herbert Marks and Robert Polzin,
general editors

INTERTEXTUALITY
AND
THE READING
OF MIDRASH

DANIEL
BOYARIN

INDIANA UNIVERSITY PRESS
BLOOMINGTON & INDIANAPOLIS

Manufactured in the United States of America

The paper used in this publication meets the minimum requirements of American
National Standard for Information Sciences—Permanence of Paper for Printed
Library Materials, ANSI Z39.48-1984.

Library of Congress Cataloging-in-Publication Data

Boyarin, Daniel.
Intertextuality and the reading of Midrash / by Daniel Boyarin.
p. cm.—(Indiana studies in biblical literature)
Bibliography: p.
Includes index.
ISBN 0-253-31251-5 (alk. paper) 1. Mekhilta of Rabbi Ishmael—Criticism,
interpretation, etc. 2. Bible. O.T. Exodus XIII-XVIII—Hermeneutics. I. Title.
II. Series.
BM517.M43B69 1990   89-45409
296.1'4—dc20   CIP

1 2 3 4 5 94 93 92 91 90

CONTENTS

This book is dedicated in loving memory to my
sister-in-law, Varda, taken before her time.

ACKNOWLEDGMENTS

There are several people whom I would like to thank for the help that they have rendered me in generating the ideas expressed here. First of all, my colleagues at Yale University in 1984-85, with whom I spent hundreds of hours in good talk: Ken Frieden, Jill Robbins, and Shira Wolosky. Next, my teacher during that year, Geoffrey Hartman, who steered me away from paths too easy. Then, my colleagues in midrashic research, Devora Dimant, Menahem Kahana, James Kugel, Chaim Milikovsky, and David Stern, all of whom have read parts of the manuscript and rendered valuable criticism. Wolfgang Iser, Dimitry Segal, and Ellen Spolsky carefully read several chapters of the work and made serious, trenchant and useful comments. Herbert Marks's work as editor was of extraordinary value. I am especially indebted to Meir Sternberg who read two entire drafts of the manuscript and devoted himself to my work as a good teacher to a student, even though I have never been formally his student. I have tried to take all warnings into consideration when I have been able to understand them and when the gain seemed greater than the loss. More and more, from my own experience I am convinced that literary production is a social practice and not an individual creative act. My brother Jonathan Boyarin has been very helpful over the years of thinking, writing, and talking that went into this book, and also has read a near final draft and made many useful comments. Ken Frieden also read the final draft and benefited me with many excellent editorial interventions. Only I am responsible for the results.

The research for this monograph was made possible in part by various grants. I would like to thank Yale University for awarding me the Horace Goldsmith Fellowship in 1984-85, the American Philosophical Society for a research grant in the same, the American Council of Learned Societies for a grant enjoyed in the Summer of 1985, and the Littauer Foundation for a grant in the fall of that year, during which period (collectively) the major research for the book was completed.

Several parts of this book have been published in earlier versions in journals or volumes, which I list here: *Prooftexts; Poetics Today; Revue Biblique; Bucknell Review; The Book and the Text*, ed. Regina Schwartz; *Representations*. I thank the editors of all of these for permission to reprint.

INTRODUCTION

One would perhaps expect that a book of this sort would begin with a definition of the subject matter of its discourse—in this case, midrash. That would be
impossible here, since the definition of midrash is precisely the issue at hand. In
a recent article, "Defining Midrash," Gary Porton has listed the different approaches to this topic, ranging from that of W. Wright, who considers it to be a
literary genre, to that of R. Le Déaut, who defines it as an "attitude."[1] Porton's
article does not offer a more satisfactory answer to the question of the definition of midrash than any of the other contradictory approaches. As James
Kugel has remarked, "since these studies have already not defined midrash in
ample detail, there is little purpose in our not defining it again here."[2]

The object of inquiry can, nevertheless, be delimited without any definition.
For the purposes of this book, "midrash" is the type of biblical interpretation
which is found in the Jewish biblical commentaries which the Jews call "midrash." The interpretations found in these several works are manifold in nature,
but all of them are more or less different from the commentary of the European traditions in that they do not seem to involve the privileged pairing of a
signifier with a specific set of signifieds. It is perhaps this characteristic that has
rendered midrash so fascinating to some recent literary critics. However, beyond that common feature, there is much that divides the several texts known
as midrashim from each other. After careful delineation of the dissimilarities
and similarities between the types of interpretation found in the several midrashim and other ways of commenting on texts, we can begin to ask more
perspicaciously how to define midrash, and whether or not it can be found in
other types of texts than those designated by the term "midrash."

The task of this book is to examine a particular portion of a particular
midrash in some detail. The claims made about the nature of midrash in this
book are to be understood as shorthand for claims made about the type of
midrash found in this particular text and perhaps others of its particular time
and place. The name of this midrash is the Mekilta. It is the earliest midrash on
Exodus, having been largely compiled of materials which belong to the Tannaitic period, the time of the rabbis who produced the Mishna, from about the
first to the third Christian centuries.[3] The section of this text that I examine
here deals with the adventures of the children of Israel from the Exodus until
Sinai, interpreting Exodus 13-18. I intend to articulate a theory of this text
which will explain its hermeneutic moves as hermeneutic—i.e., without reduc-

ing them to some other species of discourse. I have read this text with the fore-
understanding that midrashic discourse is interpretation and then asked,
"What in the Bible's text might have motivated this gloss on this verse? Can I
explain this text in such a way that this gloss makes sense as an interpretation
of the verse?" The key to this inquiry is literary theory and its questions: What
does it mean to interpret a text? Is there stable meaning in texts? If so, how is
it discovered and disclosed? If not, then what is there? The fact that such
questions are asked in the literary discipline opens up the possibility that other
types of interpretation, types with which we are not familiar, may have something to teach us about how we read and interpret. Critics convinced that we
know exactly what is meant by texts and that there are sound methods for
getting at their meaning will have no use for a sympathetic study of midrash as
an interpretive model. At most they will allow its fine ethical and spiritual
content, aside from or notwithstanding its alleged inauthenticity as a reading
practice.[4]

Since one of the underlying premises of this book is that all interpretive
discourse is positioned—situated in a historical and ideological position—I
would like to begin by situating my own work. I am a twentieth-century West-
ern-educated Jewish intellectual. That means that I am positioned between two
cultures. On the one hand, I believe in[5] and am comfortable with the discourse
of Orthodox Judaism. I study the Talmud and midrash as a part of my religious
life and find that these texts make eminent sense within the context of Jewish
faith. They embody and communicate values that are largely my values. At the
same time, however, another part of me finds these discourses puzzling—
midrash more so than Talmud. That part could be defined as the Platonic,
Aristotelian, or perhaps logocentric pole of my own inner dialogue. Questions
arise for me in the reading of midrash which I am impelled to answer.[6] How is
it possible that the Hebrew Bible can be represented as having so many meanings? Why do the meanings which are represented often seem so distant from
what appears to be the "simple" or "literal"[7] meaning of the text? These
questions are not simply posed rhetorically: in the first place, the effort of
understanding in which I am engaged here is directed at myself. I wish to have
a way of reading midrash which will make sense for me as a member of a
Western culture. In the terms of the late Hans Frei, I am ethnographer and
native at once:

> "Meaning" in a cultural-linguistic and intratextual interpretive frame is the
> skill that allows ethnographer and native to meet in mutual respect; if they
> happen to be the same person, it is the bridge over which (s)he may pass
> from one shore to the other and undertake the return journey; if they are
> natives from different tribes, it is the common ground that is established as
> they learn each other's languages, rather than a known precondition for
> doing so.[8]

For me, the bridge has been literary theory. Literary theory today is not focused on beauty but on meaning. In a sense, literary theory is the discourse where fundamental issues, once part of theology and other branches of philosophy, are being thought through: language, the Subject, the very definition and understanding of humanity. Accordingly, literary theory takes a place for me analogous perhaps to the place that Scholastic philosophy had for an interpreter of Bible and midrash in the Middle Ages. Contemporary theory opens up possibilities for reunderstanding midrash. Roughly—very roughly—speaking, the theoretical context in which this essay is undertaken is the philosophical project of Jacques Derrida.[9] Among other contributions, Derrida has demonstrated that the conception of univocity and transparency of meaning is none other than a philosophical possibility—indeed, a quite problematic possibility, not a logical necessity. I would say that this questioning of the Platonic-Aristotelian (ultimately Enlightenment) understanding of language makes possible a space for a more sympathetic reading of midrash as an interpretive act, because it puts into question all interpretive acts. Once we no longer assume that there is a single correct interpretation of the text, however difficult to achieve and prove it, then we can begin to answer the questions posed in the previous paragraph. Yet this is not a deconstructive work. The terms of reference are rather semiotic and structural. I do not speak here of "traces" and "différance," but of "signifiers" which imply (even in denial) "signifieds". The reader will realize, I hope, that the opposition between signifiers and signifieds *is* being interrogated at every point in this essay, even as the terms are being invoked. What I am attempting here involves not doing away with the sign but shifting our understanding of its structure in the light of Derrida's writing, such that a less ethnocentric semiology may be generated.

One more word on theory: My reading is not guided by any specific theory of language or interpretation. It is informed by a general climate of inquiry surrounding these. As Wolfgang Iser has remarked, "interpretation today is beginning to discover its own history—not only the limitations of its respective norms but also those factors that could not come to light as long as traditional norms held sway."[10] My use of terminology and concepts may appear eclectic to some readers. This grows out of the very nature of my project. My question is not posed as: given that we know what reading is, why does midrash deviate from it, but rather, seeing how midrash reads, what theoretical concepts are useful for understanding it? That is to say, without ascribing any theory to the rabbis, I am nevertheless attempting to determine what sort of theory would allow them to make the interpretive moves that they make in good faith. Accordingly, in my reading in literary theory, when I have found a concept that seems to help in understanding a structure of midrashic reading, I have adapted it to my descriptive system. This does not mean that I have here just a grab bag or smorgasbord, for two reasons. First of all, those concepts and terms that I use are those which make sense to me at some epistemological level aside from their aid in understanding midrash. Second, while the terms and concepts are eclectic in origin, I have molded them into a more or less self-consistent system of my own. Thus, I combine Wolfgang Iser's descriptions of gaps with Michael Riffaterre's "ungrammaticalities."[11] My disagreement with Riffaterre on certain fundamental points has not prevented me from learning much from his work and adopting it in several ways.

This essay has another meaning for me intimately related to the first. The valorization of midrash as interpretation and indeed as a model for interpretation means as well the revoicing of a Jewish discourse in the discourse of the West. The liberal term "Judaeo-Christian" masks a suppression of that which is distinctly Jewish. It means "Christian," and by not even acknowledging that much, renders the suppression of Jewish discourse even more complete.[12] It is as if the classical Christian ideology—according to which Judaism went out of existence with the coming of the Christ, and the Jews are doomed to anachronism by their refusal to accept the truth—were recast in secular, anthropological terminology. In recent theoretical writing about literature, which searches for a richer, more nuanced understanding of reading, the unique Jewish discourse called midrash has been distinguished and has even entered the theoretical canon. For someone who has devoted his life to the study of midrash (and Talmud), this is profoundly encouraging, since it means to me that I have something to say that people other than committed Jewish scholars (or scholars of Judaism) may want to hear, that my work has meaning and importance beyond a coterie of specialists.

A sympathetic reader of my manuscript remarked that it reads like a celebration of midrash, and I suppose that this is so. He asked that I attend to what is lost in midrash as well, but I do not seem yet to have the capability of doing so. My hope is that my readings of midrash are neither tendentious nor apologetic, however much they are grounded in a committed position. While I began my project with a determination to understand and read midrash in as rich and non-reductive way as I was able, I was not committed to one kind of result. I am undoubtedly blind to and suppressing much that is in these texts and much that is presupposed in my reading of them. I hope that nevertheless I have seen something in them that enriches their reception into the canon of interpretation and literary creation.

The effort of communication always involves some loss. Any comparison to other literatures is a reduction of mystery and strangeness, and therefore I would like to clearly state that midrash *is* somehow radically different. Any revelation is also a concealment. Any understanding is also loss of understanding. But making no attempt to bridge the gap seems worse. Frank Kermode has expressed this best:

For whether one thinks that one's purpose is to re-cognize the original meaning, or to fall headlong into a text that is a treacherous network rather than a
continuous and systematic sequence, one may be sure of one thing, and that
is disappointment. It has sometimes been thought, and in my opinion rightly,
that the world is also like that; or that we are like that in respect of the world.
Yet we have ways of working through the world, and ways of explaining
unfollowable texts. There are certain conditions which make the task more
comfortable: more or less acquiescent in the authority of institutions, more
or less happy that we have an acquired taste for fulfillments, for a state of
affairs in which everything hangs together, we accept a measure of private
intermittency in our interpretations—unless we are unhappy because such
acquiescence is an acceptance of untruth, and prefer antinomianism and the
unhappiness of an even more complete isolation. In any case, a sense of
mystery is a different thing from an ability to interpret it, and the largest
consolation is that without interpretation there would be no mystery. What
must not be looked for is some obvious public success. To see, even to perceive, to hear, even to understand, is not the same thing as to explain or even
the same thing as to have access. The desires of interpreters are good because without them the world and the text are tacitly declared to be impossible; perhaps they are, but we must live as if the case were otherwise.[13]

There are no words with which I could paraphrase or express more clearly or
more simply the beauty and truth of Kermode's credo as an interpreter.

   Midrash has been largely suppressed in Jewish hermeneutics, as much as it
has been marginalized in the West. The allegorical-Aristotelian tradition of
Judaism, best represented by Maimonides, has been hostile to the view of
language that midrash presupposes, and this tradition has gained hegemony in
the dominant Jewish culture. For this reason, I find unconvincing such attempts
as that of Susan Handelman[14] or José Faur[15] to speak of a uniquely Jewish way
of understanding language or texts. Jewish thought and interpretive practice
for over a thousand years has been thoroughly caught up in the logocentric
tradition, and midrash has been devalued within Judaism as much as without.
Moreover, while in some ways similar, the Kabbalistic understanding of language must be understood as significantly different from midrash and must not
be conflated with it. Reification of "Jewish" modes of thinking actually masks
the "primitive" (as opposed to "civilized") critical force of the midrashic mode.
In future studies, it will be important to deal with the ways that midrash has
been occulted in the Jewish-Christian-Moslem polysystem, and to discern the
underground channels within this system in which it was kept alive as well.

NOTE ON THE TRANSLATIONS

The language of the Mekilta, as of the midrashic and talmudic literature in general, is in the original very vivid and quite elliptical. This is perhaps owing to its status as a more or less stylized written text of oral dialogues, as they were carried on in the rabbinic academies. I have tried to retain this style in my translations, which will undoubtedly make them more difficult to follow than a smoother English rendering would have done. I hope that my commentaries on the texts will make it possible for the reader to find his/her way among them. After all, even experienced Hebrew readers need commentaries for these texts, so a translation which makes the meaning too clear is really a disguised commentary. Jacob Z. Lauterbach's translation is readily available for anyone who feels the need to have a more accessible English version, and I have included references to that version for all texts cited.

· 1 ·

TOWARD A NEW THEORY
OF MIDRASH

Reading Heinemann's *Darkhe ha'aggadah*

Isaak Heinemann's *Darkhe ha'aggadah*[1] is a powerful reading of midrash aggada predicated on a sophisticated theory of literature and history.[2] As has been often remarked in the critical literature, it is really the only serious full-scale attempt to describe midrash theoretically. It therefore constitutes the ground for any figuration of midrash to follow. Heinemann begins with a discussion of Maimonides' (Rambam's)[3] theory of aggadic midrash. It would be no exaggeration to say that Maimonides occupies a place in a specific Jewish literary history and theory analogous to that of Aristotle in the discourse of European literature. The Rambam's reflections on the nature of the Bible and the midrash are the *Poetics* of Judaism. Heinemann, accordingly, begins his work by citing the *Guide of the Perplexed*, "for the words of the Rambam must be seen as the founding type for all the discussion of [the question of the midrash aggada]" [p. 2]. He cites a passage in which Maimonides attempts to establish the genre of midrash, identifying

> the manner of *Midrashim* whose method is well known by all those who understand their discourses. For these [namely, the Midrashim] have, in their opinion, the status of poetical conceits; they are not meant to bring out the meaning of the text in question. Accordingly, with regard to the Midrashim, people are divided into two classes: A class that imagines that the [Sages] have said these things in order to explain the meaning of the text in question, and a class that holds [the Midrashim] in slight esteem and holds them up to ridicule, since it is clear and manifest that this is not the meaning of the [biblical] text in question. The first class strives and fights with a view to proving, as they deem, the correctness of the Midrashim and to defending them, and think this is the true meaning of the [biblical] text and that the Midrashim have the same status as the traditional legal decisions. But neither of the two groups understands that [the Midrashim] have the character of poetical conceits whose meaning is not obscure for someone endowed with understanding. At that time this method was generally known and used by everybody, just as the poets use poetical expressions.[4]

1

In a sequel to the quoted text, Maimonides refers to a particular midrash as "a most witty poetical conceit by means of which he instills a noble moral quality." The Rambam claims here that in order to understand the aggada, we must first have an appropriate conception of its genre. And indeed, the initial question that must be asked in order to say anything about midrash is the question of genre. What type of discourse is it that we are encountering? Is midrash hermeneutic, homiletic; or perhaps fiction? After rejecting views that propose that aggada is commentary—either bad or good—Maimonides argues that it is poetry—i.e., didactic fiction.

Heinemann's reading of this text in the Rambam is remarkable. It forms, in fact, almost an allegory in which each of the three terms of Maimonides' taxonomy of readers of the midrash are projected onto three strains in the interpretation of aggada in the *Wissenschaft Des Judentums*. Thus, Rambam's first category is described as those "who depend on the fact that the *drashot* which turn from the plain sense are not entirely without scientific value" [p. 2]. This class of readers of the aggada is then identified by Heinemann with such interpreters as Umberto Cassuto and Benno Jacob, just to take the most well known of them today, who support the midrashic understanding either from context and literary analysis or by showing that it is a survival of ancient Near Eastern literature and therefore a true representation of the intertext of the Bible. (This last, is, of course, my formulation.) In addition, Heinemann includes in this group all those who read the midrash as a response to genuine exegetic difficulty in the Torah's text. The second category of the Rambam, that is, those who "find that the [aggada] cannot be reconciled with the words quoted, and therefore reject and ridicule it," is represented in Heinemann's *pesher* by none other than the young Abraham Geiger, who wrote that the rabbis manifested a *"höchst getrübter exegetischer Sinn."*[5] The third category of the Rambam, that is, the Rambam himself, is filled in the *Wissenschaft* by Nahman Krochmal (Ranak), who indeed does seem to have made that identification himself, as the title of his masterwork, *A Guide to the Perplexed of Our Time*, indicated quite poignantly.

Against each of these three types of readers, Heinemann presents what he clearly takes to be fatal objections. Thus against the Orthodox school[6] he argues that they fail to see the woods for the trees. Although on occasion we may be able to use their interpretation of the aggada as a response to exegetical difficulty in the biblical text or as an echo of ancient knowledge, there are many cases where we surely cannot. Moreover, Heinemann argues, the rabbis themselves made a distinction between *peshat* [plain sense] and *drash*, so we cannot claim that also in the *drash* they intended simply to provide the "true, scientific" interpretation of the text.[7] Against the Reform school he only needs cite Yehuda Halevi's attack on Karaism, claiming that the same rabbis who were perfectly capable of interpreting the Mishna correctly ought to have been able to do so with regard to the Bible as well, and therefore, if they did not, it must be because they chose not to and not because they could not. Against the Conservative view of Ranak (who is, however, forgotten here), he argues that

> if the view which Maimonides rejected brought the aggada too close to the plain meaning, his answer [Maimonides'] does not take sufficiently into consideration the difference between the midrash and stories which are purely fictions. It is certainly correct that the *drash* gives greater freedom of movement to the personal character of the interpreter than does the plain sense, and the aggadic drash is "freer" than the halakic, which even Maimonides took seriously . . . but not infrequently the darshanim cited logical proofs for their midrash and also rejected the interpretations of their colleagues; also the most serious controversies between the sages of Israel and the sectarians and Christians were carried on with the methods of midrash . . . [p. 3]

Heinemann's argument means that midrash is encoded as biblical interpretation and not mainly as poetry or homiletic—on its textual surface.[8] To take it as something else is analogous to the error of taking ancient historiography as fiction, merely because the "facts" described do not jibe with our reading of documents.[9] Heinemann has accomplished through his rhetoric a "demonstration" that none of the previous theoretical understandings of midrash aggada is adequate to the subject.

It must be said that Heinemann's interpretation of the Rambam here is open to question. The claims that Maimonides is making in the passage may be much more limited in scope than Heinemann implies and perhaps best understood in the light of several other passages in the *Guide of the Perplexed*. It is beyond the scope of the present study to attempt a fuller reading of the Rambam;[10] however, the view of the aggada as a kind of praiseworthy sophistry or homiletic fiction has been common among many up until the present day, whether or not it is a correct representation of the Rambam's position. For example we can cite the following statement of Joseph Heinemann (no relation to Isaak), an influential recent student of midrash:

> Much of aggadic exegesis is, therefore, a kind of parable or allegory.
> *The aggadists do not mean so much to clarify difficult passages in the biblical text as to take a stand on the burning questions of the day, to guide the people and strengthen their faith.* But since they addressed themselves to a wide audience—including simple folk and children—they could not readily formulate the problems in an abstract way, nor could they give involved theoretical answers. In order to present their ideas in a more comprehensible and engaging fashion, the sages cast them in a narrative format and employed parables and other familiar literary means which appeal to all.[11]

This view of aggada is also the one presupposed in many studies of rabbinic thought which treat the statements of the midrash as theological or otherwise ideological utterances while tacitly denying their hermeneutical function.[12]

If we look at some of the actual interpretive work done by *this* Heinemann

on the Mekilta, we will see how the a priori adoption of an extrinsic understanding of the midrashic process deflects one from reading the' next. Heinemann actually begins his discussion by arguing *against* the facile historical
reduction of the midrash by an earlier scholar:

> The interpretation of the *aggada*, and especially the unveiling of its meaning for
> current events on the background of the circumstances of the time in which it
> was created, is a complex problem, which has no facile answer. This is because
> we cannot avoid a great deal of guesswork, when we search for the expression
> of opinions and the taking of stands vis-à-vis the problems of their own time in
> the homilies of the rabbis on verses and in their stories which expand the
> biblical text. Although there is no one who disagrees that the masters of
> aggada had *tendenzen* [i.e., conscious polemical designs] and contemporary
> intentions in many of their utterances, however, since these *tendenzen* were not
> expressed explicitly but wore the costume of biblical stories and are only
> hinted at between the lines, one cannot know with certainty whether they exist
> in a given aggada or not. And if you wish to claim that the strangeness of the
> aggada—its distance from what is said in the Scripture itself and its attempts to
> describe the events of the Bible and its characters with unexpected and appar-
> ently arbitrary descriptions, which have no basis in Scripture—this is what
> testifies generally that there is something else behind it, we are still very far
> from identifying those hidden intentions.[13]

When it comes to the actual interpretation of text, however, Heinemann
departs from the salutary caution with which he has begun his chapter. When
he reads a particular controversy in the Mekilta, one having to do with the
willingness or unwillingness of the Jews to take the plunge and jump in to the
Red Sea, he identifies one of the midrashic interpretations as generated by the
difficulties of the text, and the other as ideologically motivated.[14] When we look
at this midrashic text, we see that both of the interpreters are using precisely
the same hermeneutic techniques, whether those techniques make sense to us
or not. The important point is that Heinemann himself realized and showed
these same hermeneutic techniques in both interpretations! Why is it, then,
that one view is identified as being a response to "the burning issues of the
day," while the other is dealing with "the difficulties of the text"?

I think we would not be going too far to suggest an unacknowledged ideological background to Heinemann's own interpretive move on this midrash. Without attributing any scholarly bad faith to Heinemann, I can suggest what might
have led to his blindness to the symmetry of the two rabbinic readings and the
assymetry of his interpretation of them. Heinemann identifies the ideologically
determined reading of the text as being one that supports military activism on
the part of the Jews against their enemies, while the ideologically free reading
of the verse does not lead to such a position. The exegetic reading is moreover
identified by Heinemann with a more ancient tradition, that of the Targum
(the Aramaic translation of the Bible).[15] The later midrashic interpretation,

therefore, represents an ideologically occasioned departure from this ancient ideology-free reading. Since the author of this view, R. Tarfon, lived at the time of the great rebellion against Rome, and his interpretation praises, in effect, those who are willing to act and die for the faith, his reading must have been occasioned by that political background and stance. The paradoxical point is that this would, in fact, privilege his reading for Heinemann, because the views of the rabbis are, in traditional Judaism, more normative than early resolutions of biblical obscurities would be. I can hardly escape the thought that the atmosphere of support for Jewish political activism in the early years of the existence of the State of Israel might have led Heinemann (unconsciously) to want to identify what he read as support for such activism in rabbinic thought.

I think Heinemann really shows his hand on this issue when, in another discussion of a passage of the Mekilta, he again argues that it must represent a reading based on the difficulties of the biblical text, and not a response to current events, because "it is impossible to understand that the intention of the sages of the generation who were responsible for the creation of an aggada—at that particular time and situation—could have been an absolute attack on the Bar Kochba rebellion as an act of pride and rebellion against the will of God, an act which was justly punished by the death of all who took part in it. Whatever the attitude of that generation to Bar Kochba was, it seems that it was not an approach of absolute and righteous disapproval" [p. 140]. Why not? Perhaps because that would have had implications for the political-military activism of the Jews in our own time. Would the Hassidic opponents of the establishment of the state of Israel before the coming of the Messiah read the midrash the way that Heinemann does? Thus, owing to his theory of midrash as being unconcerned with the meaning of the biblical text, but only a vehicle for the communication of rabbinic ideology, even as sensitive an interpreter of midrash as Joseph Heinemann ends up trapped in his own ideology and cannot read the midrash.

Again, the point of this is not to attack Joseph Heinemann for dishonesty or blindness to the way his ideology may have affected his reading, but only to suggest that such blindness is a component of *all* reading and cannot be used as a taxonomic parameter for describing midrash. I wish to discredit the opposition between reading which is value-free and concerned with the difficulties of the biblical text and that which is unconcerned with those difficulties and speaks to the needs of the moment. It is clear, then, that I am not denying the reality of ideological concerns on the part of the rabbis nor that these ideological concerns may have often had an effect on the interpretive choices they made. I am asserting that we will not read midrash well and richly unless we understand it first and foremost as *reading*, as hermeneutic, as generated by the interaction of rabbinic readers with a heterogeneous and difficult text, which was for them both normative and divine in origin. Viewing the aggada through the eyes of a simplistic understanding of Maimonides results in a fatal reduction of its importance in Jewish culture, rendering it a mere decorative clothing for rabbinic thought.

Isaak Heinemann, at any rate, considered that what Maimonides was talking about was "poetic license," which he claims quite misses the point of the seriousness with which the aggada was presented as biblical interpretation. He suggests, therefore, a fourth way. We could perhaps capture it by defining it as a combination of the first and third of the Rambam's classes, that is, a poetry which nevertheless does intend to be an interpretation of the text. Citing favorably Yehiel Michel Sachs's attack on philology which "for all that it understands the demands of methodology, that much less does it understand meanings," Heinemann argues that, "aggada is not a systematic creation; so far, the approach of the Rambam is justified. However, in spite of this—perhaps, because of this—we must see it as a serious and successful effort to discover the depths of Scripture and to clearly determine the truth which is hidden from the eyes of the rationalists" [p. 41]. In order to accomplish this rapprochement, he must find a model of interpretation which does not restrict itself to the "objective," to the "plain sense of things." In order to find such a model, he turns to a strain in the literary and historiographical theory of his day (actually, as we will see, the historiographical theory of the day before his day). He argues that the most current theories of history propose a vital *subjective* character for historiography. Referring to Von Ranke's demand that the historian write things "as they actually were," Heinemann says:

> But contemporary historians do not agree to this demand. Some of them, for instance Mommsen, saw research "free of any assumptions" as an ideal goal, which no scholar ever achieved or could achieve. Some of them have even denied the ideal value of this requirement and limited its power to chronicle writing which recites individual facts . . . , whereas historiography emphasizes "the unity of events and their spiritual connection," something which is only possible with respect to the *Weltanschauung* of the author on individual and social life. Therefore, they did not compare the historian to the photographer who only creates the conditions for the objective action of light, but to the painter, the artist, whose vision and wisdom of life are recognizable from his pictures. . . .
>
> The requirement for subjective activity of the historian has been fulfilled in recent times precisely in the area which interests us: the description of heroes of the spirit. The school of Stefan George has replaced detailed studies with intuition, that is, penetration into the "typical struggle" of the described subject, which requires an inner closeness between him and the describing subject; in this fashion even the scientists of this circle intended not only to achieve more accurate pictures, but also "to make peace between life," which requires satisfaction through spiritual contact with ancient heroes, "and science," which is indifferent to our longings.[16]

Heinemann proposes then that we read the midrash aggada as historiography. Furthermore, it is a historiography which modern thought has revalidated or given us the intellectual, theoretical tools to read more sympathetically. The last paragraph, however, is written in what is practically code for the reader who does not share Heinemann's cultural context. The school of Stefan George was once an extremely dominant force in German art and thinking.[17] Moreover, this school, and particularly George's most distinguished disciple, Friedrich Gundolf[18] (he is undoubtedly the subject of the phrase "even the scientists of this circle"), had indeed very definite and widely circulated ideas about historiography.[19] Gundolf's pivotal philosophical position was that history is a series of unique occurrences. Since each occurrence is entirely *sui generis*, the analogical methods of the so-called objective historian are of no value for understanding history. "It followed that the task of the historian was its *intuitive* re-creation."[20] Gundolf's theories of historiography were based on a withering attack on the scientism and objectivism characteristic of nineteenth-century positivistic historical research, symbolized most fully in the person of Von Ranke. He held that that type of scholarship is the province of weak spirits. As G. R. Urban, a recent writer on the George school, has put it:

> Modern scholarship, he believed, mistrusts the man who, to enhance his knowledge by direct experience, seeks to re-enact for himself the events of history. Uninspired by the urge to set themselves at the centre of the flow of history or to identify themselves with its leading figures, modern scholars seize upon the secondary characteristics of historical occasions, because these appear to them to be less difficult to reduce to a familiar common denominator. . . . Too much impartiality produces a stupor of the senses; it rings the death knell of imaginative understanding.[21]

If we follow the logical implications of this statement, then the task of a true historian will be precisely to enhance his knowledge by direct experience and to seek to re-enact for himself the events of history by identifying himself with its leading figures. Those epochs which see themselves as being a legitimate continuation of history will write history which is vital and which is infused with their sense of values. Again in the words of Urban: "The search for historical objectivity, Gundolf explained, is peculiar to those epochs which have lost the conviction that in them resides, in any important sense, the legitimate continuation of history, and which, therefore, possess no universal, i.e., selective, sense of values."[22]

Up to this point, the Gundolfian theory seems to us, from the perspective of the mid-twentieth century, as not particularly radical. The conviction that historical interpretation is by definition a part of historiography and that Rankean objectivity is a "myth" has become part and parcel of contemporary historiographical theory,[23] and its attractiveness for Heinemann in his project to reach a sympathetic understanding of the rabbis is obvious. Not only will the masters of the aggada not seem naive on this view of historical understanding, but those who attack them for being subjective and their midrash for being value-laden are only revealing the poverty of their own spirits and the degeneration of their own historical sense. The rabbis certainly saw in themselves, in the most important sense, the legitimate continuation of history and their writings are the very embodiment of a transhistorical, absolute, and universal system of values.

However, this version of the validation of subjective historiography will not further too much our reading of midrash aggada, for even those historians who acknowledge the importance of aesthetics and values in the choosing of relevant facts by the historian and their arrangement into cause and effect sequences and complete stories, will not countenance the *creation* of facts *ex nihilo* by the historian. And it is this which the masters of the aggada seem to do all the time, when they tell us stories about conversations and actions which are not written in the Torah, the historical document, at all. But Gundolf's views on a proper task for the historian are in fact much more peculiar than what I have presented so far and provide an exact source for Heinemann's understanding of aggada. I am referring to Gundolf's notion, based on his reading of Goethe, of history itself as only being important owing to the legends that it produces, to the poetry to which it gives rise. "Goethe", Gundolf explained, "saw the justification of history in the historical fables to which it gave rise, because the truths which these fables expressed—though often lacking empirical basis—stimulated through their wealth and grandiosity, the imagination of mankind."[24] The only test, then, of the adequacy of historical writing for this school is in the importance of that writing for the life of the present. The method of the historian is to immerse himself in the documents of the past and achieve a oneness of spirit with their heroes, and out of that oneness fashion legends about those heroes which will be true because they are the product of deep spiritual connection between the great creative genius of the past and the great creative genius of the present. Whether or not the facts are right, this is true history because legends are the product of true apprehensions of the human qualities of the great figures which have given them rise. "The sole criterion of the historian's objectivity was whether or not he apprehended the study of history as a series of intense and personal experiences. In short, to write history was, in a very real sense, to make history."[25]

It should now be quite obvious why this historiosophy was so attractive to Heinemann, even though by the time of his writing it had long been replaced in Germany itself. This school not only provides a vindication for a subjective understanding of the writing of history—That much could have been gotten from Kant; it specifically promotes the value of the historical legend from a kind of primitive protohistory to the very Parnassus of the historical enterprise. As a philosophy of history, it does precisely the work that Heinemann wants it to, namely, to provide a theoretical model with which to understand aggada positively as a writing of biblical history. The apotheosis of Romanticism in the Symbolist aesthetic and philosophy of history characteristic of the George school has provided the very foundation of all of Heinemann's work on the aggada. It provides the source for his crucial terminology, "creative historiography." We have here the romantic theory of literary production as the creation of the individual genius, carried over, via George and Gundolf, into the realm of biblical interpretation.

We should recognize how deeply immersed all of Heinemann's thought is in a specifically German cultural context.[26] Even his formulation that the goal of the highest kind of history writing is " 'to make peace between life,' which requires satisfaction through spiritual contact with ancient heroes, 'and science,' which is indifferent to our longings" is an expression of the German ideology at its most typical. This opposition between "science" and "life" so characteristic of the George school is ultimately of Nietzschean origin.[27] It is certainly significant that the example which Heinemann cites for his theory is Dr. Faustus. "There may be no doubt," he avers, "that the play *Faust* is of more philosophical importance than the biography of the magician Johanan Faust who lived in the sixteenth century, his travels and his deceptions" (p. 5). The rabbis are the Goethes of Judaism, who with their gigantic creative abilities understand the "reality" of the salvation history and communicate this reality with their legends, the aggada. There is no small measure of irony, it seems to me, in the fact that Heinemann set out to create a theory of aggada in opposition to Maimonides' claim that aggada is poetry and ended defending a version of precisely that claim, relying on a school of thought for which everything— including any worthwhile historiography—was poetry. All of *Darkhe ha'aggadah* will proceed from this fundamentally German opposition between "second-rate, even trivial 'science,' "[28] and the vital, experienced, lived truth of legend. Even Heinemann's description of the didactic goals of the rabbis could not be more at home in the George school's theories of poetry, which imagines it as "emotional direction and liberation of a people through the artistic means of language,"[29] or as Heinemann puts it, "the aggada, and not only the aggada of the Jewish people, fills in the details [of the historical record] in an imaginative way, in order to find an answer to the questions of the listeners and to arrive at a depiction which will act on their feelings" [p. 21].

A significant example of Heinemann's Gundolfian approach to aggada can be found in his chapter, "The Bringing Near of the Distant," which begins with a strong restatement of his theoretical position:

> The popular legend [aggada]—and the aggada of the sages included—often identifies, as we have seen, the different heroes of the story with each other or with their descendants.[30] Even more important is its way of identifying to a certain extent the lives of the heroes with the lives of the narrators. For here is the difference between the aggada and the scientific historiography.

The latter emphasizes the *changes* which have taken place in the course of the generations and interprets the events particularly in accordance with one-time conditions. The organic thinking from which the popular aggada has sprung obliterates as much as possible the barrier between the describer and the described. In this sense it "erases all secondariness," in the words of a great expert.[31] But also the art of the civilized peoples and indeed even science have not always preserved, as will be shown below, the difference between times. [p. 35]

Heinemann's analogies are indeed to Shakespeare with his Julian clock and to Lessing with his theaters in the twelfth century. Just as these great poets did not care about the facts of history but its true meaning, which they perceived through their creative imaginations, so did the rabbis in presenting the biblical history in aggada. A classic example of this program in Heinemann's text is his statement that "the Abraham of the aggada who baked matzot for Passover, while he is different from the one that the Bible testifies to with regard to the details of the description, is essentially closer to the Abraham of the Bible than the one who was described by the Apostle, that Abraham of whom only faith was considered as righteousness, as if there were no value in works" [p. 39].

While it cannot, of course, be, established that Abraham actually baked matzot, the fact is unimportant. This is merely the accident of the one-time, the unrepeatable, and therefore the insignificant. What is important is that the rabbis, in touch with the spiritual reality of Abraham, have understood his true essence, while Paul has missed this truth in his reading.

There may be little doubt, therefore, that the reliance on the George school as a grounding for *Darkhe ha'aggadah* has given Heinemann theoretical tools for a very strong reading of aggadic texts. However, since that grounding is so strongly predicated on the ideology and philosophy of that school, it is prey to the same weaknesses and distortions to which Gundolf's work itself is prey.[32] One of the signal consequences of Heinemann's powerful infusion of the Gundolfian model and sensibility into his study of midrash aggada is that it leads to near total disregard for social and historical forces and meanings in the production of the texts. If the rabbis are lonely geniuses in communion with the biblical heroes and reproducing their "real" essences in the aggada, then the aggada is above and beyond time itself, belonging to the supernal world of spirit and losing all of the specificity of historical and social circumstance. Indeed, this is explicit in Heinemann's thought as he repeatedly privileges the universal and eternal over the one-time occurrence. Once more, the German intellectual atmosphere of Heinemann's writing cannot be emphasized too much, for over and over again, we find in the literature characterizations of poetry as that which is not social, indeed that which is opposed to the social. Indeed Gundolf himself depended for his theory on what is to me a bizarre Germanic opposition between the poet and the writer, holding that while the latter was subject to language and its social meanings and determinations, the former resided in a privileged ontological and epistemological space all alone and free of any contamination from his time and society. "Literature is part of society but poetry belongs to nature."[33] Aggada is, of course, poetry and not literature in this taxonomy. Considering how very heavily Heinemann's thought is imbued with the spirit of German romanticism and the George school, I find it, therefore, very understandable how he can have completely missed the social and historical factors in his theory of aggada. Any new theory will have to redress this imbalance, retaining what is valuable in Heinemann's thought and filling in its yawning gaps. I turn now to a programmatic outline of such a possibility for a new *Darkhe ha'aggadah*.

Toward a New Theory of Midrash

Repeating Heinemann's rhetoric, I would begin by saying that if the school which I have synecdochically represented by Joseph Heinemann places midrash aggada too firmly in its own historical circumstances and considers it a mere reflection of them, Isaak Heinemann removes aggada too extremely from any historical and social meanings. What is common to these theories is that they both assume the opposition between "objective" and "subjective," one privileging the objective and the other the subjective. The assumption of this distinction forces one view to assume that the rabbis did not intend to interpret at all and the other to suppose a romantic, near mystical understanding of historical interpretation. Thus, particularly in Isaak Heinemann, the binary opposition between science and aggada leads to acute structural tensions in his work. On the one hand he wishes to claim that the rabbinic midrash *is* interpretation of the biblical text, in direct opposition to what he takes to be the Maimonidean position. On the other hand his founding positivistic assumption that there is a true, objective, scientific meaning to the text which the rabbis depart from leads him again and again to compare aggada with fictional texts as such, which are not representations of the past at all, but "mouthpieces for the views of their authors" [p. 42]. In short, by not deconstructing the opposition between objective and subjective in his theory, Isaak Heinemann is led back to the very position of the Rambam which he had set out to replace. Indeed, the very argument which Heinemann mounted against the Cassuto and Jacob approach, namely, that the rabbis distinguished between *peshat* and *drash* in their text, proves to be a Trojan horse, for it tends more strongly to support the Rambam's contention that they did not intend their midrash to be interpretation than to argue against the former view.[34] Thus Isaak Heinemann argues that "the depictions of the sages are not 'interpretations' in the scientific sense, but even in the places where they supported their opinions with Scripture, in truth they were following the ways of artistic creation" [p. 23]. I, for one, am hard-pressed to find any distinction whatever between this claim and the theory of the Rambam's. It is clear from here how Heinemann's acceptance of the fundamental concept "scientific, objective truth," for all that he valued the intuitive, subjective "reality," nevertheless forced him into unthematized contradictions in his text.

In place of these approaches, I will follow much current thought in proposing that all interpretation and historiography is *representation* of the past by the present, that is, that there is no such thing as value-free, true and objective rendering of documents. They are always filtered through the cultural, socio-ideological matrix of their readers. Continuing Isaak Heinemann's own metaphor which projects a dichotomy between the painter who subjectively represents the inner truth of reality and the photographer who objectively records only what is "really" there, I would suggest that today we hold that the photographer, no less than the painter, produces a representation in which the very image is generated by what the culture encourages and constrains her to see. This understanding is an outgrowth of several currents in contemporary theory. On the one hand Mikhail Bakhtin has revealed for us the social, interactional, dialogical nature of all language use (including the romantic lyric and the scientific description—the painting and the photograph). On the other hand, theoreticians of history such as Hayden White have been exploring the ways in which all historiography is constructed by a culture.[35] Finally, in a more specifically literary context, Frank Kermode has explored how culturally and ideologically determined are all notions of "the plain sense of things."[36] These theoreticians and others of their ilk will occupy in my description of midrash the place that Stefan George and Friedrich Gundolf occupied in *Darkhe ha'aggadah.*

The sovereign notion informing the present reading of midrash is "intertextuality." This concept has several different accepted senses, three of which are important in my account of midrash. The first is that the text is always made up of a mosaic of conscious and unconscious citation of earlier discourse. The second is that texts may be dialogical in nature—contesting their own assertions as an essential part of the structure of their discourse—and that the Bible is a preeminent example of such a text. The third is that there are cultural codes, again either conscious or unconscious, which both constrain and allow the production (not creation) of new texts within the culture; these codes may be identified with the ideology of the culture, which is made up of the assumptions that people in the culture automatically make about what may or may not be true and possible, about what is natural in nature and in history.

In the first place, the analysis of literary systems shows the power of Mikhail Bakhtin's insight that the romantic view of literary creation as *creatio ex nihilo* (such as Heinemann's) cannot be sustained. Every author/speaker/human is constituted by all of the discourses which he/she has heard or read. There is, therefore, no such thing as the self-identical subject of the subject-object dichotomy, and this very distinction is revealed as a term in a specific ideological code. While recent writers on rabbinic literature have already discussed it in terms of intertextuality, I believe that a misreading of this concept often shows up in their texts, for they speak of "intertextuality" as if it were a characteristic of some texts as opposed to others.[37] Symptomatic of this misunderstanding is the vigorous attack which James Kugel's essay, "Two Introductions to Midrash,"[38] has provoked from Jacob Neusner.[39] While Kugel's text has much that is new and interesting in it about the historical origins of midrash and its connections with apocalypse, pseudepigrapha, and Philo, the aspects that Neusner attacks are more a perspicacious and elegant rendition of generally held views on midrash than they are new departures. This fact makes Neusner's text, however, all the more interesting and revealing, because of its seemingly misplaced virulence against a rather unexceptionable piece. What is interesting, then, is to try to understand what it is in Kugel's article that so stimulates Neusner's ire.

I will begin, therefore, by dealing with an egregious misunderstanding of Kugel in Neusner's text. I do not do so to point out an error on the part of Neusner, but rather because I think that this error is symptomatic, and ramified in other of Neusner's recent texts. Neusner is commenting on a passage of Kugel's which reads: "midrash is exegesis of biblical verses, not of books. The basic unit of the Bible for the midrashist is the verse: this is what he seeks to expound, and it might be said that there simply is no boundary encountered beyond that of the verse until one comes to the borders of the canon itself."[40]

I think it will be quite clear to anyone reading this passage with even a modicum of distance that "canon" here intends the *biblical* canon and all that Kugel is doing is unpacking the virtual commonplace that "midrash is exegesis of biblical verses, not books." However, in Neusner's gloss Kugel is made to say that "there is no boundary between midrash-exegesis of a single verse *and the entirety of the canon of Judaism.*"[41] The question which interests me is what led Neusner's to such a gross misreading of Kugel. I think that it would not be too speculative to suggest in the context of Neusner's recent writing that he has a kind of obsession with arguing against his misconceived notion of "intertextuality" as a characteristic of midrash (or rabbinic literature in general). He believes that the use of this term implies that all rabbinic literature is a "seamless whole" without history or contestation. Since this straw man has become his nemesis, he sees him hiding under every bed. In his zeal to attack the intertextualists on every possible front, he has opened here another battlefield against those scholars that he refers to as "Kugel and his friends" or sometimes, the "*Prooftexts* circle."[42] That this is indeed Neusner's animating obsession here is eminently clear from his having devoted an entire monograph solely to this subject.[43]

Now it is precisely on this point that I wish to address the issues. Neusner's entire discussion both in the monograph on the subject and here is founded on an entirely mistaken conception of the notion of intertextuality as it appears in myriad discussions in literary theory.[44] Intertexuality in virtually all discussions is not a characteristic of some texts as opposed to others but part of the structure of the literary text as such. One could certainly argue against the concept of intertextuality on theoretical grounds, but Neusner's attempt to discredit the concept vis-à-vis rabbinic literature on empirical grounds merely shows that he has not the slightest notion of what he is talking about, *when he uses the term "intertextuality."* Now, if the term "intertextuality" has any value at all, it is precisely in the way that it claims that no texts, including the classic single-authored works of Shakespeare or Dostoevsky, for example, are organic, self-contained unities, created out of the spontaneous, freely willed act of a self-identical subject. What this means is that every text is constrained by the literary system of which it is a part and that every text is ultimately dialogical in that it cannot but record the traces of its contentions and doubling of earlier discourses. The scholars that Neusner is attacking are certainly right in the intuition that if such be true for the texts of Wordsworth, it can only be more true of the texts of group production and redaction which comprise the rabbinic classics. Since these conceptions, in their broadest sense,[45] are, I would claim, among the virtually universally maintained positions in literary theory today, Neusner's wish to see each of the documents of rabbinic Judaism as just such organic texts and as the reflection of a worldview of "authorships" is nothing short of primitive from the perspective of precisely the discipline that he is invoking against Kugel and so-called company.[46] Far from leading to a claim that rabbinic literature is a seamless whole of harmonious views, the concept of intertexuality would suggest that not even one document of that literature (or any other) is nor could be a seamless whole that could reflect the *Weltanschauung* of an "authorship."

Not only a claim about the dialogical and social nature of all text production, the notion of intertextuality is also an extension and concretization of the philosophical position that there is no such thing as a true, objective mimesis of reality in language. Reality is always represented through texts that refer to other texts, through language that is a construction of the historical, ideological, and social system of a people. In these terms we can perhaps retrieve Isaak Heinemann's work, removing from it the mystifying encrustations of romantic ideology. In place of the hero of the spirit in communion with the true timeless essence of the heroes of the Bible, I will imagine the rabbis as readers doing the best they could to make sense of the Bible for themselves and their times and in themselves and their times—in short, as readers. The text of the Torah is gapped and dialogical, and into the gaps the reader slips, interpreting and completing the text in accordance with the codes of his or her culture. In this sense too we can retrieve Gundolf's ideas—however, in terms that he would hardly have understood or been sympathetic to. What I wish to suggest is that the legends that history produces can indeed be read as a historiography and an interpretation of the past, and the aggada can indeed then be read as an interpretation of the Bible. In other words we will return to the idea that the aggada is the most significant kind of historiography, however, not because it represents a true subjective communion with the past on the part of geniuses, but because it manifests the past as it was represented by the culture in which the aggada was produced. Midrash is a portrayal of the reality which the rabbis perceived in the Bible through their ideologically colored eyeglasses, just as Heinemann and Heinemann are reading the rabbis and the Bible through their eyeglasses—and indeed just as I am reading through mine. In place of one Heinemann's reduction of aggada to a mere reflection of the historical reality of its time and the other's ignoring of its time entirely in the name of a supertemporal psychological connection between the rabbis and the Bible, I propose a reading of aggada in which, from the distance of our time, we try to understand how the rabbis read the Torah in their time—taking seriously their claim that what they are doing is reading, and trying to understand how a committed reading of the holy and authoritative text works in the rabbinic culture. The program for a new *Darkhe ha'aggadah* is to explore and justify the view of midrash as a kind of interpretation that continues compositional and interpretive practices found in the biblical canon itself.[47] Rather than seeing midrashic departures from what appears to be the "simple" meaning of the local text as being determined by the needs of rhetoric and propaganda and rooted in the extratextual reality of the rabbinic period, or as being the product of the creative genius of individual rabbis wholly above time and social circumstance, I suggest that the intertextual reading practice of the midrash is a development (sometimes, to be sure, a baroque development) of the intratextual interpretive strategies which the Bible itself manifests. Moreover, the very fractured and unsystematic surface of the biblical text is an encoding of its own intertextuality, and it is precisely this which the midrash interprets. The dialogue and dialectic of the midrashic rabbis will be understood as readings of the dialogue and dialectic of the biblical text.

The intertextuality of midrash is thus an outgrowth of intertextuality within the Bible itself. Gerald Bruns has written that midrash is founded on the

> ancient hermeneutical insight [that] as the Rabbis, Augustine, and Luther knew, the Bible, despite its textual heterogeneity, can be read as a self-glossing book. One learns to study it by following the ways in which one portion of the text illumines another. The generations of scribes who shaped and reshaped the Scriptures appear to have designed them to be studied in just this way. Thus Brevard S. Childs speaks of "the interpretive structure which the biblical text has received from those who formed and used it as

sacred scripture." This does not mean that redaction produced a unified text
(or what we would think of as unified: a holistic text, free of self-contradiction,
a systematic or organic whole: the Bible is everything but *that*); rather it
means that the parts are made to relate to one another reflexively, with later
texts, for example, throwing light on the earlier, even as they themselves
always stand in the light of what precedes and follows them.[48]

Bruns finds a way to achieve that which Isaak Heinemann set out to do, to
explain in what sense the midrash is a reading of the Bible. We do not need the
romantic ideology of communion and creation to understand this sense; it is a
product of the very process by which the Bible was constituted as Scripture.
This perspective comprehends how later texts interpret and rewrite the earlier
ones to change the meaning of the entire canon, and how recognizing the
presence of the earlier texts in the later changes our understanding of these
later texts as well. We have here, then, an almost classic intertextuality, defined
as, "the transformation of a signifying system." This is what the midrash itself
refers to as "stringing [like beads or pearls] the words of Torah together . . .
from the Torah to the Prophets and from the Prophets to the Writings."[49]

Were I to attempt to define midrash at this point, it would perhaps be
radical intertextual reading of the canon, in which potentially every part
refers to and is interpretable by every other part. The Torah, owing to its
own intertextuality, is a severely gapped text, and the gaps are there to be
filled by strong readers, which in this case does not mean readers fighting for
originality, but readers fighting to find what they must in the holy text. Their
own intertext—that is, the cultural codes which enable them to make meaning
and find meaning, constrain the rabbis to fill in the gaps of the Torah's
discourse with narratives which are emplotted in accordance with certain
ideological structures. The type of midrashic parable called the mashal[50] is
only the most explicit of these structures, but it can be taken as a prototype—a
privileged type—of all midrashic narrative interpretation. It is here
that Hayden White's work on the theory of historiography becomes so significant,
for he is the theoretician who has most clearly articulated the role of
the intertext in historiography.

> What the historian must bring to his consideration of the record are general
> notions of the kinds of stories that might be found there, just as he must
> bring to consideration of the problem of narrative representation some notion
> of the "pregeneric plot structure" by which the story he tells is endowed
> with formal coherency. In other words, the historian must draw upon a fund
> of culturally provided mythoi in order to constitute the facts as figuring a
> story of a particular kind, just as he must appeal to that same fund of mythoi
> in the minds of his readers to endow his account of the past with the odor of
> meaning or significance.[51]

In White's theory, then, any historian who writes history as a story has perforce emplotted his discourse using the plot structures that carry the ideology of the culture. Otherwise the story will make no sense to people in the culture. These basic plots—the narratives which the culture allows one to tell—form a vital aspect of the intertext. The mashal and its congeners play a role in the present description of midrash analogous to the "eternal truths" of which Isaak Heinemann spoke. They also serve to take the biblical text out of the accidental and uninterpreted chronicle into the interpretive, value-laden structures of a true historiography; however, the eternal, unchanging verities of romanticism are replaced here by culture-bound, historically conditioned, specific ideological patterns of significance.

Combining the import of all of these insights into the role of intertextuality in the production of the interpretive text leads to the following schema. The biblical narrative is gapped and dialogical. The role of the midrash is to fill in the gaps. The materials which provide impetus for the specifics of the gap-filling are found in the intertext in two ways: first in the intertext provided by the canon itself, the intertextual and interpretive interrelations which exist and which can be made to exist between different parts of the canon, and second, within the ideological intertextual code of the rabbinic culture. The midrash is not, then, a reflex of that ideology but a dialogue with the biblical text conditioned and allowed by that ideology—and as such is no different from any other interpretation.

This story of midrash quite reverses the narrative of hermeneutic that is presupposed by the historical school. As we have seen, their assumption is that the text is clear and transparent at the moment of its original creation, because it speaks to a particular historical situation, and it becomes unclear, owing to the passing of time and that situation. In contrast to this, our conception of midrash is one in which the text makes its meaning in history. We find this insight adumbrated in a crucially important text in the midrash on Genesis, *Bereshit Rabbah*:

> Rabbi Yehuda the son of Simon opened: "And He revealed deep and hidden things" [Dan. 2:22]. In the beginning of the creation of the World, "He revealed deep things, etc." For it says, "In the beginning God created the heavens," and He did not interpret. Where did He interpret it? Later on, "He spreads out the heaven like gossamer" [Isa. 40:22]. "And the earth," and He did not interpret. Where did He interpret it? Later on, "To the snow He said, be earth" [Job 37:6]. "And God said, let there be light," and He did not interpret. Where did He interpret it? Later on, "He wraps Himself in light like a cloak." [Psalms 104:2].[52]

This is certainly a very rich and paradoxical *theoretical* statement. The Author of the Book (and indeed the Author of the world) has chosen at the time of creation—at the time of writing about creation—to hide the interpretation, but

He, through His prophets, has revealed something of this truth later on. This text bears out Bruns's understanding of midrash completely, as we will see it borne out throughout the readings of the Mekilta in this book. We see now that in this midrashic perspective all of the later books of the Bible are in a strong sense readings of the Torah, and so does the midrash continue to use them as interpretation of the Torah and develop their interpretations further. Thus we often find in midrash the phrase, "About them it has been interpreted in the tradition," [*'aleyhem meforash baqqabbalah*] before quoting a verse of the Prophets or Writings. When the rabbis of the midrash quote verses from these texts, the quoted verses are the generating force behind the midrashic elaboration and filling in of the gaps in the "historical record."

However, Bruns has even more to teach us about midrash. The gaps and dialogue and contestation of meaning which the biblical text presents to the reader act as a block—indeed a stumbling block in Bruns's words—precisely to those ideologies, whether romantic or positivistic, which set as their goal recovery of the original meaning. "The Bible always addresses itself to the time of interpretation; one cannot understand it except by appropriating it anew" [Bruns, p. 627]. Although Bruns quotes with approval precisely the language of Joseph Heinemann in which the latter proposes that the rabbis were not concerned with the meaning of Scripture, he himself proffers an understanding of midrash which is much more rich and powerful. "Midrash is not only responsive to the Scriptures as a way of coping with the text's wide-ranging formal problems; it is also responsive to the situations in which the Scriptures exert their claim upon human life. Think of midrash as the medium in which this scriptural claim exerts itself" [p. 629]. A theory of midrash for our time will have to account for the midrash's responsiveness to the "formal problems" of Scripture, which I have described as Scripture's own intertextuality, as well as for the responsiveness of midrash to the ways in which Scripture laid claim to human life in the past and lays such claim in the present as well.

In a very strong sense, if the Rambam posited two schools of readers of the aggada before him and then himself, the Aristotelian reader of midrash; and Heinemann then posited himself, the Gundolfian and Crocean reader of midrash; I come to propose a reading of midrash which is in keeping with the intellectual, critical, and theoretical movement of our times. I might indeed claim for my model that it incorporates all of the types of midrashic readers which Maimonides presented. On the one hand, I *will* claim that midrash is true reading of the meaning of the biblical text, a reading which is sensitive to literary values, echoes, contradictions, intertextuality in all of its senses within the Bible. Midrash is a reading of the "plain sense of things," but only if we recognize that the plain sense grows and changes throughout history and that this is the Bible's underlying meaning. However, I will also accept the characterization of midrash as the product of a disturbed exegetical sense, but only if we recognize that all exegetical senses are disturbed, including most certainly our own. All interpretation is filtered through consciousness, tradition, ideology, and the intertext, and the opposition between subject and object, so characteristic of the romantic ideology, must be deconstructed. Finally, midrash is literature, but all serious literature is revision and interpretation of a canon and a tradition and is a dialogue with the past and with authority which determines the shape of human lives in the present and future. The rabbis were concerned with the burning issues of their day, but their approach to that concern was through the clarification of difficult passages of Scripture. Ideology affected their reading but their ideology was also affected by their reading. The task of our research is to try to understand how. Perhaps the *nimshal* of my text is that each generation of serious readers of aggada will have to create a *Darkhe ha'aggadah* for itself. Let us begin.

The Plan of the Book

This is a much less ambitious book than its model *Darkhe ha'aggadah* in two senses. First of all the latter attempted to describe both the aggada of the tannaim and that of the later amoraim, while this book confines itself only to the earlier period and indeed to one document of that period. Second, Heinemann's book attempted to account for all of the methods of the aggada, that is, both those concerned with philosophy of history and those which have to do with the philosophy of language. This book confines itself to the first of these, and will have to be followed by a companion volume on the second. Following is a schematic plan of the present text.

In accordance with the view that all texts are a "mosaic" of marked and unmarked citations from earlier texts, the second chapter of this book is a study of the role of quotation in the midrashic text, not only the quotation of the text about which the midrash is speaking, but also the apparently subsidiary quotations of other verses, the so-called prooftexts. The third chapter discusses the Mekilta's response to the intertextuality of the Torah itself, that is, the heterogeneity of its narrative structure, which read synchronically invites dialectical/dialogical reading. This method of reading will be presented as an alternative to diachronic methods, such as source criticism.

The next chapter is an examination of the built-in ambiguity of the biblical text and the way that the midrash represents the double-voicedness of the Torah by setting up a dialectic between interpretations. I will try to show how what has been taken as homily and even allegory is, in fact, a reading of precisely the kind of textual heterogeneity exposed in the previous chapter. Certain kinds of ambiguity function by mobilizing alternative intertexts, thus generating more than one legitimate reading.[53] Also, in this chapter I pay more attention to the midrash as text, that is, to the meaning generated by the edited concatenation of the different interpretive discourses, as opposed to the individual discourses themselves. The "scandal of midrash," namely that the founding interpretations of the most authoritative text of Judaism are presented in the form of controversies, is read as a representation of this biblical intertextuality.

The next two chapters are an analysis of the particular type of midrash called the *mashal*, usually translated as "parable". In the first of the these, a theory of the mashal is presented which shows it to be a method for motivating the quotation of several verses in connection with a gapped narrative of the Torah and as a solution to that gap. The mashal, it will be claimed, provides as well an ideological model through which hypothesis formation in midrashic reading is both generated and constrained. Such ideological models are themselves intertextual in that they represent in concrete form the anonymous codes of a given cultural practice. In the second of these chapters, an extended reading of a single mashal will be presented. In the analysis of this text, I will claim that another aspect of intertextuality is revealed by the midrash, that is, the intertextuality of the Bible vis-à-vis its earlier Hebrew cultural practice and in particular the mythology of ancient Israel. Another concept of intertextuality, one drawing on the psychodynamic model of repression and displacement, will be introduced and illustrated through this text.

In the next chapter, a discussion of the crucial role of the Song of Songs in the Mekilta and in midrash in general is undertaken. The main point of this chapter is to draw distinctions between the intertextual reading practice of midrash and the other prominent type of ancient hermeneutic, allegoresis. Midrash interprets by correlating text to text, while the allegorist interprets by correlating text to "hidden meanings". The final chapter continues this theme and attempts more strongly to relate the midrash to its rabbinic culture— however, not in the way that historians have traditionally done, i.e., by claiming that midrash *reflects* its culture, but by considering complex and fateful transactions between midrash and other cultural practices.

The relationship among events, current needs, interpretation, and ideology is accordingly a much more nuanced one than the one subscribed to by the historical school. In my view, the general approach of Isaak Heinemann and Gerald Bruns, which sees *midrash as a special type of interpretive discourse which needs to be accounted for in terms of literary and historiographical theory*, provides for a much richer way of reading these texts. "Intertextuality", *because* of the polysemy of its usages, provides a powerful metaphor within which to pursue this reading. In each of the chapters, the points will be made via close readings of particular texts drawn from the Mekilta on the biblical pericope regarding Israel's deliverance at the Red Sea. This is a particularly paradigmatic moment in the self-fashioning of the Jewish People, so it provides especially rich material in which to explore the modes of rabbinic literary/historical hermeneutic. I hope by the end of this essay to have provided material for a much more nuanced and rich understanding of the interplay between history and interpretation—both in the special method of Jewish reading called midrash, and by implication, in the hermeneutics of culture in general.

· 2 ·

RECITING THE TORAH:
THE FUNCTION OF QUOTATION
IN THE MIDRASH

> . . . to uproot and stabilize simultaneously; to reject and preserve in
> one breath; to break up and to build—inside, from within, casting a
> new layer on a previous layer and welding them into one mold . . .
> Simon Rawidowicz[1]

Between Literature and Hermeneutics

Studying the Torah—interpretation—is the dominant cultural practice of
rabbinic Judaism. As such it does the work that alternate cultural practices do
in other societies. One of the tasks of a successful culture is to preserve the old
while making it nevertheless new—to maintain continuity with a tradition without freezing it. Intertextuality is a powerful instrument in the hands of culture
for accomplishing this task. As Julia Kristeva has written, "every text builds
itself as a mosaic of quotations, every text is absorption and transformation of
another text."[2] By absorbing and transforming, the textual system both establishes continuity with the past and renews itself for the future. The simultaneous rejection and preservation of tradition in midrash is shown in the all-
pervasive quotation which forms its very warp and woof. A typical page of the
Mekilta bears anywhere from ten to twenty citations of verses or parts of verses
from other biblical texts. In this chapter, I will examine how the Mekilta performs this historical work of simultaneous uprooting and stabilizing by considering in detail the function of quotation in the midrash. The regnant view is
that when a midrash like the Mekilta quotes a verse from another part of the
Bible in the interpretation of the Exodus passages, these quotations are prooftexts—texts cited in good or bad faith in support of previously determined
conclusions.[3] In contrast to this usual view of the role of these scriptural citations, I will argue that the texts cited (sometimes only alluded to) *are the
generating force behind the elaboration of narrative or other types of textual expansion in
the Mekilta's text.* That is to say, the so-called "prooftexts" are to be read as

intertexts and cotexts of the Torah's narrative, as subtexts of the midrashic interpretation. There is a tension between the meaning(s) of the quoted text in its "original" context and in its present context.[4] What is so striking (and strange) about midrash is its claim that the new context is implied by the old one, that the new meanings (Oral Torah) revealed by recontextualizing pieces of the authoritative text are a legitimate interpretation of the Written Torah itself, and indeed given with its very revelation.[5]

Midrash provides a particularly special and interesting case of the intersection of the allusiveness of poetic[6] text and the quotations of critical text. This point requires a bit of explanation, as it is crucial to understanding the present thesis about midrashic narrative. My claim is that poetic texts are understood to make free use of pre-existing linguistic material without any *necessary* responsibility to the original context in which the linguistic material appeared. That is, while the literary text may often be illuminated by reference to the context from which a quotation is taken or to which an allusion is made, no one would claim against a later poet that he/she had been somehow dishonest in quoting an earlier poet and changing the meaning of the anterior text. On the other hand, the critical text cites previously existing linguistic material openly and, at least as a convention of the genre, claims that the context of the citation reproduces and illuminates the original context. However, as we shall see, this distinction is very difficult to maintain on the theoretical level.

As has been shown in the previous chapter, according to Maimonides' theory of midrash, as well as in Isaak Heinemann's, midrash is a type of literary creation, of poetry. Poetry also creates new discourse out of fragments of quotation, allusion, and transformation of earlier discourses. The explicit claim of poetry is that it creates *new* discourse; any violations (and preservations) of the "original meaning and context" are legitimated by that authorial claim to be speaking in his/her own voice. However, various recent accounts of intertextuality have shown how constrained literary discourse is by the "discourse of the other". Bakhtin has expressed this with a biblical reference:

> The dialogical orientation is obviously a characteristic phenomenon of all discourse. It is the natural aim of all living discourse. Discourse comes upon the discourse of the other on all the roads that lead to its object, and it cannot but enter into intense and lively interaction with it. Only the mythical and totally alone Adam, approaching a virgin and still unspoken world with the very first discourse could really avoid altogether this mutual reorientation with respect to the . . . discourse of the other, that occurs on the way to the object.[7]

Since Adam, then, all discourse is dialogue with the past and all literature is therefore intertextual and double-voiced. Even those texts which most insistently claim to be the voice of the subjectivity of the author recording his or her personal experience and vision are socially and historically conditioned. The literary text in its intertextuality both continues and breaches the literary tradition of the culture; it preserves the signifying practices of a culture precisely by transforming them.[8]

Midrash, which is a stipulated post-Adamic literature, represents in this sense only a more open intertextuality than other literatures. Midrash, however, explicitly claims to be hermeneutic discourse; to be representing in its discourse the discourse of an earlier (and authoritative) text. It is not sufficient, therefore, to compare midrash to poetry; it must also be studied as a species of hermeneutic discourse. If literature often tries to hide its intertextuality by the projection of an authorial voice, the critical text typically presents the opposite fiction of voiceless subservience to the anterior text. The function of quotations in interpretation has been analyzed by contemporary theoreticians, who have shown the illusoriness of the objectivity of quotation therein. One of the most useful analyses for the study of midrash is that of Stefan Morawski. In his taxonomy of functions of quotation in modern texts, he has described

> a particularly fascinating phenomenon which deserves separate analysis, namely the selection and interpolation of quotations in such a way that they make for a reinterpretation, for instance, of the philosophical tradition on to which the investigator has fastened. . . . This phenomenon can be explained in terms of the hermeneutic interpretation of the classical texts of each school of thought. Every period of history approaches its heritage anew. By rearranging and regrading the basic elements of this legacy, it also gives it a slightly altered meaning. In such a restructuralization of a particular philosophical theory the quotation plays a double role: *it both continues and breaches the tradition*, that is, uncovers angles of inquiry which were unknown or forgotten. Hermeneutics is a corroboration and fulfillment of the vitality of the theory involved; hence quotation operates in this context equivocally. At one level it encapsulates accepted philosophical propositions, but, above all, it performs in a new whole designed to modify this acceptance.[9]

According to Morawski, then, even a philosophical hermeneutic operates equivocally, at one and the same time reproducing and radically altering the previous texts. This same equivocation, this double-voicedness, is characteristic of midrash as well. Precisely by being composed largely of quotations it both affirms and transforms the biblical text. In a sense, it is exemplary of both species of discourse, for as we have seen, the same double movement of "continuing and breaching" a tradition is found in both poetic texts and philosophical hermeneutics. The quotations of previous poetry in the poetic text cannot but maintain the tradition while openly claiming to breach it, while the quotations in the hermeneutic text cannot but breach the tradition, while openly claiming to maintain it. What is interesting, then, about midrash in this regard is that it openly takes a position between (actually never really "between," but sometimes one, sometimes the other, usually both) "freely" using the pre-existing linguistic material and quoting it with reference to its "original" context. This intersection in effect undermines the distinction that we habitually make between literary creation and hermeneutic work, by showing that all literary creation is hermeneutic and all hermeneutic is creation. Our study of the Mekilta will bear out this view that explicit intertextuality carries with it both "disruptive" and "reconstructive" features; I will argue that with reference to midrash, at least, this double movement of disruption and regeneration is precisely its *raison d'être*. I will illustrate this point with a text from our midrash:

> *And they went out into the desert of Shur* [Exod. 15:2]. This is the desert of Kub. They have told of the desert of Kub that it is eight hundred by eight hundred parasangs—all of it full of snakes and scorpions, as it is said, "Who has led us in the great and terrible desert—snake, venomous serpent, and scorpion" [Deut. 8:15]. And it says, "Burden of the beasts of the Dry-South, of the land of trial and tribulation, lioness and lion, . . . *ef'eh*" [Isa. 30:6]. *Ef'eh* is the viper. They have told that the viper sees the shadow of a bird flying in the air; he immediately conjoins [to it], and it falls down limb by limb. Even so, "they did not say, 'Where is the Lord who has brought us up from Egypt, who has led us in the land of drought and pits, land of desolation and the death-shadow?' " [Jer. 2:6]. What is death-shadow? A place of shadow that death is therewith. [Lauterbach, II, pp. 87-88]

This brilliant rhetorical piece combines scriptural and folkloristic materials to increase the vividness of the point that Israel was blindly faithful to God in this time. The passage begins by identifying the wilderness mentioned only here with a well-known desert, so well known, in fact, that there is a folk tradition of its immense size. Not only is it immense, it is also terrible, completely filled with venomous snakes and scorpions. Moreover, in the verse from Isaiah, we are told that one of the reptiles is called *ef'eh*, identified as the viper. Another folk tradition is cited indicating how terrible this viper is indeed, and even so, the Israelites did not doubt; they did not say, "Where is God," but followed Moses faithfully. This is the general meaning of this passage.

Let us look now at the very complex structure of citation in this text, for indeed it is made up entirely of quotations. First, let us note the two quotations of folk traditions, which are explicitly marked as such by the rubric, "They [i.e., the people] have told." The folklore is *quoted*: "They have told," and is accordingly part of the intertextual structure of the text.[10] The snakes and scorpions, however, are not folklore; they are explicitly signified in the verses from Deuteronomy and Isaiah, but the terrible nature, the fearfulness of the viper is greatly enhanced by the quoted legend of what happens to birds by the snake's conjoining with their shadows.[11] We have here, accordingly, a composite text whose mosaic structure is indicated openly on its surface.

The use of the verse from Jeremiah, however, most powerfully manifests the paradoxical nature of intertextuality in the midrash, for it is used here in a sense opposite to that of its original context. In Jeremiah, it is "what fault did your ancestors find in Me that they have grown far from Me, and they follow nonsense; and did not say, 'where is God who took us up,' " i.e., "they did not say" means there that they should have said it; they should have sought God. However, in the midrash, "they did not say" is to their credit, i.e., they trusted and didn't say where *is* God who took us up, now that we need Him? This placing of a verse into a new context with a different meaning is emblematic of midrash. The tradition has been breached, but at the same time, this reading of the verse is consistent with Jeremiah's own theology of the desert period. It is, after all, that prophet who says, "I have remembered for you the faithfulness of your youth, your going after me in the desert" [2:2]. In short, what is, in the context of Jeremiah, an attack on his generation, is made in the midrash an approbation of the generation of the wilderness, a sentiment with which the prophet would be in complete sympathy. The tradition is, therefore, also preserved. Only the rhetoric is new, not the ideology. The local ("original") meaning of the verse is disrupted, but the meaning-system to which it belongs, the ideology as a whole, is vivified and confirmed.

We might sum up the difference between midrashic quotation and poetic allusion by saying that while midrash is exegesis of an authoritative text, a specific type of interpretation, poetic allusion is interpretation which is not exegesis. At least the text being read is always explicitly marked in midrash by being quoted at its outset, even though the cotexts being cited are not always so. This is ultimately the difference between the intertextuality encoded in Scripture itself and the intertextuality of the rabbis as well.[12] In the next section, we will begin to see the mechanics of the hermeneutics of citation as a disruption and preservation of meanings.

Paradigmatic and Syntagmatic Citation

Midrash performs its hermeneutic work by quoting. The quoting and resituating of texts from the Torah and the Prophets and Writings, the creation of new strings of language out of the pearls of the old, is accomplished through the placing of collections of quoted verses into set structures. These structures seem to fall into two types, which I call paradigmatic and syntagmatic.[13] In the first kind, verses of the Bible are associated by features in which they are the same or different, that is to say they are substitutable one for the other as tokens of a type; hence they are shown to form a paradigm. In the second kind, verses are replaced into a new narrative structure. Let us have a brief look at an example of each of these types of midrash, beginning with the paradigmatic:

The Lord is a man of war, the Lord is His name: Rabbi Yehuda says: Here is a verse made rich in meaning by many passages, [for] it declares that He revealed Himself to them with every manner of weapon:
He revealed Himself to them as a warrior girt with his sword, as it is said, "Gird thy sword upon thy thigh, O warrior" [Ps. 45:4];
He revealed Himself to them as a cavalry officer, as it is said, "And He rode upon a cherub, and did fly" [Ps. 18:11];
He revealed Himself to them in coat of mail and helmet, as it is said, "And He put on righteousness as a coat of mail," etc. [Isa. 59:17];
He revealed Himself to them with a spear, as it is said, "At the shining of Thy glittering spear" [Hab. 3:11], and it says, "Draw out also the spear, and the battle-ax," etc. [Ps. 35:3];
He revealed Himself to them with bow and arrows, as it is said, "Thy bow is made quite bare," etc. [Hab. 3:9], and it says, "And He sent out arrows, and scattered them," etc. [2 Sam. 22:15];
He revealed Himself to them in buckler and shield, as it is said, "His truth is a shield and a buckler," etc. [Ps. 91:4], and it says, "Take hold of shield and buckler," etc. [Ps. 35:2].[14]

This text is particularly interesting to us, because it is one of the few places where we find a comment by the rabbis on their hermeneutic method.[15] We have here an explicit statement on the nature of midrashic reading. It is founded on the idea that gaps and indeterminacies in one part of the canon may be filled and resolved by citing others. R. Yehuda says that the way to interpret our verse is to consider it in the light of many other verses. This is a reflex of the general rabbinic principle that the "words of Torah are poor in their own context [lit., in their place] and rich in another context."[16] Far from being limited to interpretation in its context, *the verse is considered as impoverished in meaning when read only there.* As Goldin has put it, "the idiom and idea of this verse are made concrete and are illuminated by a number of verses in other parts of Scripture."[17] Or to put it in other terms, a metaphor describing God's nature or activities is explicated by reference to other verses from the Prophets and Writings in which the metaphor is made more specific or concrete. The collected verses form a paradigm, the paradigm, that is, of God's weapons.[18]

Syntagmatic reconstruction, in which narratives are constructed around a verse or concatenation of verses, provides an even more striking example of the way biblical references may be used to generate new/old meaning. The case at hand in the Mekilta is remarkable in that its speaker, R. Yehuda, uses precisely the same formula to introduce his interpretive discourse as above:

And the angel of God, going before the camp of Israel, moved and went behind them. And the pillar of cloud moved from before them and went behind them [Exod. 14:19].
R. Yehuda said: Here is a verse made rich in meaning by many passages. He made of it a mashal;[19] to what is the matter similar? To a king who was going on the way, and his son went before him. Brigands came to kidnap him from

in front. He took him from in front and placed him behind him. A wolf came behind him. He took him from behind and placed him in front.[20] Brigands in front and the wolf in back he [He][21] took him and placed him in his [His][21] arms, for it says, "I taught Ephraim to walk, taking them on My arms" [Hos. 11:3].

The son began to suffer; he [He] took him on his shoulders, for it is said, "in the desert which you saw, where the Lord, your God carried you" [Deut. 1:31].

The son began to suffer from the sun; he [He] spread on him His cloak, for it is said, "He has spread a cloud as a curtain" [Ps. 105:39].

He became hungry; he [He] fed him, for it is said, "Behold I send bread, like rain, from the sky" [Exod. 16:4].

He became thirsty, he [He] gave him drink, for it is said, "He brought streams out of the rock" [Ps. 78:16].[22] [Lauterbach, I, pp. 224-225]

R. Yehuda's stated purpose is to comment on the verse, "And the angel of God, etc." The reading is accomplished by bringing together other texts which relate to the same subject, the behavior of God toward Israel in the wilderness. These texts, which form a semantic field or paradigm, are reinscribed in a new narrative, in a new syntagmatic structure, by the midrashist. The new narrative specifies and concretizes the contexts in which the metaphorical statements distributed throughout the canon function.

My thrust here is not to set up a taxonomy of syntagmatic versus paradigmatic midrash, so much as to unsettle this distinction. That is to say, by identifying these two structures as realizations of the same underlying hermeneutic idea where previous scholars have not seen a structural connection between these different sub-genres of midrash, I believe that I draw nearer to an adequate characterization of the category "midrash" as a method of intertextual reading. The specifications or concretizations are essentially the same, whether the verses are organized into a story as in the second example, or into a paradigm as in the first. The essential hermeneutic moment is in both cases, "This is a verse made rich in meaning from many places," whether the enriching is by syntagmatic or paradigmatic means, and for me this is a synecdoche of midrash as a whole. Paradigmatic and syntagmatic structures are both used to accomplish the same task of quoting other verses in the context of the verse to be interpreted.

The verses of the Bible function for the rabbis much as do words in ordinary speech. They are a repertoire of semiotic elements that can be recombined into new discourse, just as words are recombined constantly into new discourse. Just as in a lexicon words are placed into juxtaposition revealing semantic similarities and differences, so in the midrashic text, semantic similarities and differences between texts are revealed via new juxtapositions. Just as the words of any language can be placed into new syntagmatic relations, so can the verses of the Bible.

Such use of higher levels of discourse as elements of further discourse has been discussed with regard to the use of the proverb in narrative by Galit Hasan-Rokem:

> It seems that the main difference between the quotation and the proverb consists of the difference in the systems to which the speaker relates when he interjects the text into the new context. All of the proverbs of one ethnic group comprise the proverb repertoire of that group. Each single proverb exists in the Saussurian *langue* aspect, that is, as a paradigmatic unit with the potential of being applied in *parole*, of being put to actual use. In quoting, on the other hand, the speaker refers to an already existing specific *parole*, which he applies to a new, intertextual *parole*. It is not possible to speak of a repertoire of quotations, since any text, poetic or non-poetic, regardless of formal, contextual, or structural characteristics, may become a quotation.[23]

Hasan-Rokem speaks of the ambiguous status of the proverb in language. It belongs to *langue* in its aspect as a unit in a paradigm of proverbial units in the culture; however, it also belongs to an already existing *parole* in that it is quoted from a previous discourse. While she expressly distinguishes between proverbs and quotations, claiming that quotations do not form a repertoire, it seems that in midrash the Bible can be understood precisely as a repertoire of quotations in this sense. The opposition between the Bible as *parole* and as *langue* is therefore unsettled. On the one hand, obviously, the Bible is a *parole*, and quotation from it appears as the injecting of one *parole* into another. On the other hand, the Bible as virtually the only source of quotations in the midrash, and a closed and well-known corpus, does take on the aspect of *langue*, in the sense that Hasan-Rokem uses the term. Quoting from the Bible resembles an act of selecting from a repertoire. The *langue*-like nature of the biblical text for the rabbis is revealed in their paradigmatic midrash, which collects verses into sets of similarities and differences, structured like the lexicon of a language. The tension between the *parole*-like nature of the verse as an element in an existing discourse and the *langue*-like nature of its possibility of being selected and combined into new discourse provides much of the fascination and power of midrash. It is in this semiotic duality that the ability of midrash to both breach and continue the Torah can be theorized.

The full meaning of a sign (never realizable, of course) is the exposure of all of the paradigmatic and syntagmatic relations into which it enters and into which it can enter. Accordingly, the re-citing of the sentences of the Bible in ever new paradigms and syntagms is interpretation. There is, therefore, no ultimate difference between these two texts of R. Yehuda's, *a point which is made explicit by the use of the same opening formula in both of them.* This enables us to perceive a generalization about midrash which has not been remarked before, namely, that the fundamental moment of all of these midrashic forms is precisely the very cocitation of several verses.[24] Both employ set structures to frame the reading-together of verses. Both understand the verses through their interaction within the frame, and both are completely new readings and yet also already existent in the Torah.

I have compared the paradigmatic midrash to a lexicon and the syntagmatic to a narrative. At first glance, the comparability of these two kinds of structure may seem very questionable. However, semiotic studies of literature have in fact revealed the commensurability of paradigm and syntagm in the making of meaning. One of the most important theoreticians of this commensurability is Michael Riffaterre. Riffaterre has shown that a narrative repeats, varies, and expands the elements of a paradigm.[25] Narrative is accordingly paradigmatic. It is related to the lexicon, in our case not a lexicon of words, but a lexicon of paradigmatic value statements. The value of narrative over a mere paradigm of values and judgments is in the rhetorical and psychological power over the reader that it retains through its development and varied repetitions. In Riffaterre's words, "narrative is interesting before it is exemplary. There is no narrative without change; no fiction without *exemplary* change."[26] It is not surprising, therefore, to find in midrash a mode of interpretation of narrative which sometimes sets up the paradigm itself *qua* paradigm, and at other times expands on the paradigmatic nature of the repetition and expansion by inscribing them in a paradigmatic story (the mashal or "parable" which will be discussed in chapters 5 and 6 below).

We can see the way these two categories interact by reading a text from the Mekilta, discussed by W. S. Towner in his book on the "enumeration of scriptural examples."[27] The type of text that Towner studied there is midrash which has the form "There are *n* who/which did so and so," or "There are *n* cases of such and such." A classic example of this form of midrash from our corpus follows:

> *And lift thou up thy rod*, etc. [Exod. 14:16]. Ten miracles were performed for Israel at the sea. The sea was broken through and made like a vault, as it is said: "Thou didst pierce with his shafts," etc. [Hab. 3:14]. It was divided into two parts, as it is said: "Stretch out thy hand over the sea and divide it." Dry land was formed in it, as it is said: "But the children of Israel walked upon dry land in the midst of the sea" [Exod. 14:29]. It became a sort of clay, as it is said: "Thou hast trodden the sea with Thy horses, the clay of mighty waters" [Hab. 3:15]. It crumbled into pieces, as it is said: "Thou didst break the sea in pieces by Thy strength" [Ps. 74:13]. It turned into rocks, as it is said: "Thou didst shatter the heads of the sea-monsters upon the water" [Ps. 74:13]. It was cut into several parts, as it is said: "To Him who divided the Red Sea into parts" [Ps. 136:13]. It was piled up into stacks, as it is said: "And with the blast of Thy nostrils the waters were piled up" [Exod. 15:8]. It formed a sort of heap, as it is said: "The floods stood upright as a heap" [Exod. 15:8]. He extracted for them sweet water from the salt, as it is said: "He brought streams also out of the rock and caused waters to run down like rivers [Ps. 78:16]. The sea congealed on both sides and became a sort of glass crystal, as it is said: "The deeps were congealed in the heart of the sea" [Exod. 15:8].[28]

Each of the verses cited here comes from a poetic text that treats the split-ting of the Red Sea. The midrashist has gathered all of these verses together, so that they may make the maximum impression on the hearer/reader. When each verse is encountered in its own place, as it were, its impact is relatively weak, but when all are encountered together, as a list of the ten miracles which God performed for the Israelites on this one occasion, the dramatic and picto-rial effect is enhanced greatly. In the words of Towner himself, this is a "device for 'setting up' the scripture so that it can be seen and heard."[29] On the one hand, we might say we have a list of all of the verses which treat a certain subject in the salvation history, a kind of archive of traditions and interpreta-tions, but it is the melding of these different texts into a single quasi-narrative that makes this passage work as midrash and ultimately that gives each of the quoted verses its maximum power. In this example of the enumeration para-digm, we can detect the synchronic transition between narrative paradigm and paradigmatic narrative. The enumeration form is not, however, the only form which has this hermeneutic function of exposing the relations of similarity and difference between verses dealing with a similar event or subject. As we have seen above, the mashal has this function; there are other such structures as well. Indeed, I would argue that *all* of the generic patterns of midrash have this function of exposing and creating intertextual hermeneutic relations between different biblical texts.

One of the most dramatic forms of paradigmatic intertextual dialogue is the realization of meanings through the confrontation of texts:

> Rabbi Shim'on ben Gamliel says, Come and see how beloved is Israel before Him-Who-Spoke-and-the-World-Was, for as they are beloved, He reversed the act of creation. He made the low into the high and the high into the low. Formerly, bread came up from the land, and dew came down from heaven, as it says, "A land of grain and wine, and His heavens drip dew" [Deut. 33:28]. But now the state of affairs is reversed. Bread began to come down from heaven and dew to go up from the land, as it says, "Behold I rain down for you bread from heaven [Exod. 16:4]—And the layer of dew went up" [Exod. 16:14].[30] [Lauterbach, II, pp. 102-103]

R. Shim'on's move here is to place these "two utterances in juxtaposition," so that they "enter into a particular kind of semantic relation which we call dialogical"[31] or intertextual. Meaning is released in this interaction of texts which neither text had on its own, in its own context. What is in Deuteronomy a poetic statement concerning the richness of the land becomes background for a high drama of cosmic intervention. What in Exodus reads as physical descrip-tion of the events of the miracle comes to have an axiological significance only latent in the original context. This miracle was so great that it involved nothing less than a restructuring of the universe. Now, this point could have been made without the quotation of the verse from Deuteronomy; we all know that normally rain falls from the heaven and bread grows from the earth. What is so striking here, therefore (and so characteristic), is not the "meaning" of the statement, but rather the way its meaning is produced. That meaning resides there already in the verses, or rather between them, that is, in the potential interaction between them. It is neither imposed on the verses "from outside," nor does it lie behind them as "intention", but is revealed/created in their coming together—in the bringing together performed by the midrashist, R. Shim'on.

What is the function, however, of R. Shim'on's "Come and see how beloved is Israel before Him-Who-Spoke-and-the-World-Was"? This is clearly an assertion that is not "literally" there in the verses as they stand in their biblical contexts. However, at the same time, this meaning emerges so powerfully from the interaction of this set of resituated signifiers that it does seem to have been always there. The invitation to come and see is a rhetorical figure through which the meanings of the verses may be read in association. It is a kind of generic pattern which enabled the midrashist, R. Shim'on, to cause the verses to speak with each other, and a kind of axiological code by which we can read the juxtaposition. It has precisely the same function, *mutatis mutandis*, as the mashal or the enumeration formula.

Let us look now at an example of a metaphorical paradigm in the *Song of Songs* that helps the midrashist to interpret the Exodus ideologically. As we will see in the next two chapters, one of the major issues facing the tannaim as they read the Exodus accounts was the evaluation of the character of Israel in the wilderness. The problem is, in brief, that the Bible seems to contain two diametrically opposed readings of the people's status at this time: one which understands it to have been the "honeymoon" of God and His bride, Israel, the other which reads the period as one of unrelenting unfaithfulness on the part of the bride. The following midrash, dated somewhat later than the Mekilta, approaches this antinomy through the collection of verses into a paradigm under the rubric of a paradigmatic verse from the Song of Songs, which we shall see below (chapter 7) was read as the hermeneutic key to the Exodus:

> *I am black, but I am beautiful* [Song 1:5]:
> I am black in Egypt, but I am beautiful in Egypt. I am black in Egypt: "And they *rebelled* against me and did not want to hear" [Ezek. 20:8]; but I am beautiful in Egypt, in the blood of the Passover and the blood of circumcision, as is written, "And I passed over you and saw you wallowing in your blood, and I said to you, In your blood you will live" [Ezek. 16:6]; this is the blood of the Passover; "In your blood you will live"; this is the blood of circumcision.[32]
> Another word: I am black at the sea, for it says, "And they *rebelled* at the sea, at the Red Sea" [Ps. 106:7]; but I am beautiful at the sea, as it says, "This is my God and I will beautify Him" [Exod. 15:2].

I am black at Mara, for it says, "And the people *complained* against Moses, saying, What shall we drink?" [Exod. 15:24]; but I am beautiful at Mara, for it says, "and he cried out to the Lord, and the Lord taught him a tree and he threw it into the water and the water became sweet."

I am black at Refidim, for it says, "And he called the place *Contention* and *Strife*" [Exod. 16:7]; but I am beautiful at Refidim, for it says, "And Moses built there an altar and called it, God is my standard" [Exod. 16:15].

I am black at Horev, for it says, "They made a calf at Horev" [Ps. 106:19];[33] but I am beautiful at Horev, for it says, "All that the Lord has spoken, we will do and we will hear" [Exod. 24:7].

I am black in the desert, for it says "How much have they *rebelled* against Him in the desert" [Ps. 78:40]; but I am beautiful in the desert, by building the tabernacle, as it says, "On the day of building the tabernacle" [Num. 9:16].[34]

The series continues through Joshua, giving four more examples along the way. This is a classic example of paradigmatic midrash. Under the rubric of interpreting the verse, "I am black but I am beautiful," a series of examples from the desert period are chosen that show the dual nature of the people—black and beautiful. The verses chosen all refer directly to the events for which they are being cited, and half of them belong naturally to those texts which regard the Jews as having been faithful at this time, half to those which regard the Jews as having been rebellious and faithless. The text is paradigmatic in two ways. On the one hand, each half of the collection of verses is a member of a substitution set of linguistic strings which belong to the semantic field, "positive or negative statements about the people in the desert." On the other hand, each pair forms a contrast set, with each half marked either positive or negative for the semantic value in question. The dialogical nature of the biblical text itself—its intertextual heterogeneity—is revealed powerfully in the citational structure of the midrash. What can be read as bifurcation in inner-biblical interpretation is here represented as a bifurcation in the actual condition of the people at each of these events in the wilderness history. Practically the whole text consists of nothing but cited verses. The verse, "I am black, but I am beautiful," is read in several situations, the "black" being substituted for by one response to that situation and the "beautiful" by another. The crucial word here is, of course, "substituted," for a paradigm is a substitution set by definition, and the substitution set thus becomes the mark of a deep structural element in the values of the biblical-rabbinic religious system. Thus, by cutting pieces of discourse out of their original context, the midrashist reinserts them into a semiotic system which is both new and old.

The rabbis were keenly aware of the radical appropriation of subtexts their midrash performs. The Talmud preserves a story[35] about the very rabbis of the Mekilta which contains a nearly explicit commentary on midrashic intertextuality:

We have learnt there: If it [a stove] was cut into coils and sand was put between the coils; R. Eliezer calls it pure and the sages call it impure. This is the stove of Akhnai. What is "Akhnai"? Said Rav Yehuda, said Shmuel: They encircled it with words like this Akhna [species of snake] and called it impure. A sage teaches: On that day, R. Eliezer used all the refutations in the world, but they did not accept it from him. He said, If the law is as I say, this carob will prove it. The carob was uprooted from its place one hundred feet. Some report four hundred feet. They said to him, One does not quote a carob as proof. He further said to them, If the law is as I say, the water pipe will prove it. The water began to flow backwards. They said to him, One may not quote a water-pipe as proof. Again, he said to them, If the law is as I say, the walls of the house of study will prove it. The walls of the house of study leaned over to fall. R. Yehoshua rebuked them, saying to them, If the disciples of the wise are striving with each other for the law, what have you to do with it? They did not fall because of the honor of R. Yehoshua, and did not stand straight for the honor of R. Eliezer. He said to them, If the law is as I say, let it be proven from heaven. A voice went out and said, What are you next to R. Eliezer, according to whom the law is in every place? R. Yehoshua stood on his feet and said, "It is not in heaven!" What is "It is not in heaven"? Said R. Yermia: Since the Torah has already been given from Mt. Sinai, we do not pay attention to heavenly voices, for You have written already at Mt. Sinai, "Incline after the majority." R. Natan found Eliahu [the prophet Elijah] and asked him, What was the Holy One, Blessed be He, doing at that moment? He said to him: Laughing and saying, My children have defeated Me. My children have defeated Me.[36]

This story has been studied from the point of view of its manifest content, that is, on the one hand, as a reflection on the nature of interpretation and the role of intention in determining (or not determining) meaning,[37] and on the other, as a manifestation of rabbinic power struggles.[38] The case of the purity or impurity of a certain type of earthenware stove is made a synecdoche for the question of the Oral Torah as a whole. What is the snake-stove? "Said Rav Yehuda, said Shmuel, They encircled it with words like this snake." For R. Yehoshua,[39] "Oral Torah" means the Torah expounded orally in the interactive process of dialectical reading for the law. Meaning is not in heaven, not in a voice behind the text, but in the house of midrash, in the voices in front of the text. The written Torah is the Torah which is written and Oral Torah is the Torah which is read.

What has not yet been shown is the structure of signification of this text itself—not what it talks about, but what it says by how it talks. R. Yehoshua suits his speech act perfectly to the word of his interpretation. "It is not in heaven" is a citation, the use of which is radically different from its meaning in its "original context."[40] R. Yehoshua is arguing with God from God's own text. You gave up Your right as author and even as divine voice to interpret Your Torah, when You said, "It is not in heaven." R. Yehoshua is, then, not only describing or making a claim about interpretation, but instituting and creating the Oral Torah. I should make it clear that I am not making the ridiculous historical claim that before R. Yehoshua there was no midrash or Oral Torah. Indeed, I am not sure that this late story reflects any "actual" historical reality at all. I wish rather to claim that in the form of narrative it *represents* the structural possibility which creates a space for Oral Torah. "It is not in heaven" is itself not in heaven. R. Yehoshua breaks it out of context and re-cites it in his own. In the Torah which is written, the verse seems to say only that the fulfillment of the Torah's commands is not beyond the reach of the human being:

> For this commandment which I command you today is not too difficult for you or too remote. *It is not in heaven*, that one should say, Who will arise to the heaven, take it and make it heard that we might do it. And it is not over the sea, that one might say, Who will cross to the other side of the sea and take it for us, and make us hear it, that we might do it. Rather, the word [thing] is very close to you in your mouth and heart, to do it. [Deut. 30:11-14]

R. Yehoshua transforms the verse through his citation into meaning that the Torah is beyond the reach, as it were, of its divine author. The nature of R. Yehoshua's hermeneutic speech act here is vital to understanding the text. If we do not perceive what he is doing with the verse from Deuteronomy, we could misunderstand him to be making precisely the opposite claim, namely that the text is autonomous and sufficient in itself, not requiring the author to guarantee its true interpretation—a version of the New Criticism. By performing the act of tesseration of the language, however, the rabbi disables any such reading of his statement. Without fanfare, R. Yehoshua creates radical new meaning in this verse, simply by reinscribing it in a new context. "It is not in heaven" means not only that the Torah is not beyond human reach, but that it is beyond divine reach, as it were.

This brings us squarely up against the dilemma of any hermeneutic theory that does not allow appeal to author's intention as a curb on interpretation. Once that control is gone, it seems that any interpretation is the same as any other, that anything at all can be said to be the meaning of the text. Such hermeneutic anarchy is clearly *not* the way that midrash presents itself. Within our text both the dilemma and an answer to it are offered. Present within the narrative is a commentary on itself, namely the sentences: "What is 'It is not in heaven'? Said R. Yermia, Since the Torah has already been given from Mt. Sinai, we do not pay attention to heavenly voices, for You have written already at Mt. Sinai, 'Incline after the majority.' "

R. Yermia's rereading of R. Yehoshua solves the problem of what constrains interpretation. The answer is surprisingly modern: the majority of the community which holds cultural hegemony controls interpretation. To put it another

way: correctness of interpretation is a function of the ideology of the interpretive community. The question is asked: What is the meaning of "It is not in
heaven"? and R. Yermia answers by supplying another subtext, namely the
verse from Exod. 23:2, which says explicitly (i.e, in its own context) that the
law is in accordance with the view of a human majority, and therefore a voice
from heaven cannot control its interpretation, but neither does hermeneutic
anarchy result. However, R. Yermia's move only enacts once more the tesseration of context which midrash performs. The whole verse which he quotes
reads, "Do not side with a majority for evil; and do not distort the evidence in a
dispute by siding with a majority to side." My verbatim translation purposely
emphasizes the syntactic difficulty at the end of the verse with its extra and
unexplained occurrence of the verb "to side." R. Yermia's solution (actually a
common midrashic reading of this verse) is to take this as a tri-colon, reading in
effect: Do not side with a majority for evil; do not distort the evidence in a
dispute; follow the majority. By taking the last clause out of its context, he then
derives warrant for the claim that God Himself has authorized the rabbis to
overturn even the simple meaning of the Torah, in order to authorize their
interpretations by majority. Once again, God the Author spoke and did not (as
it were) know what He was saying: My children have defeated Me; My children
have defeated Me.

The irony is that the hermeneutic conservative, R. Eliezer, the one who
literally has God on his side, was excommunicated and exiled for his insistence
that the Author controls the reading of His text, while R. Yehoshua, the hermeneutic radical, ended up by inevitably supporting the institutional claim over
meaning and reading-practice:

> On that day, the brought out all of the things which R. Eliezer had declared
> pure and burned them in the fire and anathematized him. They said, Who
> will go and tell him? R. Akiva said to them, I will go, for if someone who is
> not fit tells him, he could destroy the whole world. What did R. Akiva do? He
> dressed himself in black and wrapped himself in black [mourning clothes],
> and sat a distance of four ells from R. Eliezer. R. Eliezer said to him, Akiva,
> what is different about today? He said, It seems that your colleagues are
> estranging themselves from you. He then also rent his garment, and sat on
> the earth, and his eyes poured forth tears.[41]

Our story is the story of a community in which interpretation was the central,
definitive act of religion and therefore of culture. Misinterpretation (from the
perspective of that culture's practice) was perhaps analogous to the violation of
ritual and taboo in other cultures and led therefore to the removal of the
misinterpreter from the society. The paradox is, of course, that the misinterpreter is the one who had the author on his side, and indeed there is independent evidence which suggests that precisely what characterized R. Eliezer's

hermeneutic practice was an extreme fidelity to received tradition. A great deal must have been at stake here. It seems to me that it would not be too much overreading to claim that what was at stake was the ability of the Torah to survive by being renewed, an ability which the "logocentrism" of R. Eliezer and his school would have threatened.

The paradox is at the very heart of midrash; a text is being cited that is supremely authoritative for both attitudes and behaviors, and at the same time the local meanings of that authoritative text seem to be undermined. Now, any attempt to read this paradox is a kind of reduction of its meaning; there is a sense of loss. But not to read it at all seems to be an even greater loss. And to assert that midrash is merely some kind of erotic play with the text would be the greatest loss of all. I wish to claim that midrash—the Oral Torah—is a program of preserving the old by making it new. The very surprise of the new meanings that were read in (not into nor quite out of) the Bible by the rabbis was precisely the means by which the Torah was prevented from losing its ability to mold ideology and shape behavior.

> "poetic quotations" . . . function as tools for building the cultural para-
> digm, for superimposing the past upon the present, thus reversing the
> flow of time. The poet [Mandelstam] himself conceived of poetry as a
> tool by means of which the past can re-enter the present. "Poetry is the
> plough tearing open and turning over time so that the deep layers of it,
> its rich black undersoil, ends up on the surface. There are periods when
> mankind, dissatisfied with its today and yearning for the deep layers of
> time, craves, like a ploughman, for the virgin soil of time."[42]

Midrash seems to have great appeal to many people in our culture. To some, midrash is perceived as a liberating force from the tyranny of the "correct interpretation." An alternative tradition to that of Europe's metaphysics, midrash seems to provide support for the project of deconstructing that metaphysics and its "logocentric" interpretation of texts. Our study of midrash suggests that another reason that it may appeal to the postmodern sensibility is not so much for the way it liberates from cultural exemplars (that work really needs no buttressing in our culture!), but for the way that it preserves contact and context with the tradition while it is liberating. The relation between the midrash and the Bible provides not only a model of the relation between text and interpretation but between the present and the past. It is not, then, surprising that modern textuality often structures itself by an all-pervasive, radical poetics of quotation. The Acmeist poetics of Mandelstam and Akhmatova, T.S. Eliot's work, and the *critical texts* of Walter Benjamin all provide parade examples of this practice. The latter also take up a place somewhere between scholarship and critical poetry, precisely defined by a poetics of quotation, which breaches and continues a tradition. As Hannah Arendt has described this:

> From the Goethe essay on, quotations are at the center of every work of Benjamin's. This very fact distinguishes his writings from scholarly works of all kinds in which it is the function of quotations to verify and document opinions, wherefore they can safely be relegated to the Notes. This is out of the question in Benjamin. When he was working on his study of German tragedy, he boasted of "over 600 quotations very systematically and clearly arranged" (*Briefe* I, 339); like the later notebooks, this collection was not an accumulation of excerpts intended to facilitate the writing of the study but constituted the main work, *with the writing as something secondary. The main work consisted in tearing fragments out of their context and arranging them afresh in such a way that they illustrated one another,* and were able to prove their *raison d'être* in a free-floating state, as it were.[43]

These modern texts are "fragments shored up against a ruin." They are produced in the wake of the destruction of a European culture a thousand years old. The rabbis, faced with the disruption of their times, the destruction of the Temple and Jewish autonomy in Palestine, and with the necessity of appropriating Scripture for their times, found in the creation of an explicitly and pervasively intertextual literature the ideal generative and reconstructive tool, which preserved the privileged position of the biblical text by releasing it from its position of immobilized totality. The paradoxes of quotation, implicated in the "general dialectic of cultural processes," were utilized by the rabbis as a way of *avoiding* the seeming necessity of "choosing between innovation and the duplication of canonized exemplars."[44] The midrash realizes its goal by means of a hermeneutic of recombining pieces of the canonized exemplar into a new discourse. In the next chapter we will begin to look at the intertextuality encoded in the Bible itself and at how midrash is a response to that.

· 3 ·

TEXTUAL HETEROGENEITY IN THE TORAH AND THE DIALECTIC OF THE MEKILTA: THE MIDRASH VS. SOURCE CRITICISM AS READING STRATEGIES

The previous chapter has introduced one of the central issues for midrashic hermeneutics: how midrash builds its discourse out of textual fragments as a biblical mosaic. This is, of course, a kind of intertextuality. there is another sense of "intertextuality" that will be most important in my readings of midrash. In the passage cited above, Gerald Bruns remarks that, "the Bible, *despite* its textual heterogeneity, can be read as a self-glossing book".[1] I would like to go further than that formulation and claim that the Bible, *because* of its textual heterogeneity, allows for the multiple self-glossing readings of midrash. The heterogeneity—the multivocality of the biblical text itself, its hiatuses and gaps, creatively but not open-endedly filled in by the midrash—allows it to generate its meanings—its *original* meanings—in ever new social and cultural situations. It is by now practically a commonplace that the narrative of the Torah is characterized by an extraordinarily high degree of gapping, indeterminacy, repetition, and self-contradiction.[2] This sense of the fissured quality of the Torah narrative has been treated by biblical scholarship as an occasion for diachronic study of the composition of the text.[3] The Torah has been composed, according to the "Higher Criticism," by cutting and pasting between several documents without the benefit of a word processor to smooth out the resulting infelicities.[4] This view results in a reduction of the tension of the text and consequently constitutes a loss for hermeneutics. Fundamentalist interpretation, on the other hand, has often been reductive in an even more destructive way, for by harmonizing away the tension, it has been lost entirely to the consciousness of many readers. The Higher Critics may be said to have at least somehow preserved the phenomena for a new generation of readers. Such a generation is at hand. Geoffrey Hartman has reinterpreted the Higher Criticism and diverted it from a diachronic into a synchronic issue:

> Our questioning of the unity of the work of art is not so modern as it seems. It imports an older mode of study into a new context. Throughout the nineteenth century the prestige area for philology was ballad, folk song, and other forms of vernacular oral literature. When philological research extended to the Bible, Higher Criticism was born, and instead of a unity of inspiration or composition, a multiplicity of "sources" emerged, held together by an anonymous process of compilation.
>
> *The sense that authors are compilers rather than creators is strong at present.* . . . Literary theory marries philology! Not quite. . . . [5]

Let us explore this point a bit. Hartman is turning the claims of the Higher Critics on their heads in a particularly elegant fashion. These had, in effect, claimed that the Bible is *sui generis* in world literature or practically so, in that it was not written by an author but redacted by editors. The goal of literary scholarship was therefore to reconstruct the original sources out of which the Bible had been redacted. Study of the text itself became merely a pretext for studying what was hypothesized to lie behind the text, both as literature and as historical record. What Hartman claims is that in fact *all literary texts* are characterized by compositeness, and in general "authors are compilers." Moreover, this composite nature of the literary text is not an issue for diachronic study alone, although such study can be fascinating in its own right,[6] but one for reading itself.

Now this view of authority gives us, as Hartman has realized, a powerful nonreductive way of reading the Bible.[7] If gaps, contradictions, otherness, dialogue are characteristic of all literary texts, then it will not surprise or disturb us to encounter them in the text which is the very prototype of Western literature, the Bible. As argued by Sternberg in a text anything but pious, the Bible encodes a divine author. In our culture, truth claim and knowledge of what cannot be known is an oxymoron—one signals historiography, the other fiction, but "in the Bible's sociocultural context, . . . truth claim and free access to information go together owing to a discourse mechanism so basic that no contemporary would need to look around for it—the appeal to divine inspiration."[8] It follows then that God must be understood as the implied author of the Torah. This is not a theological or dogmatic claim but a semiotic one. That is to say that it does not matter for our purposes here if the inscribing of God as author of the Torah is a product of human work and therefore a fiction or an effect of actual divine authority. If God is the implied author of the Bible, then the gaps, repetitions, contradictions, and heterogeneity of the biblical text must be *read*, as a central part of the system of meaning production of that text. In midrash the rabbis respond to this invitation and challenge.

God, the implied author of the narrative of the Torah, has willingly, as it were, encoded into His text the very kinds of dialogue that all of His epigones were destined willy-nilly to encode into theirs. As with all literature, so with the

Torah, it is precisely the fault lines in the text, the gaps that its author has left, which enable reading. The argument of this chapter is that midrash enters into these interstices by exploring the ways in which the Bible can read itself. The famous indeterminacy of midrashic reading—its allowance of several possibilities equally—will be understood as a figure for the possibility of several ways of filling in the gaps.[9] In the first example of an extended reading here presented, we will see precisely how this structure can be located in the text.

Gap-Filling and Midrashic Indeterminacy

The concept of the gap is a very important one in theories which attend to the work of the reader in the processing of the narrative text. Any such text cannot but leave out much detail, including much that is vital to a construction of the story and the characters. The reader must fill in the gaps, forming hypotheses about what is left out of the text. This notion has been much elaborated in varying theoretical frameworks by several recent critics.[10] The Bible is notorious for the paucity of detail of certain sorts within its narrative. Erich Auerbach described this as being "fraught with background". The gaps are those silences in the text which call for interpretation if the reader is to "make sense" of what happened, to fill out the plot and the characters in a meaningful way. This is precisely what midrash does by means of its explicit narrative expansions. I am extending the application of the term "gap" here to mean *any* element in the textual system of the Bible which demands interpretation for a coherent construction of the story, that is, both gaps in the narrow sense, as well as contradictions and repetitions, which indicate to the reader that she must fill in something that is not given in the text in order to read it. The reason for broadening the extension of the term is that all of these textual phenomena, when read synchronically, turn out to function similarly; that is, they are resolved by assuming that something has been left out of the text which can be restored by a more or less motivated activity of the reader. There is even a native rabbinic saying for this quality of the text: "this verse cries out, 'interpret me!' "

In our first example, we will see how the apparently unmotivated exceptionality of the action of a character in one of a series of similar situations constitutes a gap which the midrash reads. The exegetical context is the unusual statement, "And Moses removed Israel from the Red Sea" [Exod: 15:22]. Since all through the Torah the travels of the Israelites were directly commanded by God, our verse seems to contradict what has gone before, thereby setting up a gap which calls for comment. The midrash offers a series of interpretations of this verse:

(1) R. Yehoshua says, This journey Israel made by the word of Moses. All of the other journeys were by none but the word of the Lord, as it is said, "By the word of the Lord they camped, and by the word of the Lord, they

traveled," but this journey was by none but the word of Moses. Therefore, it says, "And Moses removed Israel."

(2) R. Eliezer says, By the word of the Almighty they journeyed, for we have found in one place, in two and in three, that they journeyed not but by word of the Almighty.

(2a) What is then the significance of saying [*ma talmud lomar*], "And Moses removed Israel," but to make known Israel's merit, for when Moses says to them, "Arise and go!" they did not say, "How shall we go out into the desert without any victuals for the way," but they had faith and went after Moses. Of them it is said explicitly in the tradition,[11] "Go and call in the ears of Jerusalem, saying, I have remembered for you the righteousness of your youth, your going after Me in the desert" [Jer. 2:2].

In paragraph (1), we find R. Yehoshua insisting, as he does regularly in the Mekilta,[12] on a rigorously literal reading. In spite of the fact that at every other point in the narrative of the Torah, the People are represented as being led by God in their journeys, since it says here that "Moses removed" them, this journey must have been at the prophet's instigation, and not God's. It is indeed remarkable that R. Yehoshua proposes no explanation for the *sui generis* character of this particular journey, only emphasizing the more his commitment to literalism. In paragraph (2), R. Eliezer argues for a nonliteral reading of our verse. His reasoning is that, since everywhere else in the Torah we find that the journeys were by the instigation of God and since there seems to be no reason for this one to have been exceptional, we must assume it to have been the same. Now, this is followed by an expansion of the narrative (2a) to explain the apparent statement that it was Moses who led the people this time. The reading suggests that, although it was indeed God who had proposed this journey as he did all the others, it was, after all, Moses who gave the immediate order which the people obeyed without question, even entering without provisions into a trackless waste on the strength of their trust in Moses. This story is then supported by the verse from Jeremiah which indicates that in the desert, the relationship of God and the people was an ideal one, a new bride unquestioningly trusting her groom and following Him, even in the wilderness.

This passage is followed by a text that has caused a great deal of difficulty for the commentators on the Mekilta.

(2b) And so we have found that their journey returned back on itself three stations, as it is said, "And they traveled from Pi-Hahirot and went through the sea, and they traveled from Mara and came to Elim, and they traveled from Elim and camped on the Red Sea" [Num. 33:8-10].

The text indicates that the children of Israel, after having left the Red Sea and traveled for a time, returned to the place whence they came. The internal content of this comment is relatively simple. A passage from Numbers in which

Israel's journeys are rehearsed is cited. In that passage it is stated that after crossing the sea, the people journeyed to Mara and thence to Elim and from Elim back to the shores of the sea, which is taken to mean, back to the same point from which they embarked. They have thus returned three stations: Elim to Marah to the sea. The exegetical status of the comment is thus in itself clear; the question is, how does it function in this context? Several commentators, observing that returning to Egypt is a symbol of unfaithful and ungrateful desire on the part of the people—one that reappears several times in the desert wanderings—argue that this passage is cited as tacit evidence *against* R. Eliezer's reading.[13] Or alternatively, some claim that it is out of place and belongs later on, where the Jews are presented as having rebelled and wished to return to Egypt.[14] However, both of these interpretations ignore the structure of the paradigmatic midrash here. Since the following statement (2c, below) is clearly one in praise of the Jews for returning to honor and bury Aaron, and it is introduced by the formula, "similarly"—a topos of similarity in paradigmatic midrash—we must understand this one to be also praise and not blame. The philological solution of moving the text will not work either, because then again the paradigm would be broken. It is clear, therefore, that the text must stand as it is, and that the return motif is here cited as praise and not blame.[15]

In order to understand this text we must recognize that it contains a double allusion to an earlier part of the Mekilta, that which precedes the account of the Red Sea crossing. We are informed there that God Himself, on one occasion, commanded the Israelites to retrace their steps: "Speak to the people of Israel, that they shall return and camp before Pi-Hahirot" [Exod. 14:2], and in Exod. 14:4 we are told, "*And so they did.*" Now, the Mekilta, commenting on this latter verse, remarks: "*And so they did*: They said, Like it or not, we must follow Ben-Amram [Moses]." In other words: on this previous occasion, the people did not want to retrace their steps, but they did so, because Moses told them to. Now, since in our case we can prove (via the text in Numbers) that the Israelites returned again, we have evidence that this return, by analogy to the previous one, was also out of obedience to Ben-Amram. Hence, "And Moses removed them"!

The other allusion is even more explicit, in fact it is a quotation:

> Rabbi says, Sufficient is the trust that they trusted in Me that for its sake I shall split the Sea for them, as it is said, "that they shall return and camp." . . . Others say, sufficient is the trust that they trusted in Me that for its sake I will split the sea for them, for they did not say to Moses, we have no victuals for the way, but they trusted and went after Moses. Of them it is said explicitly in the tradition "Go and call in the ears of Jerusalem, saying, I have remembered for you the righteousness of your youth, your going after Me in the desert" [Jer. 2:2].

In short, the second opinion is the explanation of the merit of Israel in (2a) above, and it is associated textually with the other case of merit, namely the retracing of steps, which, as we have seen, was also out of faithful obedience to Moses! Now it is clear why a statement about the Israelites returning could be used as a support for their merit in trusting Moses blindly.

It is important that the role of the verse from Jeremiah be recognized. It has both metonymic and metaphoric aspects. On the one hand, it is a comment on the nature of the righteousness of the people in the desert, and as such it can legitimately be applied (legitimately even in modern hermeneutic theory) in several contexts as a comment or justification of a comment on the motivations of the narrative of this period. On the other hand, in both passages its use also generates the actual narrative, for it is precisely the "going after Me in the desert" which is being narrated. Moreover, even the point about the people not wondering where their food will come from is generated by this verse, as it concludes, "in a land in which nothing grows."

A similar case in which Israel gathered merit by returning is then cited in (2c), in which the contradictions between passages in Numbers and Deuteronomy are resolved, and in the resolution a moral lesson is learned—a classic midrashic technique:

> (2c) Similarly, we have found that they returned to honor Aaron and to bury him, eight stations, as it is said, "And the Israelites *traveled from the wells of the Ya'aqanites to Mosera*, and there Aaron died" [Deut. 10:6]. Now, did Aaron die in Mosera? Indeed he died on Mt. Hor! as it is said, "And Aaron the priest ascended Mt. Hor by the word of the Lord and died there" [Num. 33:38]. What then is the significance of, "And there Aaron died" but to signify that they returned eight stations to honor Aaron and to bury him, as it is said, *"And they traveled from Moserot and camped at Bne-Ya'aqan*, and they traveled from Bne-Ya'aqan and camped at Hor-Haggidgad. And they traveled from Hor-Haggidgad and camped at Yotvata, and they traveled from Yotvata and camped at Evrona, and they traveled from Evrona and camped at Etzion-Gever and camped in the wilderness of Tzin which is Qadesh, and they traveled from Qadesh and camped at Mt. Hor at the edge of Edom" [Num. 33:31-37].

In Deuteronomy it is stated that Moses died at Mosera, while in Numbers it is stated that he died at quite a different place, seven journeys (=eight stations) later. Any interpreter who is not willing to assume that we simply have two contradictory sources for Aaron's death *must* in some fashion address the contradiction between the two verses. The midrash does so by exploiting the difference in verb forms used in the two passages, such that one can only be read as "died," while the other may be read as a stative/present, something like "lies dead." The problem is resolved. In one place, Aaron passed away, but he lies dead—is buried—in another. So much for exegesis—the hermeneutic element comes in with the interpretation that the Israelites returned eight stations in honor of Aaron, to bury him in a suitable grave. The moral lesson need not be drawn explicitly, and this is the beauty of the midrash. While powerful ideological messages are being drawn from this text, this cannot be called homily. It is not exploitation of the text; it *is* exploitation of the gaps in the text, which are there, as it were, precisely to be exploited. Note that R. Eliezer's reading is supported in another way, for in Numbers it is stated that Bne-Ya'aqan is the station immediately following Mosera, while in Deuteronomy the Wells of the Ya'aqanites, apparently the same place, was the station immediately preceding Mosera; thus a reverse journey is indeed indicated in the very text of the Torah itself. This is not a political reading of the text, but it is a reading which is alive always to the ethical/ideological implications of the text and of its reading.

The import of this citation is, then, that the Israelites here also were willing to return in order to perform an act of obedience and honor to their leader. We now see the exact paradigmatic structure of the midrashic text. The Torah provides (the midrash claims) several examples in which the Israelites were prepared to follow Moses back into the dangers of the desert, the Red Sea, or Egypt. This is then the highest proof of their great trust and faith in God and Moses in this period, that immediately on Moses's order they said "Lead me and I will follow after You,"[16] and this is why it says, "Moses removed them." R. Eliezer has produced a reading of the text, filling in the perceived gap in its narrative. This gap-filling, while not controlled by the text itself, neither is wholly unconstrained, but the product of strong intertextual motivations and constraints.

In (3) we begin a diametrically opposed filling of the textual gap:

> (3) R. Eliezer [!] says, By the word of the Almighty they journeyed, for we have found in one place, in two and in three, that they journeyed not but by the word of the Almighty.
>
> (3a) What is the significance then of saying, "And Moses removed Israel," but to signify that Moses led them with a stick against their wills, for once they saw the corpses of the men who had been working them at hard labor—all of them corpses strewn on the seashore—they said, It appears that no-one is left in Egypt; "*let us make us a chief [nittena rosh] and return to Egypt*" [Num. 14:4], and let us make us an idol, and it will descend at our head, and we will return to Egypt. Now it could be *[yakol]* that they said this but didn't do it. But behold it says, "And they refused to hear and did not remember Your wonders which You did for them, and they stiffened their necks and *made them a chief [wayyittenu rosh]* to return to their work . . . and made them a golden calf and said, This is your god" [Neh. 9:17-18]. [Lauterbach, II, pp. 84-85]

First, the argument against the literal interpretation is repeated. The gap will again be filled by additional narrative material. However, the alternative explanation given in (3a) is directly opposite to the one that was offered in (2a) above, and in the name of the same tanna, R. Eliezer![17] It was not the case that the Jews followed Moses blindly, faithfully, and trustfully into the waste, but quite the opposite; they were unwilling to follow him at all. They wanted to replace him with another leader, who would return them to Egypt. Moses had literally to lead them with a stick, and this is why the verse says, "And Moses removed them." This characterization of the moral state of Israel is supported by the cited verse of Nehemiah. The very story is woven out of our verse and the verse in Nehemiah, even more rigorously than it was above in the case of Jeremiah. Our darshan has constructed a narrative to explain why Moses had to lead them with a stick, but he has not woven his text out of whole cloth; his very warp and woof are quotations. He begins by constructing a narrative context, a *new* narrative context for the verse, "let us make us a chief and return to Egypt." This was not said, or not only said, when the spies returned with tales of the giants of Canaan, but also upon exiting from the sea. Note: the verse is not cited as a *prooftext* for their desire to return but incorporated as an *intertext*, made *part* of the story itself. The justification for reading this verse in a new narrative context is its association with the verse in Nehemiah via the identical phraseology, "Let us make us a chief." Since the verse in Nehemiah implies that this was said *before* the incident of the golden calf, the midrashist is justified in assuming another such incident, in which the people wished to choose a new leader in order to return to Egypt. The very repetition of this delaration of intention to appoint a new leader and return becomes then a strong verification of the negative reading of the moral state of Israel at this time. The whole story of what they wished to do here, i.e., after the parting of the sea, is thus constructed by reading the verse in Nehemiah in our context, where it can plausibly be placed.[18] The story continues after the verse; not only did the people wish to appoint a new chief to preside over the return, but they also wished a new god, again known from the verse in Nehemiah. Then the whole narrative is validated, again, not in the form of a logical argument, a prooftext, but by the incorporation into the narrative of the midrashic intertext, namely the verse from Nehemiah. This text is made the continuation of our story, i.e., first they planned all these things and then carried them out; "They did not remember Your wonders"—the splitting of the sea; "They made them a chief"—an echo of the verse from Numbers; and they made them a golden calf—quoted in our midrash as "and let us make an idol." The narrative of the midrash is thus not arbitrary but a subtle reweaving of cotexts into a new text.

Now that the text has been glossed, its structure can be interpreted. In particular the function of the cited verses becomes clear. We have seen that the verse from Jeremiah provides two elements to the discourse. On the one hand, it contains an explicit valuation of the people in their desert wanderings. In this sense, it is paradigmatic or metaphorical; it belongs to the substitution set of verses evaluating the nature of the period. On the other hand, the narrative element in the verse itself is expanded here into a specific story, by being placed into a specific context in the Torah's text; in this sense the verse is used metonymically, as part of a narrative sequence. The narrative of the verse, its record of a movement through the desert, motivates its use here to explain a gapped text involving movement from place to place. The verse from Nehemiah functions identically in the second version of the gap-filling. It provides an explicit evaluation of the people's state at the time, one that is opposite in thrust to the one indicated by Jeremiah. It also is used in generating the narrative sequence by providing verbs which signify moving from one place to another.

Once the correct interpretation of R. Eliezer's statement in its first version has been established,[19] we can see that it is directly related to the return motif in the second version. The relation is again a paradigmatic one, but of a different sort, for here the paradigm is created by contrast and not by similarity. In both cases, the Israelites say "Let us return," but in the first, the return is a sign of faith; in the second a sign of rebellion. In the first, it is correlated with the verse of return in Exod. 14:4; in the second with that of Num. 14:4. In the first, it is supported by Jeremiah; in the second by Nehemiah. In other words, we have a balanced, rhetorical structure in which two opposing arguments are made in more or less similar form. In this sense, the two texts themselves form a paradigm in the way that we have been using the term; that is, in this case, as a contrast set of two texts marked positive and negative for a given semantic value, namely, "return." In rhetorical terms, we have here antisagoge.[20] But this is not sophistry, a study in rhetoric: R. Eliezer's antisagoge is a dialectic with himself, which only lays bare the antinomy within the "tradition" itself and the Torah. The equivocation in his interpretation is an echo of the dual voices of the Torah and of its interpretive traditions within the canon.

If we outline the structure of this complex text, we will see that there are here several paradigms and paradigms within paradigms:

I. Israelites in wilderness: praise (+)
    A. Story of willing following of Moses
    B. Jeremiah verse
    C. Support paradigm
        1. Returning to sea: faith (+)
            a. verses of forward journey
            b. verses of reverse journey
        2. Returning to bury Aaron
            a. Aaron buried in Mosera
            b. Aaron buried in Hor Hahar

II. Israelites in wilderness: blame (-)
  A. Story of Moses driving them with stick
  B. Nehemiah verse
  C. Return: rebellion (-)

In the first case, what happened here (at the leaving of the sea) is revealed as a moment of great faith and trust on the part of Israel, via its association with what happened at the beginning of the people's very journey from Egypt, and this is woven into a whole narrative, as an introduction, as it were, to a positive reading of the entire wilderness period. The phrase, "Of them it is interpreted in the tradition," a topos of midrash, is crucially important for my reading, for I take it quite literally, as a statement that the tradition [*qabbalah*], which in this context always means the Prophets and Writings, contains *interpretations* of the Torah. The import of this tradition, which even positivist philology would understand as an interpretation, is that the going through the desert was a following of the young bride after her beloved and trusted groom. This reading will serve as an introduction to a positive interpretation of the wilderness period. The second version is based on an even more prevalent tradition in the Bible that the period of desert wanderings was one of constant faithlessness on the part of Israel. It serves as an introduction to a negative reading of the wilderness time. It follows that this text bears out the claim that the quotations in the midrash are not prooftexts but a major generating force in the production of the interpretive work of the midrash. The double reweaving, *both times in the name of the same tanna*, is thus a powerful evocation of the double reading within the biblical text itself of the story of Israel in the wilderness, which we will be encountering in the next chapter. The heterogeneity of the biblical text is revealed in the heterogeneity of the intertextual web of the midrash. The voices in the midrash are a literary representation and doubling of the antithetical voices to which the Author Himself has given speech within the Torah.

We accordingly see here how the gap in the Torah's narrative, the lack of motivation for the unusual formulation, "And Moses removed" is filled in in two incompatible ways by the midrash. It is the incompleteness in the Torah's explanation of itself which provides the space within which these antithetical readings can be created. However, the material for filling the gaps is not a subjective creation of the reader but rather a strong production of the intertext, which itself provides the antithetical possibilities for this reading. Unless the double invocation of the same tanna as presenting two diametrically opposed interpretations is a mere mistake (and at some level it certainly cannot be that), then it itself is a refutation of the concept of "creative historiography" as a production of the personal ideological stance or psychological bent of the midrashist.

In summary, the biblical narrative here encompasses within itself two antithetical evaluations of the same event. How are we to respond? The solution of source criticism is simple. We do not have before us a single text but a combination of texts, and it is not surprising, therefore, to find contradictions between them. For the midrash, as for anyone who wishes to read the Torah as a synchronic unity, such a solution is impossible. If we regard the text under the rubric of prose narrative, however, we can see that a divine author (the implied divine author of a supposed reading practice) could encode in His story the same kind of ambivalent evaluations that any author can encode in his novel.[21] The point of it, *ex hypothesi*, would be to signify some very real ambivalence in the events themselves.[22] In my view, this is the sort of reading that our midrashic text presupposes, although its authors would certainly not have recognized our critical terminology and concepts. The idea of inner-textual dialogue thus enables us to read both the text and its commentary in a stronger mode— not as the arbitrary and awkward combination of documents, but as the representation of ambivalence and equivocation. Whether we adopt a secular approach and consider these voices to be the voices of different groupings within Israelite society or whether we remain within the sacral world of the midrash itself which would assert that "both these and these are the words of the Living God,"[23] reading in the gaps of the Torah is a significant challenge to the reductions of so-called Higher Critical interpretations of the text.

Reading the Repetition

Another important type of textual gapping is caused by apparent repetition or redundancy in a narrative text.[24] This type of gap is even more cavernous when a story seems to be told twice and there is, moreover, contradiction between the two tellings. Again, the solution of source criticism will be the diachronic one of assuming two separate documents. The midrash provides us with a synchronic reading of the repetition. The Mekilta has an anonymous reading of the manna story which seems at first glance to be merely a series of homiletical remarks, related perhaps to the broad context of rabbinic theology, but only very thinly to the biblical narrative. I shall try to show that it is, in fact, a profound interpretation of the biblical text. The text is a reading of Exod. 16: 3-8:

> And Moses and Aaron said to all the Israelites: Evening, and you shall know. They said to them: While you are sleeping in your beds, God is feeding you. *You shall know that the Lord took you out from the land of Egypt*: Hence you learn that the Exodus is equal in value to all of the miracles and mighty deeds that God did for Israel. *Morning, you will see the glory of the Lord*. Hence you learn that He gave the manna to Israel with a bright countenance. The quail, which they asked for with full bellies, He gave them with a dark countenance, but the manna, which they asked for appropriately, He gave them with a bright countenance. [Lauterbach, II, p. 105]

Now midrash is, by definition, a text on a text. We must begin, therefore, by looking at the explicit intertext, the passage upon which our midrash is directly commenting:

> (3). And the Israelites said to them, "Would that we had died by the hand of God in Egypt, sitting around pots of flesh, eating bread to satiety, for you have taken us out into this desert to kill us with hunger." (4). And God said to Moses, "Behold, I will cause bread to rain down for you from heaven, and let the people go out and collect daily enough for that day, that I may test them, whether they will go in my Torah or not." . . . (6). And Moses and Aaron said to all the Israelites, "Evening, and you shall know that the Lord brought you out from Egypt. (7). And morning, and you shall see the glory of the Lord, when He heeds your complaints about Him. And, as for us, what are we that you complain of us?" (8). And Moses said, "By God's giving you meat to eat in the evening and bread to satiate you in the morning, by God's hearing of your complaints—your complaints are against Him. What are we that you complain against us?"

A first reading of this passage would suggest that the events detailed in verse eight—the giving of meat at evening and bread at morning—are precisely those hinted at in verses six and seven: "Evening you shall know—by God's giving you meat to eat in the evening" and "Morning you shall see—by God's giving you bread to satiate you in the morning." The reason that this reading is natural is that it is *literal*: the reporting of events means just what it says; and *iconic*: the order of signifiers in the text is homologous with the order of events signified. This is, for example, the reading of the great champion of plain sense, R. Abraham Ibn Ezra:

> (6). *And [Moses] said*: The meaning of, "that the Lord took you out" is, since you have said [in v. 3], "You took us out," behold two miracles [signs] are done for you that you should know that it is He who took you out, one this very evening and the second on its morrow. . . . (8) *And he said.* Now he explicated to them the two miracles.

The Mekilta rejects this reading in toto. Not only is the text not iconic in the succession of signifiers according to the order of the occurrence of signifieds, but even the explicit temporal expressions are not literal but figurative. Let us go back now to the text of the Mekilta, observing how its reading of the text turns from the "natural" reading, as of Ibn Ezra.

"Evening and you shall know that the Lord brought you out from Egypt" is not read as, "In the evening [when God sends the quail] you shall know [by this sign] . . . ", as in Ibn Ezra's reading, but as "Know ye—in the evening God is feeding you [i.e., raining down the Manna], while you are sleeping." The "feeding" here must refer to the manna, because were it to refer to quail, the statement, "while you are sleeping on your beds" would be meaningless.

Therefore, we must understand that this remark specifically *denies* that there will be a sign in the evening.

It follows that "that the Lord took you out" is not read as "in answer to your charge that we took you out, in the evening God will make you a sign, and you will know that He took you out," but as a figurative assertion of the value of the miracle of the Exodus itself. The text continues in verse six, "Evening, and you shall know." Since, as we have just said, there will be no sign in the evening, therefore the text cannot mean "This evening you will see something that will cause you to know." Since nothing is to happen in the evening but the preparation of manna for the morning, this invisible event must be the object of the "knowing." Ergo, this cannot be an indicative verb, "you will know" (how would they perceive that which is not given to perception?), but must be an imperative, "Know ye that while you are sleeping God is sustaining you," But now, since the preparation of food, the object of knowing, is denoted by "that God hath taken you out from Egypt," by this metaphor it is made known that the Exodus is equal to all other miracles.

Finally, "evening" and "morning" themselves are read as signifiers not of the order of the events but of their value. Their simple mimetic and iconic signification is interrupted and a more complex figurative-symbolic signification is substituted. "Evening" no longer means "this evening, before tomorrow morning" but "unwillingly"; "morning" no longer means "tomorrow" but "willingly." We shall explore below the means by which this substitution is achieved.

How can this deeply troped reading be accounted for? Is it a reading at all or a homily attached mechanically, playfully, or in bad faith to the text? The key to understanding this midrash will be revealed via exposure of a deep anomaly within it, namely the assertion that the meat was asked for with full bellies. How is such a statement possible on a simple reading of the Torah's narrative? The people are starving and are given meat and then bread. How can the midrash claim that the meat was asked for with full bellies? The rabbis must have read the story differently indeed! Their story is that the manna was given first and the people were sated, their need for food met willingly by God. Greedily, however, they did not appreciate the gift and complained of not having meat. They were given meat, but since their request for meat was inappropriate, the meat was given with ill will. If this is the plot, the discourse must have a much more complex structure than we thought. Once we have made this assumption, then it follows that no quail was given in the evening *before* the giving of the manna, and all the swervings of the midrash from Ibn Ezra's natural reading are accounted for, and in the process, important value statements are made.

What, however, is the source of the assumption that the manna was given before the quail, an assumption that violates the simple meaning of our text? Is it the desire to articulate particular values, as per the regnant descriptions of midrash as homily? I believe that this assumption, this fabula, is itself generated by reading, for I suggest that the midrash has before it another implicit intertext, namely the story of the manna and quail in Numbers 11. The fabula set out there is the following: The Israelites sit and cry for meat, remembering the good victuals of Egypt. They complain, "Now our throats are dry; there is nothing but this manna!" God declares that He will give them meat, but eloquently shows His displeasure: "Not one day will you eat, and not two days, not five days and not ten days. For a month you will eat meat, until it is coming out of your noses, and it will be disgusting to you. . . . " And then God provides the quails—and a horrifying punishment.

There are logically two exegetical options available to solve the question of the relation of these two texts: either they are telling two different stories or they are telling the same story twice. Either way presents serious difficulties, produces gaps which must be filled. If we assume that the same events are being related, it becomes clear that we are faced with a sharp contradiction. While in Exodus, manna and quail are asked for at the same time, in Numbers it is explicitly stated that the people have been eating manna for quite some time before requesting the quail. It follows that if this is the same story as that told in Exodus, we know very well why the rabbis troped that discourse so thoroughly. By interpreting in such a way that in the Exodus account no quail is given, this seemingly intractable contradiction is resolved. Nearly all traditional commentators on the relation of these two texts have assumed, however, that accounts of two different events are preserved here. But this way is fraught with obstacles as well. To make this point, we need only examine the difficulties run into by a sophisticated commentator, Nahmanides, who wishes to read these as accounts of two different sets of events:

> It is the opinion of our rabbis[25] that the quail was with them from that day and henceforth like the manna, and so it appears to me, for they complained about two matters, and in regard to both of them He heard them and fulfilled their desire. For what would He have given them or what would He have added for them by giving them meat for one day or two? The [reason] that the text explains at length the matter of the manna is because all of its details are wonderful, and is short in the matter of the quail—"And it was at even and the quail went up"—because it is a natural happening. And as for the matter of the second quail at Qivrot Hata'avah, this is owing to the fact that now it did not come to them to satiety, as it says several times, "bread to eat and meat to satiety." Or perhaps, it is because only the mighty ones were collecting it [the meat] or perhaps it was only available to the saints, and the lowly were desirous and hungry for it. . . . But the simple meaning is that the quail was intermittent, and the manna constant.[26]

Nahmanides struggles to render the two stories a noncontradictory narrative of

two different events, in spite of the extraordinary difficulties such an interpretation raises. The answers which Nahmanides offers, indeed the very fact that he
gives several, indicate how much of a difficulty there is in assuming that the
two texts on the giving of the quail relate two different occurrences. It is,
accordingly, not surprising at all that modern critical scholarship considers
these two accounts as parallel stories of the same events deriving from different
sources. George Coats, a scholar who has closely read the "murmuring" passages, details this position:

> Yet the outline of the two is similar enough to suggest that at least the
> accounts of the quail are parallel: (1) The people remember the varied foods
> which they had in Egypt. (2) Moses hears their reminiscences. (3) The case is
> in some manner presented to . . . [God]. (4) . . . [God] responds with the
> gift of quail. (5) This process is associated with the murmuring motif. Unless
> we are to assume that two different traditions of the quail existed without
> contact but nevertheless narrated their material in the same manner, we
> must conclude that we have parallel accounts of the same tradition. The
> differences in form and content could then be explained as the peculiar
> emphases of the two sources.[27]

Coats's solution is to accept the source-critical option, i.e., to claim that we have
the *same story* in two different versions. The midrash assumes as well that only
one account is preserved, but will not, of course, simply leave it at the level of
two accounts of the same events which partly contradict each other. The Book
has only one Author. A strong reading is required, then, to bridge the gaps and
explain the repetition of the two texts.

In the Mekilta, the discourse in Exodus is made to tell the same story in
tropes and narrative figures which is told in Numbers in mimetic order. The
very brief mention of the quail in the Exodus passage only exists for the sake of
the contrast with the giving of the manna. The event does not take place here
at all, but only in the future narrative to be related in Numbers. Since at the
time of the narrative of Exodus, the events regarding the quail are only *about* to
come, what the midrash implies here is a baroque version of the biblical structure of forecast fulfillment.[28] The forecast element is made explicit in the
Mekilta via the use of predictive language: "R. Yehoshua says, God said to
Moses: Before me is revealed what the Israelites have said and what they will
say."[29]

All of the elements of the midrashic story are related explicitly in Numbers:
full bellies, complaint about the manna, and God's ill will. There is more evidence that the Mekilta is indeed reading the Numbers text together with the
Exodus text to generate its meanings. In the next pericope of the Mekilta we
read, as a gloss on the verse; "At evening you will eat meat": "You contradict
yourselves. You asked for bread. Since flesh and blood cannot live without
bread, I gave it to you. Then you went and asked for meat, with full bellies.

Behold, I will give it to you, so you won't say that I do not have the ability to give it you, but behold I give it you, and in the end I will collect from you," a dreadful hint of the plague to come. Where? At the end of Numbers 11. And if that were not enough, the Mekilta continues its interpretation with the next sequence of verses from Numbers, as a simple continuation of the interpretation of Exodus! and as if to say that those verses are part and parcel of the same story. We have, therefore, practically explicit evidence that the rabbis do indeed see these two discourses as telling the same story.[30] Since, as I have shown, there is strong textual evidence that these are indeed two reports of the same events, we do have here a structure of repetition, albeit somewhat attenuated. We could locate this repetition at a redactorial rather than authorial level to account for the attenuation of the repetitive structures, but nevertheless a synchronic reading of these texts practically requires that they be seen as repetition. The solution of the midrash is a strong way out of an apparently impassable exegetical dilemma creating the opportunity for the release of meaning (almost the explosion of meaning) at the axiological level.

We come now to the very climax of the reading, the interpretation of evening and morning in verse 8. Since they cannot be read mimetically, iconically, and literally, as ordered signs signifying the timing and order of events to take place, they must be read as symbols, whose meaning is figurative. They are, indeed, understood (as are all symbols or arbitrary signs)[31] as deriving meaning from their binary opposition. This binary opposition of night and day is homologous to an opposition in values. Why is the giving of meat mentioned in Exodus at all, since it will not actually happen until much later in Numbers, when bellies are full with bread? The answer is that only through the relation of opposition to the giving of quail in the evening does the giving of manna by morning get its meaning. The midrashic text seems to repeat itself, saying: He gave manna to Israel with a bright countenance. The quail, which they asked for with full bellies, He gave them with a dark countenance, but the Manna, which they asked for appropriately, He gave them with a bright countenance. Now the clause "but the manna" is otiose, a repeat of "He gave manna," etc., unless we understand it in the way I have posited, namely, that first the simple statement is made to the effect that from the manna being given by morning we know that it was given with a bright countenance. Then the midrash shows how we know this, namely, because of the opposition in the next verse. We have here, then, a very early adumbration of structuralist semiotic, in which signs are read through their opposition to others. The traditional commentator on the Mekilta, R. Yehuda Najara, has shown a fine awareness by saying, "Since *this* was given in the evening but *that* in the morning, it teaches that this was given with a darkened countenance and that with a shining one." In other words, one signifier would not signify and only the two together in their opposition mean anything. Now it is clear why the giving of the quail is mentioned here even though it will not happen until later; it is in order to set up the binary opposition.

However, this opposition of bright countenance/darkened countenance is not merely an arbitrary opposition, but in fact a highly motivated one. What is the nature of these linguistic signs "bright countenance," "dark countenance"? How are they signified in the biblical text, and how do they signify in the midrashic text—aside from the bare relation of binariness? The first question has been partially answered. The text tells us that the morning is when the manna was given and the evening the time of the quail. Morning, when the day is bright, is a highly motivated sign for the sign, "bright countenance." Evening, when the day darkens, is a sign of the sign, "dark countenance." But what manner of signs are these signified signs? We could say—were the rabbis pantheists—that they are signs of themselves; i.e., that the morning *is* God's bright countenance, as it were, and the evening His dark countenance. (We would still be left, however, with the problem of knowing how these signs further signify God's mood.) Knowing, however, that the rabbis are not pantheists, we are induced to seek a more complex semiotic structure. One possibility is to see the giving of gifts at morning and evening as indices of God's mood because of something intrinsic to these times. This is the strategy of Rashi, who writes that since the manna was given at a convenient time, viz., the morning, when it is easy to prepare and eat, we may understand that it was given in good cheer, as opposed to the quail which is given at a most inconvenient time.[32] However, this interpretation leaves the linguistic signs "with bright countenance," "with dark countenance" without any significance, except as dead metaphors for good and ill will. Put another way, Rashi's reading seems to be: since the manna was given in the morning, when it is easy to prepare, we can see that God gave it with a good will. The phrase for good will is "bright countenance." However, the connection that we feel so clearly between the *phrase* "bright countenance" and the morning is unaccounted for in Rashi's reading. In fact, Rashi cannot be faulted for his interpretation, because the actual text which Rashi is commenting on, namely, a parallel to our midrash found in the Talmud, seems not to have known what to do with this connection.[33] It reads, "The manna, which they asked for appropriately, was given to them appropriately," removing the very connection between the sign of giving manna in the morning and the linguistic sign of "bright countenance," for which I am trying to account.

The most satisfactory reading takes the events referred to in the words "morning" or "evening" giving, as iconic signs of God's mood; i.e., the giving of manna in the morning, when it is bright, is a motivated sign of God's bright face and the giving of quail in the dark is a motivated sign of God's dark face. Better still, the fact that the Torah tells us that the manna was given by morning is a sign of God's bright face. But having reached this point, we still encounter a difficulty, for "bright" and "dark" countenance are metaphors. A face does not literally brighten with joy or darken with sadness. These metaphors are being radically literalized, as if to say that God's actions in the world can be interpreted through the metaphorical code of human speech. In other words, the rabbis make a theosophical inference based on their intuitive understanding of human language—indeed, a radical new meaning for the proposition that the Torah speaks as in the language of men! God gave the manna in the morning and the quail in the evening, *because we say* "He gave it with a bright countenance" to mean "He gave it willingly." Another way of putting this would be to say that such verses as "May God shine His countenance upon you" are being activated intertextually to render ideological meaning to a "historical" event, the giving of manna in the morning.[34]

In fine, then, we see that what at first glance are sharp distortions in the Mekilta's reading of Exodus 16 are in fact the results of its authors' attempts to interpret a seemingly contradictory repetition of the narrative in Numbers 11. A repetition (especially, but not exclusively, a contradictory one) creates a gap, then, just as surely as do details left out of a story. The repetition of the narrative in the Torah sets up an interpretive gap; this gap must be read, if the unity of the text is to be maintained. What is perhaps so special about midrash is the way that value is insistently *implied* through the filling of the gap, without, therefore, there being a need to explicitly paraphrase or translate the values of the story into a nonnarrative discourse.

Summary

If we re-examine now the structure of reading in the two examples discussed here, we can perceive the similarities between them in spite of differences. In both cases the midrashic reading is a gap-filling. In the first case, the gap arises from the ambivalent evaluation of the Israelites' behavior in the wilderness together with the unexplained anomaly of the Torah's narrative indicating that Moses initiated the move in but this one instance. The struggle for the text generates two mutually exclusive readings of the narrative, actually two mutually exclusive reconstructions of the very events. In the second case, the gap arises from the fact that what is apparently the same story is told twice in the Torah and the two narratives seem to contradict one another. In both situations, the interpreter who is not willing to adopt a diachronic reading strategy of dissolution of the text is forced to interpret—strongly or weakly. My claim is that midrash (as practiced at least in the Mekilta) is a method of strong reading of the gaps of the text, filling them, as it were, by inserting the intertext into them. In the next chapter, I shall further explore the specific workings of ambiguity in the Torah's narrative and how they are represented and dealt with in the Mekilta.

· 4 ·

DUAL SIGNS, AMBIGUITY, AND THE DIALECTIC OF INTERTEXTUAL READINGS

The previous chapter dealt with the Mekilta as a reading of the gaps and heterogeneity in the Torah's narrative. In this chapter, I would like to continue that discussion, focusing on the precise semantics and semiotics of ambiguity and the way that the midrash responds to it. I will here read closely the Mekilta's interpretation of a particular narrative of the Torah, in order to show that the midrash seems to be responding to ambiguity in the discourse itself. Moreover, I will try to show that the resolutions of the ambiguities which the midrash presents are not merely appropriations or preemptions of the text but rather choices made from interpretive options that the canon itself offers.

Michael Riffaterre has provided precise analyses of ambiguity and intertextuality in literary production. His most powerful notion is that of the "ungrammaticality," the awkwardness of a textual moment, at any linguistic or discourse level, which by its awkwardness points semiotically to another text which provides a key to its decoding. This notion takes us one step beyond "gaps" as the intertextuality of the production of the narrative text and into the possibilities of reading that text and its intertextuality. I am interested here in a particular kind of such ungrammaticality, the "dual sign," which by calling up two intertextual codes generates two possible decodings of the text:

> . . . the dual sign works like a pun. We will see that the pun in poetic discourse grows out of textual "roots." It is first apprehended as a mere ungrammaticality, until the discovery is made that there is another text in which the word is grammatical; the moment the other text is identified, the dual sign becomes significant purely because of its shape, which alone alludes to that other code.[1]

> The dual sign is thus the lexical equivalent (and because of its ungrammaticality, the hyperbolic equivalent) of two simultaneous, synchronized expansions generated parallel to each other, but separately. . . . Separated in the text, they are again united in the portmanteau word, whose hybrid morphology arouses the reader's curiosity so as to better guide him to the significance.[2]

This description of two expansions which grow out of the hybridity of a single sign in the biblical text is an almost perfect description of the midrashic text with which I will be dealing here. However, this type of midrashic ambiguity and its connection with intertextuality goes beyond the duality of a single sign, i.e., word, and reaches into the duality and ungrammmaticality of an entire narrative as a syntagm of many signs. Since I am explicitly dealing here with ambiguity and its intertextual decoding, I will put forth the midrash as a text *representing* acts of interpretation and implicitly commenting on them and not only the acts of interpreting that are represented. Accordingly, I shall here adduce a complete running text of the Mekilta on a whole narrative, in order to give more of the special flavor of a midrashic commentary. (My strategy will be to discuss the issues relevant to the main thrust of my argument here in the body of my text and leave other interpretive issues to the notes.) Specifically, I shall be reading here two examples in which the midrash, in its most typical discursive style, presents a narrative of the Torah in two directly opposed interpretations. I propose to interpret the "scandal" of the fact that the authoritative commentaries on the holiest text of Judaism are presented as a series of controversies in which each of two or more interpretations contradicts and undercuts the other(s). My claim is that the Mekilta is a metacommentary that through its organization provides an implicit theory of reading and of the biblical text. I shall try to show through this reading that the Mekilta is aware of true ambiguities in the biblical narrative, and that while each of the readers it presents work in their readings toward reduction of the ambiguity, the cumulative effect of the midrash as compiled is to focus on the ambiguity and the possibilities for making meaning out of it.

Verbal Ambiguity, the Dual Sign, and the Double Reading

The first passage involved is the story of the bitter waters of Mara [Exod. 15:22-26]:

> (22) And Moses led Israel from the Red Sea, and they went out into the desert of Shur, and they went three days in the desert, and they did not find water. (23) And they came to Mara, and they could not drink water from Mara, for it was bitter [*marim*]; therefore its name was called Mara. (24) And the people murmured against Moses, saying, "What shall we drink?" (25) And he cried out unto the Lord, and He taught [*wayyorehu*] him a tree, and he threw [it] into the water, and the water became sweet; there He gave him a statute and an ordinance, and there He tested [*nissahu*] him. (26) And He said, if hearing you shall hear[3] the voice of the Lord, your God, and do that which is straight in His eyes, and listen to His commandments, and keep His laws, all of the disease which I put on Egypt, I will not put on you, because I, the Lord, am your physician.

There are several ambiguities which can, I think, be located quite securely in this discourse itself. The first three are on the level of the lexicon. The adjective *marim*, here translated "bitter," is very similar to a verb which means "rebellious." This usage is, moreover, quite frequent in descriptions of the behavior of the Jews in the wilderness. Syntactically, this adjective can refer either to the (bitter) water or to the (rebellious) people. Another meaning, therefore, echoes ambiguously behind the surface reading. Next, the verb *wayyorehu* is quite surprising in this context. It generally refers in the Bible to verbal instruction and not the kind of pointing out that seems to be required by the context here. That would generally be expressed by *wayyar'ehu*, an entirely different verb. The similarity between the two verbs and the incongruity of the one actually used sets up rich ambiguous possibilities. Finally on the lexical level, the verb form *nissahu*, while unambiguously meaning "He tested him" in its written form, orally is homonymous with a verb form meaning "He exalted him." On the level of the narrative itself, it is extremely unclear what the nature of Israel's act is here. On the one hand, it seems to be presented as unwarranted rebellion, but on the other, wouldn't such murmuring be expected in a situation where, having been led into a desert, people seem threatened by death of thirst? Next, there is a major gap between the story of the water and its recapitulation in the verse, "There He gave him a statute and an ordinance." Where has the giving of law been mentioned or hinted at? In the same vein, the reference to the "diseases of the Egyptians" and God as a healer seems to be a non sequitur. Attempting to join the story and its moral creates various possibilities for interpretation, thus again giving rise to ambiguity.

The first series of comments on our passage deals with the nature of the water signified and with the cause of the failure to find water:

> *And they went three days in the desert and found no water.* R. Yehoshua says: According to its sound.

R. Yehoshua insists on a "literal" reading of the verse. The text says they did not find water, and that is what it means. This sort of reading is characteristic of R. Yehoshua, as presented in the Mekilta.[4]

> R. Eliezer says, But indeed there was water under the feet of Israel, for the land floats on water, as it is said, "To Him who spreads the earth on the water" [Ps. 136:6], so what is the significance of saying, "and found no water," but it was to exhaust them.[5] Others say: The water which Israel took from among the clefts was finished at this moment. What is, then, the significance of "and they did not find water?" Even in their vessels they did not find, as in the matter where it says, "And their mighty ones sent their youths for water; they came to the wells; *they did not find water*; their vessels came back empty" [Jer. 14:3].

This midrash is an echo of another one. Among the miracles which God performed at the Red Sea, according to the Mekilta, was "He extracted for them sweet water, from the salt."[6] It seems therefore that they were supplied with water at least for the first part of the journey. We must understand, then, that what happened is that they ran out of this water at the end of three days. However, this interpretation renders the language difficult. "They went three days in the desert and did not find water" seems surely to imply that they were walking for the three days without water and searching for it. So why does it say, "they did not find water," instead of saying something like, "the water ran out"? The Jeremiah verse is then cited to support the use of "they did not find" with the meaning that their vessels turned up empty.

Up until now, at any rate, both tannaim have read the water as literal water. However, the next reading takes the water metaphorically as a symbol for the words of Torah:

> The interpreters of *reshumot*[7] said, "They did not find water": The words of Torah which are symbolized by "water." And from whence [do we learn] that the words of Torah are symbolized by "water," as it is said, "Ho, anyone who is thirsty, go to water" [Isa. 55:1]. Because they separated themselves from the words of Torah for three days; that is why they rebelled. Therefore, the elders and Prophets decreed that they must read the Torah on the Sabbath, Monday, and Thursday. How so? They read on the Sabbath and skip the day after; they read on Monday and skip Tuesday and Wednesday. They read on Thursday and skip Friday.

In the discussion below, I shall attempt to account for the reading of the *dorshe reshumot* as a response to the several ambiguities of the Torah's text.

We find the axiological ambiguity of the biblical story sharply encoded as dialectic in the Mekilta in the next series of interpretive exchanges:

> *And they came to Mara.* R. Yehoshua say Israel came to three places at that time, for Scripture says, "And they came to Mara, etc." R. El'azar of Modi'in says, they came only to one place.

The basis for R. Yehoshua's view is the threefold repetition of Mara in the verse. R. Yehoshua reflects here the same literary sensibility as the modern commentator, Umberto Cassuto, who remarks on our verse, "The name of Mara occurs three times in the passage, for emphasis, corresponding to the period of three days, which underlines the length of time during which they found no water."[8] Both the ancient and the modern reader sense that the rhythmic, almost ponderous repetition of the word "Mara" in the verse heightens the growing desperation of the three-day search for potable water. R. Yehoshua, to be sure, renders this sensibility in midrashic fashion indirectly by narratizing it, while the modern interpreter remarks it directly. We can focus more precisely, however, on R. Yehoshua's interpretation. As we will see in the next section of this chapter, this tanna consistently reads the wilderness period as the one of God's honeymoon with the Jewish people. When the Torah's text seems to contradict this view, he interprets this contradiction away, occasionally with nothing short of hermeneutic violence. By reading the verse as saying that they were disappointed three times in their search for water, coming three times to Bitter Springs, R. Yehoshua certainly justifies, at least partially, their cry, "What shall we drink!?" Rabbi El'azar, on the other hand, is represented throughout as emphasizing the faithlessness and constant rebellion of the people in this period. He therefore insists that the complaining about the water here took place after only the relatively minor disappointment of not finding potable water in one place. We find the same bifurcation of their views represented even more explicitly in the next exchange:

> *And the people complained against Moses, saying, etc.* R. Yehoshua says, Israel should have taken counsel with the greatest among them first, saying "What shall we drink?"; instead, they stood and said angry words against Moses. R. El'azar of Modi'in says, Israel was schooled in angry words against Moses, and not against Moses alone, but against the Almighty. That is why it says, "*saying* what shall we drink?"

The tannaim are addressing a very real exegetical problem here. Why does the text pejoratively call their natural question here a complaint or murmuring? What could be more natural than this question for a people being led three days in a desert only to find bitter waters? R. Yehoshua answers by saying that they should not have been so quick to complain, but should have first taken advice of the greatest of their number (is Moses himself meant?); instead they immediately spoke angrily. This is the import of "stood and," i.e., immediately. R. El'azar says they were schooled, ready and waiting with angry words against Moses, and the question of water was not asked in good faith at all. Moreover, we see from the apparently superfluous word, "saying" ("they complained" is already a *verbum dicendi*), that they complained against Moses and even blasphemed. R. Yehoshua's explanation deemphasizes the pejorativity of the verb, "they murmured," while R. El'azar's emphasizes it. They are each solving the exegetical problem in accord with their readings.

> *And he cried out unto the Lord.* Hence, the righteous are not difficult of acceptance (or "complaint").[9]
> *There He proved him.* [R. Yehoshua says] There He made him great, as it says, "Ewil-Merodach raised the head of Yehoiachim" [2 Kings 25:27], and it also says, "raise the heads of the Gershonites" [Num. 4:22]. R. El'azar of Modi'in said to him, But indeed "greatness" is dependent on "shin" and here it is written with "samekh." What is then the significance of, "And there He proved him"? There God tested Israel.

The disagreement of the rabbis requires exegesis for the English reader. R.

Yehoshua takes "He proved him," *nissahu*, as if from the root *nsa*, "to raise," and interprets, accordingly, that God at Mara magnified Israel, as in the cases of aggrandizement in the prooftexts. R. El'azar counters that *nsa*, "to raise," is always spelt biblically with the letter "shin," but here the letter is "samekh," so it must derive from *nsy*, "to try" or "test." We see that these two views are again in accord with the general interpretive tendency of these two tannaim in reading our text. R. Yehoshua is presented as stretching for an interpretation which is favorable to Israel, while R. El'azar is emphasizing the negative aspects of these narratives. R. Yehoshua, who certainly was as aware as his colleague of biblical orthography, nevertheless exploits an ambiguity at the oral level of the text,[10] in order to maintain his "praise" interpretation.

The Mekilta next focuses its reading on the nature of the tree. By identifying the tree, it seems, a key to the resolution of the meaning of the story can be found.

> *And the Lord taught him a tree.* R. Yehoshua says it was a willow. R. El'azar of Modi'in says it was an olive, for there is none more bitter than the olive. R. Yehoshua the Bald says it was oleander. R. Shim'on ben Yohai says, He taught him a word from the Torah, for it says, "And He taught him [*yorehu*]"; "And He showed him [*yar'ehu*]" is not [written] here but "He taught him," as it is said "And He taught me and said to me" [Prov. 4:4]. R. Natan says it was a cedar, and some say the root of a fig and the root of a pomegranate. The *dorshe reshumot* said, 'He showed him words of Torah, which are symbolized by a tree, for it says, "It is a tree of life to those who grasp it" [Prov. 3:18].

Among these several identifications of the tree, we can discern two competing schools of interpretation of our text. One school identifies the tree as an actual tree, while the other reads it as a metaphor for Torah. Let us focus first on the "literal" reading. R. Yehoshua, in accordance with his general practice as presented in the Mekilta, argues for the simplest possible interpretation of the verse, reading the tree as the willow which would normally be found aboriginally growing near the water in an oasis. The other tannaim, however, identify the tree more specially. While it is not certain that this is true of all of the readings, it is certainly the case that R. El'azar (explicitly), R. Yehoshua the Bald, and very likely the "some say" are concerned to explicate the tree as one which is bitter to the taste. The oleander, in any case, is not only bitter but deadly poison.

The motivation for this interpretation of the tree, as well as its justification, can be found in the continuation of the Mekilta's discourse:

> Rabban Shim'on ben Gamliel says: Come and see how different are the ways of the Place from the ways of flesh and blood. Flesh and blood uses sweet to cure the bitter. Not so He-Who-Spoke-and-the-World-Was. He uses bitter to

cure the bitter. How so? He puts something which spoils into something spoilt, in order to perform therewith a miracle.

Similarly you will say, "And Isaiah said, let them take a cake of figs and spread it on the boils" [Isa. 38:21]. But is it not so that when you place a cake of figs on raw flesh, it spoils immediately? How so then? He puts something which spoils into something spoilt, to perform therewith a miracle.

Similarly, "And he went out to the water-source and threw in salt, and said, Thus saith" [2 Kings 2:21], but is it not so that if you put salt into sweet water, it goes bad immediately? How so then? He puts something which spoils into something spoilt, in order to perform therewith a miracle.

R. Shim'on cites two cases motivating his interpretation. Whatever we make of the story of Hezeqia and the cake of figs, in the case of Elisha and the waters of Jericho the explicit meaning of the biblical text is that Elisha is to "cure" the salty waters with salt. R. Shim'on has adopted a classic formula of paradigmatic midrash. In this form, a series of incidents or texts are cited under the rubric "similarly" or a variant thereof with a view to exposing the similar features of each case, thus establishing, as it were, a theosophical truth—in this case, God's paradoxical, supernatural behavior emphasizing His ability to perform miracles. In the passage from Isaiah, we find Hezeqia sick with boils. The prophet tells him to place figs on his eruptions, and he will be well. The rest is clear. In the passage from Kings, the verse continues explicitly, "And he threw therein salt saying, 'Thus saith the Lord: I have healed these waters.' " I rather suspect that the third case is the keystone of the whole construction, thus showing the value for exegesis of "paradigmatic" midrash. In other words, we learn to interpret the incident of the figs and our incident at Mara from the case where the paradoxical "cure" is explicit. Moreover, as Cassuto acutely points out, there is a series of verbal echoes in the Elisha episode which suggest that it is intended as an imitation (or interpretation, from the hermeneutic perspective) precisely of the Mara incident. "The passage dealing with the healing of the water by Elisha draws upon our narrative (see ii Kings ii 19-22); there, too, we find *and he threw*, as well as the verb *heal*."[11] If Cassuto is correct, and it seems that he is, R. Shim'on's exegesis, as well as that of the other tannaim who argued for a bitter tree, was already current at the time of the Prophet. We have here an elegant demonstration of how what appears to be homily is really exegesis of Scripture by Scripture. Even more to the point, this reading via the story in Kings solves the several interpretive problems that we have exposed in the Mara narrative. The "law and ordinance" are taken on this view to be the law of God that He cures the bitter with the bitter. I suggest also that R. Shim'on ben Gamliel's reading solves as well the puzzle of the unusual form *wayyorehu*. It is attractive to interpret the lexical ungrammaticality of *wayyorehu* "and He taught" as precisely a reference to the teaching, "Come and see how different are the ways of God from the ways of man." This interpretation of R.

Shim'on's midrash has already been offered by a very early interpreter of our passage, the author of the somewhat later midrash, *Tanhuma*:

> You find that flesh and blood smites with a knife and cures with a poultice, but the Holy One, blessed be He, is not so, rather, that which He smites with, with that He cures. And so you find that when they came to Mara they could not drink water from Mara, and Moses believed that the Holy One, blessed be He, would tell him to throw there honey or figs and the water would become sweet. But see what is written there, "And he cried out unto the Lord, and the Lord taught him a tree." It does not say, He showed him, but He taught him, He taught him His ways.[12]

R. Shim'on's reading is thus an elegant solution to the problems of coherence within the Mara narrative. All of the ungrammaticalities are accounted for. The form *wayyorehu* is explained precisely by the paradox of God's act; this is what God teaches here: His ways which are different from those of man. Moreover, this provides a solution to the question of the "law"; it is God's unnatural law to which reference is made.[13] Finally, the strange reference to God as healer is explained by the echo in the Kings passage where the waters are "healed."

R. Shim'on's interpretation of the story, together with that of the other tannaim who insist on the bitterness of the actual tree, thus chooses and activates the meaning "bitter" for *marim*. The contextual choice made by these readers is to interpret the story in the light of its nearly explicit intertext in Kings. This interpretation resolves several other ambiguities in the text as well, by providing a narrative coherence which the bare biblical narrative lacks. (This coherence is so clearly lacking that modern biblical scholars of the Higher Critical school split the text at the caesura of verse 25 into two allegedly incompatible documents.)[14]

The other interpreters, that is, R. Shim'on ben Yohai and the *dorshe reshumot*, interpret the tree metaphorically as the "tree of life," the Torah. Let us see how their reading works on the ambiguity of the text. As we have read above, the Torah line of interpretation begins by taking the "water" of the Torah's narrative not as literal physical water but as a symbol for Torah. This interpretation certainly looks on the face of it like an allegory, that is, an interpretation founded on the assumption that the text is about some "idea" (in the Platonic sense) external to the text itself. The outside idea would be, in this case, the idea of Torah. However, it seems to me that closer reading will show that this is not the only, nor indeed the most attractive, analysis of what is going on here. A crucial clue is that the several statements which make up the metaphorical reading of the narrative all cite verses from a single passage of Proverbs as their "prooftexts." That is, the *dorshe reshumot* cite the explicit metaphor about Torah: "It is a tree of life to those who grasp it" [Prov. 3:18], and Rabbi Shim'on ben Yohai cites "And He taught me and said to me" [Prov. 4:4]. Moreover, in a further interpretation of the "healing" as words of Torah, Rabbi El'azar of Modi'in cites, "They [words of Torah] are life for those who find them, and to all of his flesh a curative. It [the Torah] will be a cure for your flesh" [Prov. 4:21 and 3:8]. The claim that I am making is that these several citations of verses from the same passage of the Proverbs are not accidental, and amount, in effect, to a tradition that the difficulties and ungrammaticalities of the Mara account are to be resolved by reading them in the light of the figurative usages of Solomon's texts, which, as I will argue below (chapter 7), were taken by the rabbis as hermeneutic keys to the Torah.

This semiotic process can be described quite precisely. The entire interpretation is generated by the lexical ambiguity of *marim* and *wayyorehu*. Syntactically, the first reading of verse 24 takes the adjective as referring to the water. However, it is also quite plausible to read it as referring back one more clause to the "they" of the beginning of the sentence. Since "water" is a plural noun in Hebrew, the adjective agrees either with "they" or with "water." This secondary reading sets up a whole set of intertextual resonances. First of all, this adjective is almost identical in sound to one commonly used to describe the rebelliousness of Israel in the wilderness. Thus we read, "And they *rebelled* against me and did not want to hear" [Ezek. 20:8], "And they *rebelled* at the sea, at the Red Sea" [Ps. 107:7], and "How much have they *rebelled* against Him in the desert" [Ps. 78:40]. In all of these verses, forms of the verb *mry*, paronomastically related to *marim*, are used. Even more pointedly, in a parallel narrative of a rebellion concerning lack of water, Moses addresses the people in the following language, "Hear O you rebels (*hamorim*)" [Num. 20:10], using a word almost identical to our *marim*. Moreover, in other cases of etiologies for names of places in the desert, it is the historical event and not the natural condition that provides the naming; specifically, the name carries with it a memory of the rebellion of the people at that place. Thus, for instance, in the very similar story of a rebellion concerning water at Exod. 17:1-7, the place is renamed "Strife and Contention" because of the rebellious behavior of Israel. Accordingly, all of these subtexts provide strong motivation for reading the verse as, "They could not drink water from Mara, because they were rebellious, and that is why it is called Mara."

As I have indicated above, the verb *wayyorehu* also has two meanings, "to show" and "to teach," but the latter meaning is by far the more common one in the Hebrew lexicon. It is, moreover, the culturally dominant one, by virtue of its being the root of Torah. On the other hand, it is the unusual sense of the verb, namely, "to show," which is initially mobilized by the narrative context in the Mara story. We have, therefore, a kind of syllepsis in the Riffaterrian sense of a special kind of pun which calls up an intertext by the very awkwardness of its form. Following Riffaterre's description, we can see that the use of *wayyorehu* here is so unusual, in fact, as to form a dual sign. The dual sign is dual precisely because, by way of referring to two intertexts, it generates two meanings for the text being read. What happens in our text conforms precisely to Riffaterre's description. We begin to read the text by mobilizing the sense of the verb which the context calls for, that is, as a story of physical thirst in the desert, but the power of the other sense intrudes. The unusual usage of the verb *wayyorehu* comes to be read as an intertextual signpost to the passage in Proverbs, which then provides the rest of the solution to the mystery of Mara by supplying us with the metaphor of "tree" for Torah, as well as the explicit statement that the words of Torah are "healing"—that is, precisely the further difficult elements of the Mara narrative. These gaps and the success of the intertextual reading in filling them become a convincing authorization for taking the whole story in accord with the double reading of the verb *wayyorehu* itself. In effect we have two stories—one derived from the meaning "to show" and the other from "to teach". The second story is then to be read in the following fashion: They went three days in the desert and they did not find water=Torah (as in the Isaiah verse), and they came to Mara, but they could not drink water (study Torah) in Mara, because they were rebellious. Moses prayed and God taught him a word of Torah, which is a "tree of life," and the bitter waters (rebellious, Torah-less people) became sweet. There indeed, He gave them law and ordinance, and there He tested them, saying, "If you keep the Torah which I have, this day, given you, then I will not place upon you any more plagues like the plagues of Egypt, for the words of Torah that I give you are healing for you and prevent you from being rebellious and requiring such chastisement." All of the ungrammaticalities and infelicities of the Torah narrative are thus elegantly resolved when it is read as a series of metaphors, decoded through their intertextuality. Again, it seems to me that while there is a choice for the reader of *what* context to animate in order to provide some resolution of the ambiguities of the text, the requirement that *some* such activity must be undertaken is given by the text itself. The ambiguity is, therefore, in the discourse. Moreover, the particular choices of contextualization involved, while they are not necessary ones (quite obviously in the narrative at hand, since there are two of them), neither are they arbitrary, but rather seem to be actualizations of genuine interpretive possibilities that the canon offers.

The Mekilta continues its interpretation through to the end of the story. (Commentary to this section not strictly relevant to the argument of the chapter will be found in the notes).

> *And the threw into the water.* Others say, the Israelites were pleading and prostrating themselves before their Father in heaven at that time, like a son who pleads before his father and like a disciple who prostrates himself before his master, so did Israel plead and prostrate himself before his Father in heaven, saying, Master of the Universe, we sinned before you when we murmured about the water.[15]

And the water became sweet. R. Yehoshua says, It became bitter for a time and then sweet. R. El'azar of Modi'in says, It was bitter from the start, for it says, "the water, the water," twice.[16]

There He gave them a statute and a law. "Statute" is the Sabbath, and "a law" is honoring one's parents; the words of R. Yehoshua. R. El'azar of Modi'in says, "Statute" is forbidden sexual relations, as it is said, "Not to behave according to these abominable statutes" [Lev. 18:30]; "and a law," these are the laws of robbery, the laws of fines and the laws of torts.[17]

[Here follows the controversy on the meaning of "And there He proved them," which I have discussed above.]

And He said, if hearing you will hear. Hence, they said, If a man hear one commandment, he is given to hear many commandments, as it is said, "If hearing, you will hear." If a man has forgotten one commandment, he is made to forget many commandments, as it is said "If forgetting, you will forget" [Deut. 8:19].[18]

The voice of the Lord, your God. These are the ten words which were given mouth to mouth in ten voices [sounds]. *And do what is straight in His eyes.* These are the praiseworthy interpretations which everyman can understand. *And you will hearken unto His commandments.* These are the decrees. *And keep all of His statutes.* These are the *halakot.*[19]

I will inflict upon you none of the diseases that I have inflicted on Egypt, for if I should inflict them, *indeed I am the Lord your healer.* [These are] the words of R. Yehoshua.

This last paragraph is also difficult. It seems to involve a self-contradiction. I will not inflict, but if I inflict. . . . R. Yohanan's reading of this verse in the Talmud provides insight into his meaning: "Said R. Abba to Rabba bar Meri, It is written 'I will not inflict upon you any disease which I inflicted on Egypt, for I, the Lord, am your healer.' Now since He does not inflict, why should I need a healing? Said R. Yohanan, This verse explains itself. 'If you will hear the voice of the Lord'—if you will hear, I will not inflict; if you won't hear, I will inflict, and even so, indeed, I the Lord am you healer" [Sanh. 101a].

R. Yohanan expands the verse according to simple logic of implicature. According to this, R. Yehoshua's statement is merely elliptical, not contradictory. He reads the verse like those verses in which the most terrible curses are mentioned but assurance of ultimate salvation is promised. I will not inflict— but should you force me to—even then I will heal you in the end. The value of this reading is that it recuperates the whole narrative as a covenant institution in minature, with both the giving of law and a structure of blessings and curses (however elliptical) at the close. Just as in the other great covenant texts there is an explicit promise that even should Israel fail, in the end God will redeem them, so is there here.

R. El'azar of Modi'in says, *If you will hear* [=obey]. It could mean optional. Thus the significance of saying, "you *will* hear."[20] It is obligatory and not optional. [Another interpretation: *you will hear*; this is a principle in which the whole Torah is included.]

The voice of the Lord, your God. Scripture says that anyone who obeys the voice of the Almighty, it is accounted for him as if he were standing and serving in the presence of Him who lives and subsists forever. *And do what is straight in His eyes.* This refers to business. It teaches that anyone who conducts business in good faith and people are pleased with him, it is accounted for him as if he had kept the whole Torah. *And hearken unto His commandments.* These are the *halakot. And keep all His statutes.* These are the laws of sexual morality.[21]

I will inflict upon you none of the diseases I have inflicted upon Egypt. What is the significance of saying "for I, the Lord, am your healer"? God said to Moses, Say to Israel: The words of Torah which I have given you are a medicine for you, as it is said, "They are life for those who find them, and to all of his flesh a curative. It will be a cure for your flesh" [Prov. 4:21 and 3:8].

R. El'azar picks up here the metaphorical recuperation of our narrative, taking the "healing" to refer not to the sweetening of physical water but to the healing effect that words of Torah have on the spiritual and physical body. As noted above, his interpretation cites the same intertext for this metaphor as the other interpreters, R. Shim'on ben Yohai and the *dorshe reshumot*, who adopt this line of reading.

In a recent book, exemplary for its thoughtful and powerful synthesis of scholarship and theory, Lee Patterson denies that there is any such thing as textual ambiguity per se:

> Ambiguity is usually recognized as a characteristic possessed by the text, an uncertainty of meaning in fact present in discourse itself. But like other kinds of verbal meaning, whether fixed or indeterminate, ambiguity is also a function of reading: a text is ambiguous only to someone. As recent medieval criticism witnesses, there are many readers to whom no poem is ambiguous. Nor are these readers wrong in ascribing the meanings they do to the poems they interpret: indeed, correctness is clearly a misleading criterion to apply to criticism. Disambiguating is always, and properly, a process of deciding not what a text means but what we want it to mean. We do this, basically, by locating the text in an interpretive context, such as an authorial intention or a genre (e.g., Christian instruction, courtly lyric), that organizes meanings into primary and secondary. Put simply, by privileging one context at the expense of others we decide how the text's ironies should be read, whence they derive their authority, and against whom they are directed.[22]

According to Patterson everything in the text, including its very ambiguity, is a function of hermeneutic preemption.

Not surprisingly, Patterson's model reader is Augustine. Remarking that, "One of the great achievements of Augustinian hermeneutics is to make the preemptive nature of interpretation explicit,"[23] he cites very approvingly that Saint's claim that "whoever, therefore, thinks that he understands the divine Scriptures or any part of them so that it does not build the double love of God and of our neighbor does not understand it at all. Whoever finds a lesson there useful to the building of charity, even though he has not said what the author may be shown to have intended in that place, has not been deceived, nor is he lying in any way."[24]

Taking Augustine's rule of charity as merely making explicit the nature of all interpretation seems to me too extreme. Patterson seems to postulate that there are only two possibilities for theorizing ambiguity and disambiguation: either they are located entirely in the text or entirely in the reader. Are these two extremes really the only possibilities? Midrash is often portrayed as precisely the kind of radically preemptive reading that Augustine calls for and Patterson theorizes as the only available option for readers; that is, an interpretation the results of which are given wholly in advance and for which any distortion of the text is permitted to achieve those results. Indeed, both of the readings of the Mara episode in our Mekilta passage have been so characterized. Thus, for R. Shim'on ben Gamliel's reading a Realpolitik appropriation has been suggested by Ira Chernus:

> R. Simeon, too, obviously thought that the tree Moses threw in the water was bitter, but he went on to generalize the principle implicit in this detail and show its applicability to other biblical incidents. Here again we have a paradoxical pattern of divine action in history; did R. Simeon intend it to be a paradigm by which contemporary events could be understood as well? As the highest ranking political leader of his community he surely must have been deeply concerned with the political situation of his day, and it seems fair to hypothesize that this concern would be a major factor in his midrashic activity. Such an hypothesis sheds interesting light on this particular midrash, for it accords well with R. Simeon's political position and political concerns. Certainly R. Simeon found the rule of Rome a bitter reality; he is reported to have said of the Jews' sufferings under Rome: "If we had to write [them] we would never finish." Nevertheless he was against any further attempts at rebellion and urged his people to acquiesce in Roman rule. His motives were apparently compounded of political prudence, a concern to maintain his own position of leadership, and a desire to avoid further war. Thus he opposed any attempt to replace the bitter Roman rule with something "sweet"— either a conquering Persian government or a renewed independent Jewish government in Palestine. Rather he hoped to work through the existing government to improve the lot of the Jewish community; he hoped to use something bitter to cure the bitter situation.
>
> It seems plausible that R. Simeon stated the general principle implicit in the Mara episode to prove that he, in pursuing this political course, was acting according to the ways of God rather than man.[25]

Chernus assumes that the interpretation of the tree as bitter precedes logically and chronologically the association of our passage with the other ones and particularly with the curing of the waters by Elisha. He accordingly suggests that R. Shim'on's reading of the passage is externally motivated by his political concerns. However, I have tried to show through my reading that our narrative is one that *requires* strong interpretation if it is to be readable at all, and that it is precisely the passage from Kings which provides one possible and indeed very plausible line of interpretation for it, for the story of Elisha and the water seems to have been generated by reading our story. If my suggestion is at all convincing, then the ambiguities of our text and their resolution via the intertexts provide sufficient motivation for reading the tree paradoxically as a real and bitter tree. This does not argue, of course, that there is no correlation between R. Shim'on's political concerns and his reading of the Torah here. Quite the opposite. Chernus's hypothesis remains very possibly correct (whatever correct can mean here), but the relation between the midrashic practice and the other social, historical practices implied by texts about R. Shim'on ben Gamliel would be considerably more complicated than the simple one of genealogy that Chernus hypothesizes.

A similar case can be made for the other interpretation. This is generally read as the parade example of allegoresis in midrash, of a reading wholly controlled and motivated by an external ideological construction, the typically rabbinic ideology of the moral and spiritual efficacy of the study of Torah and the destructive effects of dereliction therefrom. And, indeed, there may be no question but that this reading of the Mara story is located in that cultural realm. The question is again one of explanatory models for that location. If previous scholars have read the midrash as radically preemptive of a simple and literal meaning in order to make its ideological point, I would propose, in the light of my reading, that the Torah authorizes such a spiritual reading of itself, via the gaps, ambiguities, and ungrammaticalities of its narrative discourse, although I will admit that the particular inflection of the midrash's reading in which all that is spiritual is referred to as Torah is a particularly rabbinic move.

Close reading of the Mekilta's interpretation of the story of the waters of Mara has led me to the claim that the ambiguities and gaps of that narrative are to be located in the discourse and not as a pure function of reading. Moreover, while the strategies employed to foreclose and reduce the ambiguities of the story are clearly an effect of reading, these are also not merely an arbitrary choice on the part of the rabbis of what they want the text to mean. These processes of foreclosure of ambiguity are also authorized by choice of different controlling contexts or intertextual allusions given within the textual system for resolving the local narrative and its axiological meanings. While the choice of context involves a complex interaction with ideology, that is, it may function as a moment in ideological production, the possibilities themselves for such choice are not merely arbitrary nor imposed from outside. They arise, once more, from ideological tensions which the Torah (and the Hebrew Bible as a whole) make manifest.

Voices in the Text

In the next passage which I shall be reading here, the Mekilta interprets the story of the giving of the manna. The Mekilta here again and on the immediately following narratives consists of the running commentaries of Rabbis Yehoshua and El'azar of Modi'in.[26] We shall find these two interpreters adopting consistent attitudes in the reading of this text—consistent attitudes which are diametrically opposed to each other. This seems to be a counterexample to my claim above that the Mekilta's reading practice is not radically preemptive in the Augustinian sense. It would appear that each tanna has decided *in advance* what the text must mean on ideological grounds and is now reading in a way that fits the idea. However, I will again read this consistent disagreement as a response to ambiguity that plays within the text, now not on the lexical level, but on the level of the *evaluation* of the entire narrative situation. The two alternative readings are generated once again by referring the current text to two possible intertextual codes which it calls up through its own heterogeneity.

The narrative and its interpretation begin with Exod. 16:2.

> *And the whole congregation of Israel murmured.* R. Yehoshua says: They ought to have consulted the greatest of their number, "what shall we eat?" but instead Israel stood up and said angry words against Moses. R. El'azar Hammoda'i says: Israel was schooled in saying angry words against Moses, and not against Moses alone did they say, but against Aaron, for it says, "And the children of Israel said to *them*, 'Would we had died, etc.' " They said: Would we had died in the three days of darkness of Egypt. (Lauterbach, II, pp. 100ff)

Both tannaim are faced here with the same interpretive problem as above. The verb "murmured" has a strong pejorative connotation, of rebellion and ungratefulness, but why should the question of the congregation have been characterized as such? After all, the people are indeed hungry, and what could be more natural for them than to ask, "What shall we eat"? R. Yehoshua answers this difficulty by minimizing and explaining away the pejorative aspect of the words; their fault was essentially one of protocol. Before complaining to Moses in an angry fashion, they ought to have asked their wisest man what they would eat. R. El'azar, on the other hand, enthusiastically activates the pejorative connotations of the word "murmured," and even enhances them dramatically. He claims that it was in the nature (or at any rate the nurture) of the people to be rebellious, and this act, therefore, was merely a manifestation of that tendency. Moreover, he even adds to the extent of the murmuring by arguing that they rebelled against Aaron as well as Moses. The two interpreters have thus taken diametrically opposed positions. One has read the text in a way least unfavorable to Israel and its actions, while the other reads it in a most unfavorable way.

We will see the same patterning of their interpretations also in the continuation:

> For you have taken us out into this desert, *to cause this congregation to die of starvation.* [*bara'av*]. R. Yehoshua says, There is no death which is more painful than death by starvation, for it says, "Happier are those who were killed by the sword than those killed by hunger" [Lam. 4:9]. R. El'azar Hammoda'i says, Ba ra'av[27] "Comes starvation": there comes upon us starvation upon starvation, plague upon plague, darkness upon darkness.

Again, R. Yehoshua reads in a way that reduces the pejorative feel of the verse. This accusation which the people are bringing seems both unnecessarily harsh and unjustified; the people have been cared for until now. R. Yehoshua justifies their tone as owing to panic in the face of starvation, which he calls the worst death known to man. R. El'azar, on the other hand, reads this statement as one of the most incredible of false accusations. Again and again you have starved us, sent plagues upon us, plunged us into darkness! What, in fact, are the events to which these people are referring? They are nothing but the plagues sent against their enemies, the Egyptians, which they now turn into the basis for an accusation against God and His vicar, Moses! R. El'azar accomplishes this hermeneutic feat by his characteristic move[28] of dismantling the word *bara'av* [of starvation] into two: *ba ra'av* [starvation comes].

The story continues with God's response to these requests or importunities of the people:

> *And the Lord said to Moses: I hereby rain bread from Heaven for you.* R. Yehoshua says, I hereby reveal Myself immediately; I do not tarry. R. El'azar Hammoda'i says, He says "hereby" only to mean by the merit of your ancestors.

The word translated "hereby" in legal contexts has the sense of volition, of entering into an obligation to perform an action in complete free will and good spirit, without any duress. As R. Yishma'el is reported to have said, "Wherever it says *hineni* [hereby] it is none other than an expression of joy."[29] Therefore, R. Yehoshua's reading of *hineni* as an expression of volition (for, as Yohanan Muffs has proven, that is what alacrity symbolizes)[30] reads as a straightforward interpretation of the verse, which is consistent, of course, with his entire reading of the passage. R. El'azar uses his "anomalist"[31] methods to make the verse consistent with his whole reading as well. He reinterprets the word *hineni* in such a way that he takes away its positive connotation of will and joy (as referring to the present situation) by taking it to be an allusion to the *hineni* pronounced by the righteous ancestors, as in the following texts:

> "And it was after these matters that God tried Abraham, and said to him: Abraham! And he said *hineni*" [Gen. 22:1]. Here I am, ready to do your

bidding.[32] "And God said to Israel in a night vision, Jacob, Jacob! And he said, *hineni*" [Gen. 46:2].

So God's response here was not at all joyful and willing, but grudging in the extreme. Only by virtue of the "merit of the ancestors" does God meet the murmuring of the people at all.

Again in the next passage we find the same two interpretive stances:

> For you: R. Yehoshua says, Indeed it is {not} coming to you. R. El'azar Hammoda'i says, He says "for you" only by the merit of your ancestors.

If the emendation of R. Yehoshua's statement is correct,[33] he is saying that the words "for you" in the verse are a further indication of God's good will in giving the gift of the manna. R. El'azar, on the other hand, turns "for you" into an apostrophe to those very ancestors alluded to by *hineni*, as if to read (taking the two comments together): O *Hineni*! it is for *you* that I rain down bread from the heavens, and not for these unworthy descendants.

In the next series of comments by the two tannaim, the distinction between their views is again quite clearly drawn in the midrash:

> *And Moses said to Aaron: say to all the congregation of the Children of Israel, Draw nigh unto the Lord!* R. Yehoshua says, "draw nigh," for the Mighty One is revealed. R. El'azar says, "Draw nigh" to be judged.

The positions here are very clearly delineated. R. Yehoshua interprets that the people are being bidden to draw nigh to receive this wonder, to behold the glory of the Lord, but R. El'azar holds that this drawing nigh is for judgment (and possible punishment is implied, of course) of their sins. The differing evaluations of the whole episode are thus sharp and complete.

This theme is continued in the next comment as well:

> *And they turned to the desert.* R. Yehoshua says, They turned only because the Almighty revealed Himself. R. El'azar Hammoda'i says, They turned only to the deeds of the ancestors, for it says, "the desert"; just as the desert has in it neither iniquity nor sin, so too the first ancestors have in them neither iniquity nor sin.

Both rabbis seem troubled by the turning. Why did the Israelites turn? They had been asked to draw nigh! Moreover, they are in the desert; how can they turn toward it? (This is a question which troubles current commentators on Exodus.)[34] R. Yehoshua's solution—characteristically—is that they turned to observe the wonder that was happening: "And they turned . . . for behold, the Glory of the Lord was seen in the cloud." R. El'azar—just as much in character—reads figuratively and relates the events to the ancestors and their merit. This turning was spiritual—to the deeds of these ancestors; it may signify repentance or appeal. The interpretation is "proven" by the figurative interpretation of "desert," similar to the other figures by which R. El'azar reads the ancestors in all these events.

Together the two readings produce the following picture. According to R. Yehoshua, the people were hungry, legitimately so. They asked for bread (admittedly committing a minor violation of protocol or etiquette in the process), and God answered them swiftly, generously, and willingly. According to R. El'azar, on the other hand, the story is quite different; the rebellious people acted according to their wont and rebelled. God would have punished them for this act of little faith, but the ancestors interceded on their behalf, and for the sake of these holy ones God not only desisted from punishing them but answered their prayers as well.

What could possibly motivate such radically divergent readings of the same text? Here we have a kind of crux for the interpretation of the midrash in general, a crossroads in which the nature of the questions that we ask will determine the nature of the answers we receive. One type of interpretive move would be to attempt to isolate a theological or ideological issue which divides the tannaim, having its origin, as it were, outside of the text, and assume that they are each pushing an interpretation in order to justify this theological position. The climax of this mode of understanding of midrash is E. E. Urbach's classic study, *The Sages: Their Beliefs and Opinions*, where he understands that R. Yehoshua's motivation here is opposition to the principle of the "merit of the fathers" (the principle that one receives undeserved benefits from God, owing to the meritorious behavior of one's ancestors), while R. El'azar Hammoda'i is firmly committed to this idea.[35] The weakness of this traditional research paradigm seems to me to be that it does not account for the role that interpretation of Torah plays in the formation of ideological and theological positions. Like literary research that considers the text to be a reflection of history, the literature itself is not perceived as one of the practices that *creates* that very history. We can exemplify this issue in our context by having a look at a passage we have not considered as yet. On Exod. 16:4 ["And let every person gather a day's portion on the day, in order that I may test them whether they will go in my Torah or not"], we have the following controversy in the Mekilta:

> *A day's portion on the day*: R. Yehoshua says: This means a person may gather on one day the portion for the next day, just as is done on the eve of Sabbath for the Sabbath. R. El'azar Hammoda'i says: This means that a person may not gather on one day the portion for the next day, as is done on the eve of Sabbath for the Sabbath. For it says, "A day's portion on the day"; He who created the day created its sustenance. From here, R. El'azar used to say, He who has enough to eat for today and says, "What will I eat tomorrow?" is one of little faith. For it is said, *"That I may test them, whether they will go in my Torah or not."* R. Yehoshua says: If a person studies two *halakot* [paragraphs of the Torah] in the morning and two in the evening and the whole day occu-

pies himself with his trade, it is accounted for him as if he had fulfilled the whole Torah. [Lauterbach, II, p. 103]

The tannaim differ in their interpretation of the ambiguous "a day's portion on the day." R. Yehoshua takes it to mean that one may provide today for tomorrow's needs, while R. El'azar understands that one may only provide for today today and have faith that tomorrow will be taken care of. Their interpretations are immediately reflected in their prescriptive practices. R. El'azar, in accordance with his view, claims that one who has enough for immediate needs, and not being sure of tomorrow, continues to exert himself in searching for sustenance rather than studying Torah, is one of little faith. Such a one has failed the test of "whether they will go in my Torah or not," analogously to one who in the days of the desert wanderings would have gathered manna for tomorrow. R. Yehoshua, on the other hand, holds that one should devote oneself to livelihood, even beyond immediate needs, and the test is that, after having one's needs provided for will one find some time for Torah or not, just as in the desert, the Jews had their needs provided for tomorrow as well, and the question was will they *then* "walk in my Torah" or not. Now, we can adopt two approaches to this disagreement. We could assume that the attitudes held by the two tannaim derive from external ideological positions which force their readings, or we could assume that something within the text stimulates the different readings (or at any rate, the very fact of difference in readings) and promotes the different practices. At any rate, it should be noted that the midrashic text itself claims that this reading was the *source* and not the *effect* of R. El'azar's position. The two positions here are certainly in concord with the two readings of the whole story. R. El'azar projects a very extreme pietistic requirement which would make any complaint of hunger into a rebellion, while R. Yehoshua's position regarding livelihood would mitigate strongly any pejorative connotations in the request for bread. We see, therefore, that the disagreement here is embedded in a consistent bifurcation of their readings of the whole complex of narratives in this section of the Torah.

But what generates that bifurcation in the reading? I would like to suggest that the difference of the tannaitic readings, far from being an extratextual issue situated, as it were, in tannaitic times, is a profound response to and doubling of a tension within the biblical text itself.[36] Brevard Childs, along with many other modern commentators, has noted this tension. Childs begins by establishing that the tension is not only in one narrative but in the canon as a whole:

Perhaps the most basic traditio-historical problem of the wilderness tradition has to do with the role of the murmuring motif, which, although it is completely missing from some of the stories [Exod. 17:8ff.; 18:1ff.], increasingly becomes the rubric under which these stories were interpreted [Deut. 9:22ff.; Ps. 78]. The problem arises from the apparent divergence within the Old Testament in the understanding of the wilderness period. . . . On the one hand, both within the Pentateuch and elsewhere, the wilderness period was condemned as a proof of Israel's early disobedience and repeated rebellion against God. On the other hand, there are strands within the Pentateuch [Exod. 16] and explicit references in the prophets [Hos. 2:16, EVV 14; Jer. 2:2] which give an apparently positive interpretation of the period.[37] Indeed, it is characterized as a "honeymoon" before the corruption of idolatry set in, caused by contamination with the Canaanites.[38]

These data provide in themselves a powerful explanation for the tannaitic controversy here documented. Our text, Exodus 16, is unique in the Pentateuch, in Childs's view, in manifesting the positive interpretation of Israel in the wilderness, and there are strong and unambiguous voices in other texts which hold the exact opposite position: "You have been rebellious against the Lord from the day that I knew you" [Deut. 9:24]. And even more to the point: "And they tried God in their hearts by asking for bread for their throats, and spoke against God, saying, 'Will God be able to set a table in the desert?' " [Ps. 78:18-19]. We can thus interpret that R. Yehoshua, responding, as he often does, to the indices within the local text, reads the story as positive, while R. El'azar takes more account of the larger narrative and axiological context. Can we go further in accounting for the two contrary readings?

To answer this question, we must look again at the exegeses of the two tannaim on the micro-level of the individual verses. The key is that each of them has read some verses in what appears to be a simple and straightforward manner while adopting apparently forced readings of other verses. Thus, on the one hand, in order to support his reading, R. Yehoshua troped the usual interpretation of the word "murmured," with its strong negative connotations of conspiracy and rebellion, and moreover felt bound to provide apologetic for the ungrateful accusation that Moses had taken the people out of Egypt to kill them by starvation in the wilderness. On the other hand, in order to support his reading, R. El'azar was forced to read such words as "*hineni*" and "for you," seemingly a gracious and free-will response on the part of God to the people's prayer, in a completely anomalous fashion, i.e., by totally ignoring their syntactic contexts. Since, in order to read it harmoniously, this biblical text seems to force any reader to distort the language of some of its parts, it can be said to contradict itself in its evaluation of these events. To be sure, the narrative of Exodus 16 leans heavily toward the positive interpretation of the events (and, therefore, R. El'azar's readings are so much more heavily troped than his colleague's), but nevertheless, there is a tension within it between indications of a positive reading and those which suggest a negative reading. This tension has been felt by many commentators, including Nahmanides, who writes:

> *I have heard the murmurings of the children of Israel. Say to them, at evening* [16:12]: This discourse has already been said by Moses to Israel [above in verse 8], but it is repeated because He said, "I have heard the murmurings of the children of Israel," for in the beginning He said, "I hereby cause bread to

rain down for you," as one who does a favor for them, or because of their
merit, and now He says that it is accounted for them as a sin, and because of
this murmuring He will do thus with them, that they should know that "I am
the Lord your God," for until now you do not believe.

Our story of the manna, in Exodus 16 (and indeed all of the texts to a
greater or lesser degree) is heterogeneous.[39] On the one hand, there are the
ample indices of a story of need, complaint, prayer, and miracle, which
dominate the text; on the other, the initial murmuring with its strong over-
tones of exaggeration and rebellion ("If only we had died by the hand of the
Lord in the land of Egypt, when we sat by the fleshpots and ate our fill of
bread. For you have brought us out into this wilderness to starve this whole
congregation to death"). Looked at from a literary-critical perspective (syn-
chrony), rather than a literary-historical perspective (diachrony), the text is
polyphonic.[40] Built into its very structure is contradiction and opposition.
Here and all through the canon, there is a dialogue of voices evaluating the
wilderness period, a voice which proclaims that it was the time of the greatest love of Israel for her God and a voice which cries out that under the very
marriage canopy, as it were, Israel was unfaithful to her Groom. Each tanna
hears only one of these voices.

The double-voicedness of the Exodus narrative doubly inscribes itself in two
different genres. On the one hand, there is a series of narratives in the Torah,
which tells a story of the people's need in the desert, their (or Moses's) prayer,
and God's fulfilling of the need. These narratives are ideologically consistent
with the view of the Israelites' behavior in the desert as praiseworthy. The use
of the language of free-willed gift of the manna in our story seems to place our
text within the intertextual code of this genre. On the other hand, there is
another collection of narratives which tells a story of unwarranted complaint
on the part of the people and God's answering the complaint by ironically
fulfilling the false need together with a terrible punishment. Our story seems to
belong to the first pattern. As Childs has insightfully remarked, the verb "murmured" in both of our narratives creates a contradictory or ambiguous moment within the narrative by referring intertextually to the blame series. Each
of the tannaim may be said, therefore, "to smooth 'the troubled passage between text and reader' by soothing the contradictions within the text."[41] The
midrash, however, as an edited text, does not soothe these contradictions.
Quite the opposite, by presenting two diametrically opposed views, it manifests
a powerful awareness of ambiguity as built into the text itself and not as a pure
function of reading.

Each of the tannaim indeed hears only one of the "voices in the text." The
Mekilta, on the other hand, hears both voices. We do not have only two antithetical views of what the Torah means, as if in two separate books. What we

have is one text, *Mekilta Wayyassa*, in which both of these views are articulated together. The midrash is thus heterogeneous in the same way as the Torah is. Rabbis Yehoshua and El'azar can be read as hypostases, as personifications of the voices that *we* hear within the Torah itself.[42] It becomes unnecessary to reduce their controversies to polemics and ideological differences grounded in their historical circumstance—even in this most explicitly value-laden of substantive hermeneutic controversies—when we see that these controversies arise from within the text as encoded by its very Author Himself, and we are no more (or even less) justified in such a reduction than we are in reducing the different readings of a great work of secular literature[43] to the political differences of its readers.[44] The interplay between the hermeneutic practice and other cultural/social/political ideologies and practices is complex and dynamic, with each area of practice affecting the others and affected by them.

Patterson seems then to be confuted by this text in his claim that ambiguity is located only in the reader's work. This ambiguity can, it appears, be located in the text. However, it could be argued as well that my analysis *confirms* Patterson's theoretical point, since each of the readings in the Mekilta denies ambiguity. Put in other words, I believe that Patterson is arguing that since "for some readers no text is ambiguous," this puts into question the very idea of a *textual* ambiguity as such, placing my (perhaps by now, our) perception of ambiguity on precisely the same epistemological level as those readings which foreclose that ambiguity. I think that I can counter that argument in two ways. First of all, the energy which the tannaim must expend in order to read the text, the penetration and boldness of the hermeneutic moves required to rationalize the ambiguity, serve not to hide or deny that ambiguity but rather to dialectically reveal it. Thus Geoffrey Hartman has argued that "the heterogeneity of poem or original text by no means disappears in the older hermeneutics, but it appears only by way of the daring interpretation that is startling and even liberating in its very drive for harmony."[45] Each of the tannaitic interpretations, in order to drive toward a harmonious understanding of the nature of Israel in this time, is forced to distort the local meanings of certain passages. The strength of these harmonistic readings is placed into relief by contrast to the weak harmonistic way in which later midrash deals with these contradictions. The later tradition almost invariably assigns the positive indices within the Torah to the "true Israel" and the negative ones to the "mixed multitude." The refusal of the Mekilta to adopt this reading is a strong affirmation of the complexity and polyphony of the Torah.[46] Thus R. Yehoshua, usually presented in the Mekilta as a proponent of "plain" reading, here presents several very daring interpretations in his desire to understand the story in the light of the "honeymoon" tradition of Israel and God at this period, while R. El'azar works to emphasize the evil of their ways, e.g., by turning their murmuring against Moses into a full-scale blasphemy against God. Each of these interpretations, by the very distortion necessary for its maintenance, forces us to recognize the ambiguity encoded in the narrative. Sternberg has remarked on the function of such ambiguities in the Bible:

> The coexistence of two (or more) mutually exclusive hypotheses—concerning action, motive, character—always enables the author to kill two birds with one stone, using the same materials for different ends. Above all, it enables him to base sequence and effect on the tensions between the two possibilities. Each reading may serve to balance and ironize the other. The emergence of such a hypothesis in a text that equally validates its contrary renders each quite unlike a similar hypothesis appearing unchallenged.[47]

If this is true of the literary text itself, then it is true, as well, of the midrashic text, which doubles the ambiguity of the Torah's narrative with its own dialectic. Thus, each of the tannaitic interpretations in the Mekilta can be said to balance and ironize the other, and it is certainly the case that the presentation of one interpretation in a commentary that equally validates its contrary renders each quite unlike a similar interpretation appearing unchallenged. The effect of the midrashic text as a whole is to present a view of textuality that occupies neither the extreme of assuming a univocal "correct" reading of the text, nor the extreme of "whoever finds a lesson there useful to the building of charity, even though he has not said what the author may be shown to have intended in that place, has not been deceived, nor is he lying in any way." Rather, the midrash seems to present the view of an ancient reader who perceives ambiguity encoded in the text itself with various dialectical possibilities for reducing that ambiguity, each contributing to but not exhausting its meaning(s). Our midrashic text here is, in effect, occupying the position of Sternberg the critic himself, observing and commenting on the too single-minded resolutions of the text's ambiguity. It is in that sense that I have referred to it as "metacommentary." Moreover, the Mekilta does not speak discursively and abstractly in metalanguage *about* the ambiguity of the Torah. It represents the tension and inner dialogue of the biblical narrative by tension and inner dialogue of its own, providing us with an elegant precursor of Harold Bloom's famous remark, "*All interpretation depends upon the antithetical relation between meanings, and not on the supposed relation between a text and its meaning.*"[48] However, intertextuality is a much more complex notion than this. It is also a matter of the deep-seated ideological codes which determine and allow for any cultural practice. In the next chapters, I will begin to locate the workings of the intertext in this latter sense in the Mekilta's reading.

· 5 ·

INTERPRETING IN ORDINARY LANGUAGE: THE MASHAL AS INTERTEXT

Up to this point, I have tried to show how midrash can be understood as an intertextual reading practice, founded on the intuition that the Bible is a self-glossing text. The Mekilta uses other parts of the Bible to read the Exodus in several different ways. I have suggested that these structures can be read as manifesting the two basic organizing principles of language—paradigms and syntagms. In this and the next chapters, I will be reading the major genre of syntagmatic midrash. This kind of midrash, the mashal, does its hermeneutic work by recasting diverse texts into a narrative, which then frames and contextualizes the verse to be interpreted.

The term "mashal" is often glossed "parable", and indeed there is good reason for this. First of all, as has been conclusively shown by David Flusser, the parables of the Gospels belong certainly to the same tradition as the mashal in rabbinic literature.[1] Second, the very term *parabole* translates the Hebrew in the Septuagint and the Gospels. However, there are also very great differences in semiotic structure between the parable of the Gospel and the mashal of the midrash. In order to show better the structure of the mashal, I will begin by discussing its differences from the parable.

Susan Wittig has written a very clear analysis of the semiosis of the Gospel parable and its congeners in later Western literature.[2] Her thesis is that in normal denotation a sign vehicle refers to a *denotatum*, "which has or could have physical existence in the extralinguistic world (e.g., 'The householder went out early in the morning to hire workers for his vineyard')." In the parabolic system, however, the denotatum, in turn, becomes a sign in itself, "designating an *unstated designatum*, a conceptual referent which exists only in a world of moral and physiological abstraction, which cannot be perceived in the extralinguistic world, and which must be supplied by the perceiver of the sign (e.g., 'The spirit of God at the beginning of time began to seek out righteous men')":[3]

> The structure of this duplex semiotic gains its energy and effectiveness from the nature of the semantic relationships which link its components. The first order linguistic sign vehicle is linked *conventionally* and *arbitrarily* to its de-

notatum, as are nearly all linguistic signs; the second order material sign vehicle, however, is linked *iconically* to its object in the same way that the structure of a diagram formally exemplifies and exhibits the structure of its object.[4]

In Wittig's description the parable is allegorical in its structure. A structure is created in language which is interpreted through the reference of its signified to another signified that resembles it in some way or other. Moreover, Wittig argues that the parable is, in the phrase of Wolfgang Iser, an indeterminate text, one marked by "*hiatus*—the lack of syntactic or semantic connections—and 'indeterminacy'—the omission of detail—and which invite(s) the reader to establish his own connections between the lines of the text, so to speak, and to create his own significant detail, when the text does not offer it."[5] The parables of the Gospels are in Wittig's view just such texts. The "indeterminacy" of meaning is suggested by the fact that the "second order denotatum" is not stated in the text. (It should be made clear, incidentally, that this analysis is governed by the assumption—common but nevertheless an assumption—that the applications of the parables in the Gospels are not an original part of the text. If the application is an original part of the parable, then it can hardly be described as an open text.) The reader, by being forced to interpret such texts, comes up against his/her own "expectations and preconceptions—his own meaning-system."[6] Then:

> In semiotic terms, such texts are self-reflexive in a metacommunicative di-
> mension, calling to our attention not their syntactic or semantic structures,
> but the variety of ways in which those structures are actualized in our minds
> [and] are made to yield their potential meanings. When we read a text
> characterized by the quality of indeterminacy, as the parables are, we are
> reading ourselves as well as the text, and are being forced to an awareness of
> the creation of meaning in our own minds, as well as to an awareness of the
> meaning itself.[7]

Now, whether or not Wittig's characterization of the Gospel parables as "indeterminate" texts is successful[8] in any case the midrashic mashal manifests a completely different structure—which is not, of course, a criticism of her work. Let us go back to the example that I have discussed briefly in chapter 2 and see the differences which this text shows from Wittig's description (and from the parables, if she is correct). I will quote the text again:

> *And the angel of God, going before the camp of Israel, moved and went behind them.*
> *And the pillar of cloud moved from before them and went behind them* [Exod. 14:19].
> R. Yehuda said: This is a Scripture enriched from many places. He made of it
> a mashal; to what is the matter similar? To a king who was going on the way,
> and his son went before him. Brigands came to kidnap him from in front. He
> took him from in front and placed him behind him. A wolf came behind him.
> He took him from behind and placed him in front.

Brigands in front and the wolf in back he [He] took him and placed him in his [His] arms, for it says, "I taught Ephraim to walk, taking them on My arms" [Hos. 11:3].

The son began to suffer; he [He] took him on his shoulders, for it is said, "in the desert which you saw, where the Lord, your God carried you" [Deut. 1:31].

The son began to suffer from the sun; he [He] spread on him His cloak, for it is said, "He has spread a cloud as a curtain" [Ps. 105:39].

He became hungry; he [He] fed him, for it is said, "Behold I send bread, like rain, from the sky" [Exod. 16:4].

He became thirsty, he [He] gave him drink, for it is said, "He brought streams out of the rock" [Ps. 78:16].[9]

A semiotic analysis of this text will reveal how far it is from the description of the Gospel parables we have been summarizing. Let us begin by questioning "mashal" itself. The term translates as "likeness" in English, a translation expanded as well by the phrase, "to what is the matter similar?" in the introductory formula to the midrashic mashal. The very semantics of the mashalic terminology seem therefore to support at this level Wittig's analysis of the parable as an iconic sign. However, this support is only apparent, because the mashal is not iconic of an abstraction, of a *designatum* which is not present in the text itself as in Wittig's account, but precisely of other signs which are present and even primary. Moreover, that of which the mashal is a sign is itself a narrative, and indeed a narrative which is *more* concrete in reference than the narrative in the mashal. There seems to be some kind of a reversal of structure here. While in the parables of the Gospel, a story is told which, in Wittig's words, does or could have real reference in the world and designates another meaning which is not referential, in the midrashic text, it is the biblical narrative which is being interpreted by the mashal. Now, the biblical narrative certainly makes referential claims—much more strongly than that of the denotatum of a parable. It not only claims that something could possibly have happened out there in the world, but that it certainly *did* happen. Moreover, the mashal makes no such claim in its discourse that something did or even really could have happened. It usually, in fact, is either quite schematic in its characterizations and plot or even quite unrealistic. Finally, the mashal, as an interpretive structure, is anything but indeterminate. There is indeed hardly any room for interpretation at all of the mashal. Its meaning is rigidly controlled by its textual form. Insofar as any text can be closed, the mashal is a closed text, not an open one.

Let us see then what this text actually does. The narrative in the verse upon which R. Yehuda is commenting is gapped. The motivation for the movement of the angel of God which was accustomed to go before the people is not made clear. Moreover, there is a doubling in the verse. "The angel of God who was accustomed to go in front of the Israelite army, moved and went behind them. And the pillar of cloud shifted from in front of them and took its place behind them." The Higher Critics identify a juncture between J and E in the middle of this verse.[10] R. Yehuda puts in his story. The story which R. Yehuda puts in and which answers to the gapping in the verse is built up entirely out of materials drawn from other parts of the biblical canon itself. The mashal provides a structure (genre/code) which enables and, at the same time, constrains the possibility of the production of new narrative to fill in the gap. This point requires further discussion.

The midrash has itself described the function of mashal as interpreting the hermetic Torah, not by any means of being hermetic itself. The Torah is encoded; the mashal is the code book by which it was encoded by its Author, as it were, and through which it may therefore be decoded. In the introduction to the midrash on Song of Songs, which the rabbis read as a mashal itself,[11] we read:

> Another interpretation: Song of Songs. This is what Scripture has said: "And not only that Kohellet was wise" [Eccles. 12:9]. Had another man said them, you would have had to bend your ears and hear these words; "and not only that"—it was Solomon who said them. Had he said them on his own authority, you would have had to bend your ear and hear them; "and not only that"—he said them by the Holy Spirit. "And not only that Kohellet was wise, he moreover taught knowledge to the people, and proved and researched, and formulated many *meshalim*"—"and proved" words of Torah; "and researched" words of Torah; he made handles[12] for the Torah. You will find that until Solomon existed, there was no *dugma*.[13]

Kohellet is, of course, Solomon. According to biblical tradition, that wise king wrote three books—Song of Songs, Proverbs, and Ecclesiastes [*Kohellet*].[14] Therefore, the verse of Ecclesiastes that tells us of his intellectual activity in general is appropriately referred to all three of his works. Now, this activity is characterized as "teaching knowledge to the people," which for the rabbis ineluctably means teaching Torah. It follows that he "proved and researched" the words of Torah. And this interpretive activity is designated by the verse itself as "making of many *meshalim*," this last glossed by the midrash as *dugma*, that is, figure, simile, or paradigm.[15] The interpretive activity which Solomon engaged in was the making of figurative stories that are "handles to the Torah"—stories, as I shall argue, which render the axiological meaning of the narratives of the Torah accessible.[16]

We see, therefore, that on the rabbis' own account, the mashal is not an enigmatic narrative. Its central function is to teach knowledge to the people, to make "handles" for the Torah, so that the people (not an elect) can understand. The filling in of gaps as a major force in midrashic reading has been documented above and certainly seen before me. My claim here concerns the role of intertextuality in this process. The material for the filling in of the gaps in midrash is generated by the intertext in two ways. First of all, as we have seen, the narrative material is created often (if not always) out of other scriptural materials having a more or less explicit reference to the narrative at hand. Second, as already pointed out, the plot—the narrative action—and the characters of the narrative gap-filling are also given in the intertext. They are the mashal. The mashal provides the connections which enable the rabbis to associate texts from different parts of the canon by assigning relations to these texts, by allowing them to be placed into a plot together. This is what the midrash above means when it characterizes the mashal as *dugma*, paradigm, an icon of a narrative.

In order to understand better the function that I am claiming for the mashal I would like to discuss it in the light of Frank Kermode's *The Genesis of Secrecy*, although not with reference to his chapter on parable, but rather to the one in which he discusses the generation of the Gospel narrative. In an extraordinarily elegant and lucid discussion which I can hardly hope to reproduce well in shortened from, Kermode presents something like the following model by which the Gospel story has been generated. There was or is a primitive fable underlying the *récit* as we have it today. Kermode discusses the Passion narrative as having been generated from such a primitive fable. His theory is that originally (diachronically or synchronically understood) the fable existed. The fable is a series of actions—a plot:

> The primitive "ado" must, insofar as it is a series of actions, have agents, and these agents, insofar as ado or fable acquires extension, must transcend their original type and function, must cease to be merely Hero, Opponent, and so on, and acquire idiosyncracies, have proper names. The more elaborate the story grows—the more remote from its schematic base—the more these agents will deviate from type and come to look like "characters."[17]

The fable underlying the Gospel has, according to Kermode, an appearance quite similar to the deep structure of the folk tale as told by Propp or Greimas. "Let us then presuppose a *fabula*, progressively interpreted: first by Mark, then by Matthew and Luke using Mark, and by John, who perhaps used a not dissimilar but not identical original." Kermode calls this process of narrative elaboration interpretation because "the redaction of an existing narrative was, in these circumstances, a pre-exegetical interpretative act; instead of interpreting by commentary, one does so by a process of augmenting the narrative."[18] This primitive gospel fable had the following narrative acts: Leavetaking, Arrest, Trial, Execution, and Reunion. Now, this narrative sequence requires that there be a betrayer. In Kermode's words:

> The necessity, in a circumstantial and history-like story, of having a character to perform the Betrayal is obvious enough. Depending how one looks at it, he plays the role of Helper or Opponent; by opposing the Hero he serves the logic of the narrative, as Satan did in Job. Satan's name means "adversary" or "opponent"; so here, when, as Luke and John report, he entered into

Judas, we have a case of a character being possessed by his narrative role. Of course by opposing he helps; his evil act, like Satan's, is permissive, ultimately a means to good.

So Betrayal becomes Judas. . . . And for Mark, that is the end of Judas. He has done his narrative part. So in this gospel there is not a great deal to distinguish Judas from a more abstract agency—he might be called simply "the Betrayer," or "Betrayal," as in some morality play . . . [19]

For Kermode, then, the characters of the narrative are fleshings-out of underlying narrative functions which are the province of the underlying fabula. I propose that in the midrash text which includes the Written Torah story, the mashal, and the narrative filling which the midrash provides, the mashal itself (the schematic story) is the (necessarily synchronic) *fabula* underlying the narrative elaboration of the biblical text together with its midrashic expansion. The mashal accomplishes its work by assigning a deep-structural description to the elliptic narrative of the Torah, which enables the completion of its syntactic structure. Moreover, since structural description on the syntactic level is also semantic description, this assigning of an underlying structural description to the narrative declares its meaning as well. In order to make this point clearer, I would say that the relation of the schematic story—the mashal proper—to the "real" story, is analogous to that of deep structure to surface structure in syntax. That is to say, surely, that the "real" story is *not* by any means to be understood as the solution to the mashal, but almost the opposite. The mashal allows for the structuring of this "real" story in the sense that it prescribes what kinds of characters and narrative functions will be appropriate in filling out the ellipses of the biblical text, and, moreover, it assigns value to these characters and events by assimilating them to a cultural icon which incorporates the culture's values. The mashal, on my view, corresponds, then, to what Wittig has called "the 'meaning system,' the organized stable gestalt of beliefs and values held by the perceiver,"[20] except that I would prefer to locate this system not in the individual perceiver but in the cultural code. The mashal proper, that is, the schematic story of the king and his retainers, when combined textually with the "real" story which the midrash weaves out of the Torah's narrative and other biblical texts, creates a powerful twofold semiotic object. The mashal gives to the Torah narrative a clear ideological value, without reducing the vitality and vividness of the representation of character and event in it. Both the complication and interest of the narrative surface and the clarity of meaning of the narrative deep-structure are combined and embodied in one textual system. We have here historical interpretation at its very intersection with fiction. As Hayden White has taught us:

A historical interpretation, like a poetic fiction, can be said to appeal to its readers as a plausible representation of the world by virtue of its implicit appeal to those "pregeneric plot-structures" or archetypal story forms that define the modalities of a given culture's literary endowment. Historians, no less than poets, can be said to gain an "explanatory effect"—over and above whatever formal explanations they may offer of specific historical events—by building into their narratives patterns of meaning similar to those more explicitly provided by the literary art of the cultures to which they belong.[21]

In White's view, then, there is a stock of "archetypal story forms," which are the bearers of the ideology of the given culture. When a historian, including the most modern and "scientific" of historians, reconstructs the past, this is always done in conformity to the plots which the intertext of the culture allows. This is what endows the narrative he or she creates with both plausibility and significance. What is the mashal if not such a narrative pattern of meaning?

We see this semiotic structure in another text from the Mekilta, where the authoritative and axiological power of the mashal is explicit:

> *And Amaleq attacked* [Exod. 17:8]. R. Yehoshua and R. El'azar Hasama say, This scripture is unclear[22] and it is interpreted by Job, where it says, "Can the rush grow without a swamp; can reeds wax large without water?" [Job 8:11] Is it possible for the rush to grow without a swamp; or is it possible for the reed to grow without water? So it is impossible for Israel to exist unless they busy themselves with the words of the Torah. And because they separated themselves from the Torah the enemy came upon them, because the enemy only comes because of sin and transgression. [Lauterbach, II, p. 135]

The text of Exodus is declared unclear, because the connection between this passage and the immediately preceding one is not explicit in the biblical text. The immediately preceding verses tell a story of the arrival of the Israelites in a place called Refidim, where they have no water to drink. The people become rebellious, and even threaten violence against Moses until God intervenes and sends water miraculously. The narrative finishes with the statement "He called the name of the place Trial and Strife, because of the strife of the Israelites and their trying of God, saying, 'Is God among us, or isn't He?' " [v.7]. And then immediately, "And Amaleq attacked." What is the connection between the two events, or rather, what is the meaning of the second following hard on the first? This is the gap that the midrash wishes to fill here. The text of Job is invoked as a solution to this hiatus or indeterminacy. In my reading of this text, the actual words cited from Job are only part of the text mobilized here in the interpretation. In order to understand how the text works, we ought to have a look at the quoted verse of Job in its context:

> Can the rush grow without a swamp; can reeds wax large without water? While it is still in its youth, will it not be cut down, and be dry before any grass? *So* are the ways of those who forget God, and the hope of the scornful will be lost.

Now it can be seen that the text from Job is itself a simple parable, so by utilizing this parable to solve the indeterminacy of the Exodus text, the rabbis are performing precisely the same sort of hermeneutic operation that we have been considering until now. The explicit meaning of the Job text is that sinners will be punished and the implication is that those who do not sin will not be, as is, indeed, the message of the whole speech from which this is a quotation. This message is inserted into the gap of the Torah text which is now no longer unclear. The attack of Amaleq is a direct result of the previous events. Since they were forgetters of God ("Is God in our presence or not?"], therefore they were doomed to early death, and the connection is explained. However, we can go even further than this. In the story of the Torah, the problem has to do with water. The people have arrived at a desert place and there is no water for them to drink; they complain and ask for water. Now this narrative presents problems of its own, for if they are indeed in the depths of the desert, and there is no water for them to drink, their desperation and crying out for water is quite understandable. This problem has exercised interpreters of Exodus up to the present day. Our midrash, by using the mashal of Job, solves this problem as well. The lack of water which is spoken of is itself to be understood figuratively as lack of Torah, just as in the Job text those who forget God are compared to a stand of reeds whose water has dried up. Note again the interpretation of "water" as a symbol for Torah. Accordingly we see that it is the neglect of Torah which leads to the forgetting of God and then to sin; and the punishment for sin is "the hope of the scornful will be lost."

The semiotic structure here is identical to that of the previous texts. A gapped narrative in the Torah is explicated by the application to it of a mashal, which is composed of verses from another part of the canon. The narrative gap-filling is structured both in plot and ideology by the mashal. Again as Hayden White perceives, "What the historian must bring to his consideration of the record are general notions of the *kinds of stories that might be found there*."[23] The mashal structure therefore has the function of intertext—it controls the possible messages which can be sent and received in the midrashic culture; it is an explicit representation of the culturally specific "meaning system," making reading possible. The mashal itself has either the authority of Scripture or that of an anonymous code.

Another text about the mashal in the introduction to the midrash on Song of Songs makes this idea clearer:

> The rabbis say: Do not let this mashal be light in your eyes, for by means of this mashal one comes to comprehend the words of Torah. A *mashal* to a king who has lost a golden coin from his house or a precious pearl[24]—does he not find it by means of a wick worth a penny? Similarly, let not this *mashal* be light in your eyes, for by means of this *mashal* one comes to comprehend the words of Torah. Know that this is so, for Solomon, by means of this *mashal*,[25]

understood the exact meaning of the Torah. Rabbi Judah says: It is to teach you that everyone who teaches words of Torah to the many is privileged to have the Holy Spirit descend upon him.[26] From whom do we learn this? From Solomon, who because he taught words of Torah to the many was privileged to have the Holy Spirit descend upon him and utter three books, Proverbs, Ecclesiastes, and Song of Songs.[27]

This passage gives us some very important insight into the nature of the mashal. It is figured here as something which does not cost much, but nevertheless has great value. What is the meaning of this figure? I suggest that it designates the fact that the meshalim (plural of mashal) are themselves a corpus of well-known narrative themes, characters, and actions. The same relations and events recur over and over: There was a king who had a son; the son angered him and was banished; the king regretted his action. There was a king with a beloved bride, etc. These stories are even more conventionalized and schematized than fairy tales. This point about the meshalim themselves has been made before,[28] but it has not been argued that this is essential to the signifying structure of the mashal form of interpretation. Our text does make this clear. The mashal is a wick worth a penny; it is "common coin" and this is precisely its value. Since it comes from the common stock of possible characters and possible actions and motivations, it provides the possible, legitimate ways to fill in and understand the hidden biblical narrative. This wick which is so common that it is worth only a penny is an excellent figure, it seems, for the intertext in the sense of the cultural code, the anonymous cultural code which is available to everyone.

Our analysis up until now suggests that the mashal is not truly a narrative at all, but a narrative structure or scheme. Lest I be misunderstood, I am making this claim not about the genre, but about the tokens. I claim that the schematic story of a king and his associates is not a story at all, but a metalinguistic statement about another story. It is not analogous to the telling of a fairy tale, but rather to the analysis of the tale by an interpreter. What the mashal-interpretation reveals is a code which allows for the creation of narrative within the culture. The mashal does not stand beside the concrete situation but creates it, or allows it to be created. The very story did not exist before the mashal; it is enfolded within it. The mashal is the matrix or code out of which the narrative of the Torah is generated; it is both syntactic and semantic structural description, and necessarily, then, as conventional and schematic, as fixed, as the morphology of the folk tale described by Propp. Thus it has properties of Kermode's *fabula*.

Kermode sums up his theory in the following way:

The matter of this chapter is really quite simple. Of an agent there is nothing to be said except that he performs a function: Betrayal, judgment. . . . The

key to all this development—from fable to written story, from story to character, from character to more story—is interpretation. At some point a narrative achieves a more or less fixed form; in the case of the gospels this was
the formation of a more or less fixed canon. There were many other gospels,
but their failure to achieve canonicity cost them their lives; four remain, and
each illustrates in its own way the manner in which precanonical intepreta-
tion works. Some of the differences between them are no doubt due to the
varying needs and interests of the communities for whom the evangelists
originally wrote, and to their own diverse theological predispositions; but
many are induced by the pressure of narrative interpretation, not independent of these other pressures, but quite different from the kinds of institutional
commentary and exegesis that typically constitute post-canonical interpretation. For these early interpretations take the form of new narrative, whether
by a reorganization of existing material or by the inclusion of new material.
In the first stage this new material characteristically derives from texts—Old
Testament texts tacitly regarded as somehow part of the same story. . . . [29]

Now, in some ways Kermode's description applies directly to midrash. Here
also, as we have amply seen, we have narrative expansion derived from other
texts, tacitly—or not so tacitly—regarded as part of the same story. As such,
however, his system presents several paradoxes. The most obvious is that
Kermode claims this type of interpretation to be characteristic only of the
precanonical situation whereas midrash is obviously postcanonical. Moreover,
Kermode's description wavers on the very crucial point of the status of the
"primitive fable." Although Kermode himself presents them as if they were
equal alternatives,[30] it is in fact one thing to state that there was an early,
historically accurate account which was elaborated by midrashic techniques or
other sorts of narrative expansions and quite another to claim this fabula as the
underlying scynchronic structure of the Gospel stories without positing its or
their historical reality. Just how fraught this issue is will become clear when we
pursue our application of Kermode's analysis to the mashal a little further. It is
clear that the mashal can only fit the synchronic version of the primitive fable
theory; there is no possible claim that there was a historical story about such
agents as a king, his son, and robbers which was somehow elaborated into the
Torah's account. But the whole genre of the Torah requires that it be taken
seriously as a "true" story. This point has been made by Sternberg, who ob-
serves that the narrative "illegitimates all thought of fictionality on pain of
excommunication. . . . "[31] If the midrashic reading is a claim that the mashal
represents the ideological/narrative matrix from which the Bible text is synchronically derived, how can that text claim—in the view of the midrash—to
be true? It would seem at first glance that only a fiction in the sense of a made-
up story can have an underlying, synchronic structure, but history cannot.
Stated baldly, how can a true story have a primitive fabula underlying it?

What we need here is a model that accounts for two structures, each answering to one of the alternatives which Kermode has raised. The issue is not

whether we consider the biblical narrative as fiction with its synchronically underlying fabula or as historiography with the fabula as diachronic "kernel of truth" or ancient eye-witness account, but something much more complex and sophisticated. The Bible must be read as historiography; that much has been made clear by Sternberg, but it is ideologized historiography, as also shown by him. Indeed, according to Hayden White all historiographical narrative is structured by plots and genres in ways that are controlled by the personal and social ideology of the writer of the history.[32] Historical narratives are, for White, "metaphorical statements which suggest a relation of similitude between such events and processes and the story types that we conventionally use to endow the events of our lives with culturally sanctioned meanings." Writing history is the articulation "of a complex of symbols which gives us directions for finding an icon of the structure of those events in our literary tradition," in a word, a mashal. I claim, therefore, that if the Bible is historiography, then midrash is precisely metahistoriography. The biblical narrative, at least as much as any historiography, is structured by metaphor at its very heart; it could hardly be a mere transparent chronicle of events. The midrashic mashal is to be understood as a raising to consciousness of the unstated tropics of the biblical history. It is the schematic statement of the icons of the structures of events in the literary tradition, the Prophets and Writings. As the midrash says, "of them it is *interpreted* in the tradition," which means, as we recall, the Prophets and Writings.

Louis Marin in an essay on a parable of Pascal's has brilliantly addressed precisely this use of the parable form. In Pascal's text, the speaker is addressing a young nobleman and in trying to teach him some truth about his place in the world tells him a classic sort of parabolic tale about a man who is stranded on an isolated island, where he discovers the people have lost their king. Since he has the appearance of the king, he is taken as such by the people, and after a period of some hesitation accepts the role, remembering however that it is only a role. Now, on one mode of reading we could take this as a moral parable of a fairly simple semiotic structure. You are the castaway, young friend. Know that you have no more right by nature to be a nobleman than did that man, but accept your role and perform it with self-knowledge. Indeed, on one level, Pascal's text authorizes such a straight reading. Marin does much more. He shows how the parable is not merely analogously related to its application, to an interpretation of its meaning, but that it is the underlying structure of the biography of the narrator's interlocutor. Thus:

> One perceives how narrative and code function in relation to each other in the construction of Pascalian discourse: the first narrative is (in its textual manifestation) the figural development of the notion of chance occurrence contained in the second code. This notion appears in the narrative only in the form of an "image," without being expressly manifested: the tempest, the

disappearance of the island's king, the shipwreck, and finally the castaway's corporal and facial resemblance to the lost king, are all so many figures of contingency, the notion of which permits the deciphering of the parabolic narrative by another narrative which is unveiled in its turn, as it comes into contact with the "parable," at a point of articulation marked by the term "chance occurrence." *This other narrative is the biographical "structure" of the interlocutor: his birth as son of a duke, his finding himself "in" the world, the marriage of his parents and all those of his ancestors, a thousand unforeseen events which left their mark on his family and whose narration would constitute the family tradition.*[33]

The analogy to our midrashic meshalim is precise. In these as well, it is a "family tradition" and a "biographic structure" which are being interpreted. This tradition and biography are real stories, just as they are in the case of Pascal's young duke. However, by themselves they have no meaning. They are merely data. *They must be made into fictions before they can signify,* fiction here not being used in the sense of a text which is not true, but in the sense of a text which has been structured so as to mean, an artifact. The function of the mashal is to reveal the fictionality of the true story of the Torah, that is, to take its recital of events, gapped as it is, and by assigning it a place in the cultural codes articulated by simple narrative functions and structures, to allow it to be completed and to signify. That is why until Solomon created the mashal, the Torah was like a thicket into which no one could enter, or like a basket of fruit which no one could carry.[34] Again in Marin's words: "The function of the parabolic narrative therefore appears through an ambiguity which gives it great practical efficacy: the parable designates in its fiction a real narrative (situation, position) that it assimilates to itself in the process of showing that this narrative is the revealing figure of one term of the code by which the parable was encoded into a fictive narrative."[35]

The parable in Marin's analysis has as its designatum not an abstraction but the "true story" itself. The "real narrative" is interpreted by being shown to be an element in a paradigm, "the revealing figure of one term of the code," through its attraction to the parable. The entire then forms one signifying system—"the parabolic narrative." This is precisely what I have claimed for the midrashic mashal as well. Its designatum is the very biblical narrative. This narrative is assimilated to the mashal—the history itself is shown to be a figure of the code which the mashal represents. The mashal then stands in an ambiguous position similar to the one that Marin discusses. Is there a story or is there not? Is it history or is it fiction? This ambiguity is greatly heightened in the story of the king and his son, wherein the two narratives are physically assimilated to each other. Ostensibly R. Yehuda begins by telling a fictive narrative of a king and a king's son, which we would expect to be placed beside a real narrative of God and the people, but as soon as he begins, it becomes clear that only one story is being told at all, for God *is* the king and Israel is the son. This ambiguity is embodied in such sentences as: "He [the son] became hungry, He [who, the king or God?] fed him, as it says, 'Behold I [God] will rain bread down' "! This is not, in my reading, merely a shorthand, owing to the perpetual nature of the metaphorical transfer king=God, son=Israel, but rather a matter of the inherent logic of the mashal's essence. There is no story of a king and his son at all, but only an interpretation of the relation of God to His people as being that of a king to his infant child, so that the gapped, unmotivated movement of the angel from in front to in back of the people can be motivated and understood. Moreover, the assigning of this narrative to the underlying structure, king and son, allows for the collection of the other verses which relate to this structure and their re-emplacement in a narrative sequence.

At this point, we can return to our overall characterization of the mashal as a type of midrash. The biblical text as written is characterized by hiatus and indeterminacy at many points. The work of midrash, similar to all reading of narrative, is the filling of the gaps. The way that midrash works is by introducing into the fissures in the text new narrative material, largely created out of other biblical texts. This practice is founded again on the insight that the Bible is a single semiotic system—in hermeneutic terms, a self-glossing text. However, this work is not—at least in midrash—a free, individual response to the text, but one which is constrained by a very specific ideology.[36] Only certain plots and certain associations of text to text are allowed. I would suggest that this is true of any reading in any culture, but it is usually unconscious and suppressed, while the rabbis have often represented on the surface of their hermeneutic texts precisely the ideological codes which allow and constrain their interpretation. The mashal is the most clearly defined of those codes which generate interpretation by narrative expansion. The mashal is a basic narrative structure whose characters and actions belong to the common coin of the intertext. These basic narrative structures are thus the carriers of values and ideology in the culture. The biblical story, referential and historical in its generic claims, is made to signify by being read with its rabbinic intertext.[37] By this practice, history becomes parable.

·6·

THE SEA RESISTS: MIDRASH
AND THE (PSYCHO) DYNAMICS
OF INTERTEXTUALITY

The text, however, as we possess it today, will tell us enough about its own vicissitudes. Two mutually opposed treatments have left their traces on it. On the one hand it has been subjected to revisions which have falsified it in the sense of their secret aims, have mutilated it and amplified it and have even changed it into its reverse; on the other hand a solicitous piety has presided over it and has sought to preserve everything as it was, no matter whether it was consistent or contradicted itself. Thus almost everywhere noticeable gaps, disturbing repetitions and obvious contradictions have come about—indications which reveal things to us which it was not intended to communicate. . . . the difficulty is not in perpetrating the deed, but in getting rid of its traces. We might lend the word *Entstellung* [distortion] the double meaning to which it has a claim but of which today it makes no use. It should mean not only "to change the appearance of something" but also "to put something in another place, to displace." Accordingly, in many instances of textual distortion, we may nevertheless count upon finding what has been suppressed and disavowed hidden away somewhere else, though changed and torn from its context. Only it will not always be easy to recognize it. Sigmund Freud[1]

As pointed out in an important recent paper by Christopher Johnson, Freud is here drawing a powerful analogy between text-work and dream-work. In typical nineteenth-century fashion he projects an "original" pure text which has been distorted through the conscious efforts of repressive scribes. In the present climate of thought, I find it hard to imagine this originary purity of the text (except as an article of religious faith), but Freud's remarks are, nevertheless, very suggestive. If we transpose (displace) them, as Johnson does (and, as he claims, Kristeva does), from the realm of textual transmission to that of textual production, we arrive at intertextuality—intertextuality as the traces within the text, the bumps on its surface, which mark the suppressions, conflicts, and transformations of earlier signifying practices of which it is the site.

93

Intertextuality is, in a sense, the way that history, understood as cultural and ideological change and conflict, records itself within textuality. As the text is the transformation of a signifying system and of a signifying practice, it embodies the more or less untransformed detritus of the previous system. These fragments of the previous system and the fissures they create on the surface of the text reveal conflictual dynamics which led to the present textual system. Now, it is, I would claim, precisely these gaps in the text which the midrash reads,[2] and the rabbis very early drew the connection between dream interpretation and hermeneutics of the Torah.[3] It is, then, perhaps, not altogether unexpected to find the psychodynamic model a useful one for the understanding of some aspects of midrash and its relation to the biblical text. The Torah itself, even as it is generically identified as God's work, nevertheless indicates its own belatedness with respect to earlier texts: "Therefore it says in the book of the Wars of the Lord 'and Waheb in Sufa and the rivers of Arnon' " [Numbers 21:14]. Other markers of the presence of earlier signifying systems within the biblical text are less explicit but nevertheless discernible in the "noticeable gaps, disturbing repetitions and obvious contradictions" to which Freud referred. Indeed, all those fissures in the Torah which diachronic scholarship figures as evidence for a plurality of sources, our present reading practice will re-figure as indications of intertextuality.[4] These intimations of intertextuality are part of what gives the Bible its continuing power to fascinate, and the rabbis could not fail to mark and interpret them in the midrash-work. In analyzing a text from the Mekilta, I will try to show that it constitutes an interpretation of these intertextual fragments of earlier repressed but not utterly expunged cultural practice. The claim that I wish to make about this midrash is that it enacts in very important ways the conflict in Jewish culture between its pagan past and its monotheistic present. Putting this in psychic terms, the midrash makes manifest the repressed mythic material in the Bible's "textual subconscious." More specifically, much of the Bible records openly the conflict in its culture between paganism as the old religion of the people and the new religion of the Torah and the Prophets. The remnants of that conflict, and indeed the remnants of the suppressed culture, are to be found in the allusions which the Bible makes, willingly and willy-nilly, to the content and images of the earlier mythology. One of the important dynamics of midrash as reading is that it makes manifest the hidden dimensions of that mythic intertext by gathering together these fragments of allusion and figural language and reinscribing them into narratives.

This idea is not entirely new. Samuel Loewenstamm already pointed to an example of this process in the very text we are studying here, the Mekilta:

> As for the wind [which drove back the water of the Red Sea], the midrash has already focused on it very precisely and remarked that it is not accidental

that God here acted by means of an *east wind*, but indeed this wind is counted as one of the traditional weapons of God. [The midrash] cited evidence for this in its interpretation of Exodus 14:21 from the verses: "With the east wind I will scatter them before the enemy" [Jer. 18:17]; "With the east wind You have broken the ships of Tarshish" [Ps. 48:8]; from the verse in Hosea [13:15], which dubs the east wind, "the wind of the Lord"; and from the verse in Isaiah [27:8] about the War of the Lord, "With His strong wind, on the day of the east wind." . . . It is clear that the east wind was singled out from all the winds in the mythological tradition of Israel.[5]

As Loewenstamm has acutely realized, the Mekilta,[6] by gathering all of these verses into a paradigm (under the rubric, "And you also find that God punished the generation of the flood and the people of Sodom, only by means of the east wind. . . . And you will also find in the case of the People of the Tower . . . "), has revealed that which perhaps the biblical authors sought to hide, the actual mythic background of the description of the east wind as a weapon of God. In the rest of this chapter, I would like to analyze a much more complex text from the same midrash, which thematizes both this mythological intertext and the conflict with it:

> *And Moses stretched out his hand over the sea* [Exod. 14:21]. The sea began to resist him. Moses said, 'in the name of the Holiness,' but it did not yield. The Holiness, blessed be He, revealed Himself; the sea began to flee, as it says, "The sea saw and fled" [Ps. 114:3].
>
> Its *mashal*; to what is the matter similar? To a king of flesh and blood, who has two gardens, one inside the other. He sold the inner one, and the purchaser came to enter, but the guard did not allow him. He said to him, "In the name of the king," but he did not yield. He showed him the signet, but he did not yield until the king came. Once the king came, the guard began to flee. He said, "All day long I have been speaking to you in the name of the king and you did not yield. Now, why are you fleeing?" He said, "not from you am I fleeing, but from the king am I fleeing."
>
> Similarly, Moses came and stood at the sea. He said to him, "in the name of the Holiness," and it did not yield. He showed him the rod, and it did not yield, until the Holiness, blessed be He, revealed Himself in His glory. The sea began to flee, as it is said, "The sea saw and fled" [Ps. 114:3]. Moses said to him, "All day long I have been speaking to you in the name of the Holiness, blessed be He, and you did not submit. Now, 'what has happened to you, O sea, that you flee? [Ps. 114:5]' "He answered him, "Not from before you am I fleeing, son of Amram, but 'from before the Master, tremble earth [progenitor of the earth],[7] from before the God of Jacob [Ps. 114: 7-8]' ".

This midrash fits the formal structure theorized in the previous chapter. We begin with the Torah verse to be interpreted, "And Moses stretched out his arm over the sea—and God moved the sea with a strong east wind all of the night . . . " The verse provides a gap. Aside from any theological problem which this verse raises, it is problematic from the point of view of narrative logic. If Moses has been empowered to split the sea with his hand, as implied by God's command to him in the previous verse, "Stretch out your hand over the sea and split it," then why does God intervene directly and perform the splitting Himself? Alternatively, if Moses has not been thus empowered, then for what purpose does he stretch out his hand? The oddness of this verse can be shown by comparison with others, e.g., "Then the Lord said to Moses, 'Stretch out your hand toward heaven that there may be darkness upon the land of Egypt'. . . . So Moses stretched out his hand toward heaven, and there was a thick darkness . . . " [Exod. 7:21-22]. Or in the continuation of our very story, "So Moses stretched out his hand over the sea, and as morning broke, the sea returned to its normal course" [14:27]. The effect of our verse is so jarring that the Higher Critics have placed a juncture between two sources in its caesura.[8] In fact, many Bible critics regard the whole account of the splitting of the sea as the interweaving of two contradictory traditions or documents.[9] The rabbis who composed the midrash, unwilling, of course, to adopt such diachronic solutions, read the text synchronically, that is, as a system of gaps.[10] They resolve the contradiction of the two halves of the verse by narrating a set of events which took place between them and which motivates the change in subject from Moses to God Himself as director of the sea's split. The plot of this narrative expansion is structured by a mashal. It is the text of Psalm 114, however, which provides the primary material for the narrative. The solution of the midrash is produced by reading the text of Psalm 114 as a commentary on the Exodus passage. The text of the psalm, which generates the story of the sea's opposition, is thus introduced precisely into the middle of the original verse, precisely into the split where the Higher Critics see the junction of sources and for exactly the same reason.[11] The dialogue of the psalm is inserted right into the middle of the verse between "And Moses stretched out his arm" and "And God moved the sea."

Let us have a look now at the psalm itself, a text well known for its personification of natural entities:

[1] When Israel went out from Egypt; the house of Jacob from a foreign nation.
[2] Judah became His holy one; Israel His dominion.
[3] The sea saw and fled; the Jordan turned back.
[4] The mountains danced like rams; the hills like lambs.
[5] What has happened to you, O sea, that you flee; O Jordan, that you turn back?
[6] O mountains, that you dance like rams; O hills, like lambs?
[7] From before the Master, tremble earth, from before the God of Jacob.

The midrash projects a world in which the Red Sea is not a personification, but a personality; not a metaphor, but a character. It will be easier to sense the radicality of the midrashic reading of the psalm by considering first a road not taken. As read by Sir Philip Sidney, the personifications of nature in David's psalm are a figure, an *enargeia* of the God who cannot be seen by eyes of flesh: "[David's] handling his prophecy . . . is merely poetical. For what else [are] . . . his notable *prosopopeias*, when he maketh you, as it were, see God coming in his majesty, his telling of the Beasts' joyfulness and hills' leaping, but a heavenly poesy: wherein almost he showeth himself a passionate lover of that unspeakable and everlasting beauty to be seen by the eyes of the mind, only cleared by faith?"

Commenting on this passage in Sidney, Murray Krieger remarks:

> The prosopopeia is a form of personification which gives a voice to that which does not speak and thereby gives presence to that which is absent. Through this figure, Sidney argues, God enters David's poem (we are made to "see God coming in his majesty"). It is as if this figure is made to serve the larger objective of *enargeia*, the verbal art of forcing us to see vividly. Through the "eyes of the mind"—an appropriately Platonic notion—we are shown the coming of God and his "unspeakable and everlasting beauty." Here, then, are words invoking a visible presence, though, of course, to "the eyes of the mind" alone. Though God's may be only a figurative entrance through His personified creatures, the poet makes us, "as it were," see this entrance. He is there, in His living creation, and absent no longer.[12]

In Sidney's/Krieger's reading, then, the personification of the sea, the rivers, and the hills in the psalm is not truly a representation of nature at all, but a poetic means of making the reader see the coming into the world of the unrepresentable God by evoking the reaction of imaginary witnesses to this event. Nature—that is, that which is properly apprehended as a *res*—is *personified*; the very terminology of trope reveals the reification of nature implied and assumed. As Jon Whitman has remarked, "it is only when the 'personality' is a literary fiction separate from the actual condition that we have a personification."[13]

The midrash, in contrast, reads the psalm as literal, i.e., as the record of an actual colloquy which took place at a specific moment in history, that moment being the moment suspended between the two halves of our verse in Exodus. The psalm completes perfectly the gap of the Torah text. The speaker addressing the sea is Moses and not (as has been suggested) some anonymous Jewish poet wondering at the miracles of the Exodus and evoking the presence of God.[14] Nor is the sight which the sea perceived and from which it fled left as the unspoken/unspeakable presence of God, but the actual self-revelation of God.[15] The rhetorical question and answer of the psalm—"What has happened to you O sea that you flee? Before the Lord, Creator of the Universe, tremble earth"—is turned in the midrashic text into an actual colloquy between Moses and the sea.[16] That is to say, the figurative usage of the poem, the personification of the sea, is contextualized historically and dramatized. This minidrama is then correlated with the verse in Exodus which is the subject of the midrash, and that verse is situated dramatically as well. Out of the two texts is created a third, a new text, which has qualities, both semantic and aesthetic, which neither had alone. The verse in Exodus is now motivated. An answer has been given to the question of why Moses stretched out his hand, if God was to be the motivating force behind the movement of the sea. Furthermore, the text of the psalm has been sharpened. We now understand what the sea saw. It saw God! The half-hidden memory of this event is recorded also in Ps. 77:17, "The waters saw You, O God, the waters saw You and *trembled.*" Instead of a vague "When Israel went out from Egypt," we have a specific moment. Instead of the somewhat enigmatic "What has happened to you, O sea?" we have a more specific question: Why did you flee now and not before?

It is important to note that vis-à-vis the earlier ancient traditions of biblical interpretation, this rabbinic sea as an actual sentient subject represents a reversal of a conventional historical-cultural development. The earliest interpretive tradition, and very likely the Bible itself, had already arrived at a rationalized perception of the world as nonsentient and wholly different from man. While the Bible, as Cassuto has shown, contains allusions to the ancient myth of a primeval battle between God and the sea, these allusions are all reduced from their narrative fullness and have only figurative force.[17] The prophets and poets of the Bible, we may imagine, were very wary of even suggesting that the sea had a personal nature because of the real danger that, with the polytheistic world around them, they would be misunderstood, and the misunderstanding would lead to polytheistic belief.[18]

Sidney's interpretation, then, is solidly in the older mainstream of interpretation of the psalm, and also seems close to what may have been originally meant by the psalm, as far as that can be guessed. The rabbinic reading therefore seems at first a sort of step backward in history. Midrash reverses all of these processes of demythologization. In our example the relevant process is "depersonalization," which is, according to Benjamin Uffenheimer, "to alter myth in such a way as to remove the personal nature of its protagonists. The sea and other depths became geographical concepts . . . " In our midrash, the "geographical concept" becomes once again a person. Inserting the psalm into the historical context of a dialogue with Moses reanimates its meaning and by doing so reanimates the sea. In short, metaphor becomes myth.

The gap in the text of the Torah corresponds to a fault line between ideologies. One half of the verse represents God as the only controlling force over nature in the world, while the other half allows that there may be human intervention in nature. The ambivalence of the verse is thematized in the midrash in the ambivalence of the sale of the garden to the king's friend. On the one hand, the Torah tells us that Moses has been given power over the sea to subdue it and split it; the inner garden has been sold to him. I read this not as magic, but as a reduction of the status of the universe to a will-less nonsubject, a mere object of human desire, the reification of nature. On the other hand, owing to the contradiction in the verse and the "evidence" of the psalm, we see that will was not taken away from the sea. He still had the power, and perhaps the right to resist; the outer garden was not sold. The garden which is sold and not sold then can be read as representing a kind of liminal moment in cultural history (indeed, in materialist terms, in economic history). However, it also plays a concrete function in the interpretation of our biblical narrative. It represents a deep-seated inner contradiction in the very situation of Moses's having been commanded to split the sea. One who sells an inner garden without selling the means of access to it is, after all, creating a self-contradictory moment. This self-contradiction parallels the contradiction between God's placing "an *eternal* border for the sea from which it will not pass" [Jer. 5:22], and His command to Moses to now make the sea pass from that very border.[19]

On my reading of the Mekilta's story of the encounter between Moses and the sea, there are really two conflicts being enacted within this textual gap, one between two characters and one between two ideologies. The first is the conflict between Moses and the sea and the second is the conflict between monotheistic myth and polytheistic myth, and the two conflicts are perfectly isomorphic in the midrashic text. On the one hand, we have the sea realized as a fully conscious and free-willed creature, a person—not a personification, a person who can resist the person Moses. This is, I submit, a reflection of a myth-like view of the landscape, one in which nature has not yet been reified. However, the moment *God* appears the sea does begin to flee. There is no battle between the sea and God. The conflict between Moses and the sea, then, is paralleled in the midrash by the conflict between a monotheistic myth and a polytheistic one lurking, as it were, in the intertextual unconscious. The mythic dimension is evoked by the conflict between Moses and the personal sea, and the defeat of polytheism by the absolute dominance of the presence of God over the sea. Were the sea to have any power to withstand God, we would no longer have Judaism at all, but a polytheistic regression. Accordingly, our midrash—notwithstanding its personal sea and once-more visible God—makes it, nevertheless, absolutely unambiguous that the sea has power against a man, but only against a man. The unquestioning and immediate capitulation of the sea to the revelation of God is at the same time, then, an enactment of the defeat of the *myth* of the battle between a god of heaven and a god of the sea, the famous hydromachia. This point is underlined heavily by the mashal in which the sea is figured as an employee of the king and no more, one who is bound upon hearing the king's word to immediately obey. When God appears, there is no contest; the sea immediately obeys, like a faithful servant and no more. The fact that the sea could be insubordinate (and there is no reason to suppose that it could not happen again) verifies the mythic reading of the landscape which is still alive for the rabbis, but at the same time the text renders it crystal clear that the sea is not a god or a rival to God. The mashal, then, serves as an aid in the interpretation of the "dangerous" material by containing it within safe limits, a function the rabbis themselves figured by comparing the Torah to "a pot full of boiling water, which had no handle to carry it, and someone came and made it a handle [the mashal], and it began to be carried by its handle."[20]

A later midrash on our midrash[21] brings to full explicitness both the mythic and dialectical[22] conflicts which are latent in the earlier one:

> Thus, when Moses came and stood against the sea, he said in the name of the Holiness, God has spoken to you, make a path and the redeemed ones will pass. The sea answered and said to Moses, Ben Amram, behold, Adam was not created first, but at the end of the six days of creation, and I was created before he was. I am greater than you; I will not be split for you. Moses answered to God, Thus and so said the sea; Master of the Universe, he is right; the sea will not be split before me; rather You speak to him with Your word, and he will be split. The Holiness, blessed be He, said to Moses, if I speak to the sea and he is split, he will have no healing for ever and ever,[23] but indeed, you speak to him and he will split, in order that he will have healing by your hand. Here is a fount[24] of strength with you. Immediately, Moses came with strength going on his right side, as it says, "He causes His glorious arm to go on the right of Moses, splitting the sea before them, to make him an eternal name" [Isa. 63:12]. When the sea saw the strength, standing to the right of Moses, he said to the earth, Earth, make me channels and I will enter into your depths, before the Master of Creation, may He be blessed, for it says, "The sea saw and fled." And when Moses saw the sea fleeing before him, Moses said to him, All day I have been speaking to you in the name of the Holiness, and you did not yield; I showed you the staff and you did not yield; now "what has happened to you, O sea, that you flee?" The sea answered and said to Moses, Ben-Amram, Ben-Amram, do not give greatness to yourself; I flee not from before you, but from before the Lord of Creation, may His name be made sanctified in His world, as it says, "From before the Lord, Creator of the earth/Make channels,[25] O earth, from before the God of Jacob." [*Exodus Rabba, ad loc.*]

This text makes explicit much that is implicit in the earlier version, and again we have the same double movement: revivification of the mythic universe simultaneously with the neutralization of its polytheistic content. On the one hand, the claim of the sea against Moses has a very human note; it is not an abstract philosophical or theological argument that would signal an allegorical reading of our text, but a claim of priority and seniority. We are still here in the realm of what I have called the mythic. Moreover, the mythic potential of "He causes His glorious arm to go on the right of Moses" is vividly realized, again by literalizing Isaiah's metaphor and rendering it a necessary element in the logic of the narrative. But on the other hand, the very content of the sea's response ("I was created first"), emphasizing its and the man's mutual status as creatures of God, enacts once again the total defeat of polytheism. The process of a monotheistic mythic reading of the landscape is thus continued and deepened in the midrash on the midrash.

Reading the landscape in this way is of great cultural significance, as it implies a certain situation of the human subject as one among many in nature, and not as qualitatively and absolutely unique. Isaak Heinemann has already noted this fundamental ontological reorientation of the rabbis, their "primitivity" both with regard to what came before them and what came after them as well:

> The medieval philosophers, with Rabbi Saadya Gaon at their head, depended on figures, such as "the eye of the earth," the "mouth of the earth," to prove that the Torah, even where it spoke of the eye of God and His mouth, "spoke in human language," that is, in metaphor. They assumed, therefore, as self-understood that all that was said about the bodily parts of the earth, was not intended literally. And indeed in all of the Apocrypha and certainly in the ancient philosophical literature, there is no sign of anyone who understood these verses literally. The midrash is entirely different: "All that God created in man, He created similarly in the earth. Man has a head and the earth has a head, as it says, 'the head of the dusts of the earth'; man has eyes and the earth has eyes, as it says, 'and it covered the eye of the earth.' " . . . To all of these anthropomorphic metaphors, we can apply the dictum, "A metaphor is none other than a reduced myth." And even if the rabbis did not go so far as the realm of real myth, which sees the earth as a woman and a goddess, . . . for the rabbis there functioned the anthropocentric necessity to find "our brothers" even in non-human nature and to bring it close, therefore, to our senses and understanding.[26]

Heinemann bases his description on his conception of the rabbis as belonging to one of those romantic peoples who are closer to the earth than the peoples of culture, but the point is well taken nevertheless. There is something different in the way that rabbinic literature regards the world of nature. It is hard for me to imagine precisely what it "felt like" to live in a world peopled by a personal earth, a personal sea, and a personal desert, but it is not hard to imagine in general how different an orientation to the world this provided. Certainly it is difficult to see people who have such a consciousness acting toward nature as if it were only there to be exploited and spoiled for human purposes—as if it had no ontological importance of its own. If we cannot recover fully the sense of an earlier and other culture, we can nevertheless, it seems to me, have some sensation of it by paying close attention to practices within our own culture which seem somehow closer to that other one. I have found certain passages in romantic poetry strikingly evocative in that regard. For one example, among many possible, I will cite a famous passage from "The Prelude":

> I dipped my oars into the silent lake,
> And, as I rose upon the stroke, my boat
> Went heaving through the water like a swan;
> When, from behind that craggy steep till then
> The horizon's bound, a huge peak, black and huge,
> *As if with voluntary power instinct*
> *Upreared its head.* I struck and struck again,
> And growing still in stature the grim shape
> Towered up between me and the stars, and still,
> *For so it seemed, with purpose of its own*
> *And measured motion like a living thing,*
> *Strode after me.*[27]

The poet, even the high romantic, locates the space of nature which is not a thing, in the no-place, the utopia of childhood, and from the point of view of the adult, the "working" poet,[28] it must all be displaced into the realm of "as if" and "seeming," marginalized, however longed for. In a sense, we might say that in the absence of an active (however repressed) cultural unconscious, the only resources for the recovery of the unreified nature are in the individual psyche and its childhood memories.

If my reading has any historical validity, the true inheritors of midrash are the kabbalists, for whom the world is populated with anthropomorphic entities, from animals to trees to books. Thus Gershom Scholem refers to a "classical period" in the development of religion, "in which the scene of religion is no longer Nature, but the moral and religious action of man and the community of men, whose interplay brings about history as, in a sense, the stage on which the drama of man's relation to God unfolds," and then jumps to a "romantic period" of mysticism, which "strives . . . to bring back the old unity which religion has destroyed, but on a new plane, where the world of mythology and that of revelation meet in the soul of man."[29] In my reading of this midrash, however, we have a third term, mediating between these two, in which nature itself is projected into history and into moral and religious action in a community of man and nature. In such a world, it is irrelevant to speak of "personification" altogether—as it would be irrelevant to speak of the portrayal of George Washington in a history book as personification; the world is already personal. It is reification which is the trope.

I have interpreted the midrashic text as bringing to consciousness, as it were, repressed elements of cultural history which are scattered throughout the biblical text. Both the repression and its interpretation belong to a kind of psychic repression within the collective (that is, socio-ideological) consciousness of the people. By putting it in these terms, I have already signaled a kind of homology that I see between psychical and political repression and return of the repressed. It is intriguing that this homology or ambivalence of the psychological and the cultural-political in the conflict with polytheism has already been recorded in the Talmud:

"And they cried out unto God in a loud voice" [Neh. 9:4]. What did they say? Rav (and some say Rabbi Johanan) says, "Woe is us; this is the one who destroyed the temple, and burned the holy place, and killed all of the righteous ones, and exiled Israel from their land, and still he dances among us. What is the reason You gave him to us? Is it not to receive reward [for resisting him]? We don't want him or his reward!" A sherd fell from heaven with the word "truth" written on it. . . . They sat in fast for three days and three nights, and he was given over to them. A figure like a lion of fire went out from the Holy of Holies. A prophet said unto Israel: "That was the inclination to worship strange gods, as it is said, 'That is the evil.' [Zech. 5:8]"[30]

This rather obscure legend requires some exegesis. After the return from the Babylonian exile, the book of Nehemiah tells us of a great revival of religious fervor. The Talmud asks here what was the burden of the prayer which they prayed on that occasion and answers that they prayed to be delivered of the desire to worship idols, recognizing that it was this desire which had led the Israelites into exile and all of its terrors. We see here an amazing confluence of political and psychic imagery. The "evil inclination," that is, the temptation to worship idols, is understood to be both a collective and an individual force—or better, a collective force realized within each individual. This dual nature is depicted by being referred to in psychological terms but dealt with in political ones. The activity against it is that of the "Men of the Great Assembly," the semi-legendary governing body of the Jewish people at the end of the second temple period. Their prayers being answered, the evil inclination is delivered into their hands. As Saul Lieberman has argued, this is an etiological legend; it explains the fact that, while the ancient Jews were inclined to idol worship, the ones of rabbinic (talmudic) times were not.[31] It thus provides evidence that the rabbis considered the temptation of polytheism a dead issue. It indicates memory, as well, of the historical struggle that killed that temptation.

We can offer now a model for the "regression" of the rabbis, and account for this reversal of an apparent progression in the history of consciousness. As Frederic Jameson has argued, "strategies of containment are not only modes of exclusion; they can also take the form of repression in some stricter Hegelian sense of the persistence of the older repressed content beneath the later formalized surface."[32] In this model, the Bible's allusions to the ancient myth of the rebellion of the sea are precisely the older repressed content beneath the formalized surface of the Bible. I would suggest, therefore, that given that the rabbis had no fear of the Jews succumbing to polytheism, they were able to allow the barely repressed mythic intertext of the Bible to resurface, as it were, into textual consciousness. If, as I have suggested, Sidney's figurative reading is responding to the textual surface of Psalm 114, the literalized midrashic reading is going below this surface and touching the repressed mythic intertext. In the midrash, the coming of God into the world and the psychological effect which it had on the sea need no longer be reduced from myth to the figure of prosopopeia, which gives voice to the voiceless-by-nature, but can be given full-fledged narrative and visual representation, representing nature as having its own voice.

This text and its reading can offer us insight, then, into the general dialectics of cultural history. History is not a one-way street. Older formations remain. They manifest themselves in the social body as dissident groups, in the individual as hidden and partly repressed desires, in the texts of the culture as intertextuality. Since the fragments of such older cultural forms are not entirely expunged from the "textual unconscious," cultural history can, as it were, regress, transforming and recovering older orientations to the world. While this textual unconscious is perhaps only a metaphor, it seems to be one of great heuristic value. Reversing the Lacanian dictum, we can say that language is structured like a psyche and the reading of sign systems can have the same dynamic dimensions as the reading of the negotiations of the conscious and the unconscious in the individual.

· 7 ·

THE SONG OF SONGS,
LOCK OR KEY:
THE HOLY SONG AS A MASHAL

Pseudo-Saadya, an anonymous Jewish commentator of the tenth century, characterized the Song of Songs as a "lock to which the key has been lost."[1] Some few centuries earlier the rabbis of the midrash regarded the holy song as a mashal, a hermeneutic key to the unlocking of the Torah. *However, both the rabbis and Saadya interpreted the Song of Songs itself in essentially the same fashion*, as a poem on the love between God and Israel. The question immediately rises: how can it be that opposite theories can lead to the same interpretation? What is the meaning of this opposition of theory? What happened, historically, to generate this difference in the apprehension of the very nature of the text? These are the questions I would like to explore in this chapter, with a particular view toward achieving greater understanding of midrash and of rabbinic thought about interpretation and meaning.

As portrayed in the midrash, Solomon, the author of the Song, is the very prototype of the rabbinic reader. In the sequel to the passage quoted above in chapter 5, the rabbis give us no less than five meshalim, through which we can get a double handle—through the content and the form—on the meaning of Solomon's interpretive work:

> Rav Nahman gave two [parables]: It is like a great palace with many entrances, and all who entered it would lose the way to the entrance. A wise man came and took a rope and attached it to the entrance, and all would enter and exit by following the rope. Thus until Solomon came, no man could understand the words of Torah; but once Solomon had come, all began to understand the words of Torah. Rav Nahman gave another version: Like a thicket of reeds, and no man could enter into it, and a wise man came and took a sickle and mowed, then all began to enter and exit by way of the mowed [path]. So Solomon. Said Rabbi Yose: It is like a basket full of fruits, which had no handle, and it could not be carried, and someone wise came and made for it handles, and it began to be carried by its handles. So until Solomon came, no one could understand the words of Torah, but once Solomon had come, everyone began to comprehend Torah. R. Shila said: It is like a pot full of boiling water, which had no handle to carry it, and someone

came and made it a handle, and it began to be carried by its handle. R.
Hanina said: It is like a deep well full of water, and its waters were cold and
sweet and good, but no one could drink of them. Someone came and provided a rope [tied to] a rope, a cord [tied to] a cord, and he drew from it and
he drank. Then all began to draw and drink. So from word to word, from
mashal to mashal, Solomon comprehended the secret of Torah, as is written,
"The meshalim of Solomon the son of David, King of Israel" [Prov. 1:1.]—by
virtue of his meshalim, Solomon comprehended the words of Torah.

These little narratives are themselves meshalim of the mashal and give us
accordingly a clear insight into the midrashic reading of Song of Songs. The
mashal is a story whose meaning by itself is perfectly clear and simple, and
because of its simplicity enables one to interpret by analogy a more complex,
difficult, or hermetic text. Of recent writers, it seems that only Gerald Bruns
has realized the crucial import of this text for the theory of midrash:

> The passage is essentially a litany of parables giving the theory of the parable
> as a hermeneutic rather than (as we would figure it) a literary form: the
> parable is a vehicle of instruction in the meaning of Scripture—but notice
> that it is a vehicle of a special kind. It does not convey a meaning to an
> audience, rather it conveys the audience to the meaning. The meaning of the
> Torah is, after all, a hidden meaning and is meant to remain so: it is not to be
> carried out of the Torah, that is, its hiddenness is not to be dispelled by
> understanding but requires to be preserved, for hiddenness is an essential
> part of that which is to be understood.[2]

Bruns draws a distinction between a literary and a hermeneutic form, and
indeed the function of the mashal as it is described from within the culture is
that it is interpretive. I am less in agreement with the general description that
he draws of the nature of this hermeneutic. It does not seem to me obvious
that this text is claiming that the meaning of the Torah is hidden and meant to
remain so. Indeed, in my reading, such propositions as that the Torah was in
the past like a thicket into which no one could enter, but now one can enter,
indicate that there has been a fundamental change in the status of the Torah as
a result of the interpretive activity of Solomon and his rabbinic followers. I am
not certain, moreover, that Bruns has paid enough attention to the differences
between the different images of the mashal conveyed in these meshalim. Thus
in R. Yohanan's first version, the people can get in but not out, but in the
second, they cannot even enter. In R. Yose's mashal, the basket which cannot
be carried has sweet and good things; in R. Shila's, it holds something dangerous, which if it cannot be carried properly can kill. Finally, R. Hanina's image is
similar to R. Yohanan's second one, except that it adds the image of the Torah
itself as water, as the goal, and not as the space into which one has to enter;
furthermore, it speaks of conveying the goal to the people and not the people
into the goal. The exact hermeneutic analogues of these metaphorical differ-

ences are difficult for me to grasp, but they do not seem to support Bruns's claim that the meaning of the Torah is meant to remain hidden. However, one point is clear and should be amplified, for it will be of some importance in my whole argument: the mashal is not a text which is itself enigmatic; it is a text whose declared function is to interpret.[3] I will cite again a passage which I have discussed in chapter 5:

> The rabbis say: Do not let this mashal be light in your eyes, for by means of this mashal one comes to comprehend the words of Torah. A mashal to a king who has lost a golden coin from his house or a precious pearl—does he not find it by means of a wick worth a penny? Similarly, let not this mashal be light in your eyes, for by means of this mashal one comes to comprehend the words of Torah. Know that this is so, for Solomon, by means of this mashal understood the exact meaning of the Torah. Rabbi Judah says: It is to teach you that everyone who teaches words of Torah to the many is privileged to have the Holy Spirit descend upon him. From whom do we learn this? From Solomon, who because he taught words of Torah to the many was privileged to have the Holy Spirit descend upon him and uttered three books, Proverbs, Ecclesiastes, and Song of Songs.[4]

Solomon's texts are figured here as a source of light which illuminates the dark places of the Torah. This characterization is explicable in terms of the ancient taxonomy of texts into "light and dark." Bruns has pointed out

> a commonplace distinction between light and dark sayings, or between proverbs and enigmas, where the one is a truth which circulates widely and which everyone can recognize, whereas the other requires study, reflection, investigation, and the assistance of the sorts of special insight possessed by unique individuals such as Tiresias or even Oedipus: people who are required to cope (often as a matter of life or death) with riddles and prophecies.[5]

We have, therefore, an ancient topos which divides texts into two categories: those whose meaning is available to all—light sayings or proverbs, and those whose meaning is reserved for an esoteric elect—dark sayings or enigmas. This typology is certainly relevant here, and the rabbis are clearly placing Song of Songs into the category of *light* sayings—proverbs and not enigmas. Indeed the Song is a "proverbial" text whose very function is to illumine the dark sayings of Torah. By reading Song of Songs, Proverbs, and Ecclesiastes as meshalim, then, the midrash is claiming that they are not hermetic texts, "locks to which the key has been lost," but hermeneutic keys to the unlocking of the hermetic Torah, or, in the words of the midrash itself, "the secret of Torah." I would suggest that the rabbis read the Song of Songs as a mashal written by Solomon to be hermeneutic key to the unlocking of the book of Exodus. In this chapter, I would like to show *how* the Song of Songs has been read as such a mashal by the Mekilta. I will consider as well the relation of midrashic reading to allegoresis—particularly with regard to that classic of allegoresis, the common tradition of Song of Songs interpretation.[6]

This characterization of the midrashic interpretation of the Song as an interpretive mashal, similar to the meshalim of the midrash which I have analyzed in the last chapter, is not the generally accepted one. The most often encountered approach understands the midrash on Song of Songs to be an allegorical reading similar in kind to the later Jewish interpretations of the poem as well as the Christian readings. The claim is made, in effect, that the hermeneutic method is the same; only the specific allegorical identifications are different, with God and Israel the male and female protagonists, rather than Christ and the Church. One finds this view in nearly every hand-commentary or introduction to the Song of Songs.[7]

However, it seems to me that we must clearly distinguish the midrashic reading of the Song from that of allegorists such as Origen. Aphoristically, we might say that the direction of Origen's reading is from the concrete to the abstract, while the direction of midrash is from abstract to concrete. Or, using Jakobsonian terminology, at least heuristically, we could say that allegorical reading involves the projection of the syntagmatic plane (metonymy) of the text onto a paradigmatic place of meaning, while midrash projects paradigms (metaphor) into a syntagmatic plane of narrative-history. Thus, while seemingly similar strategies of reading (and often genetically connected ones),[8] Origen's allegoresis and midrash are really quite different from each other. I would like to add two clarifications at this point. The first is that the category of "allegory," both as a genre(?) of text production and as a reading practice, is a notoriously slippery one. Therefore, it should be clear that when I say allegoresis in this text I mean allegorical reading of the Philonic-Origenal type, which has a fairly clear structure as well as explicit theoretical underpinnings. The other point is that I am *not* contrasting Jewish with Christian modes of reading. The Gospels themselves, Paul and even much later Christian literature, contain much that is midrashic in hermeneutic structure (more, in my opinion, than is currently recognized, e.g., *Piers Plowman*). Moreover, much authentic Jewish hermeneutic is allegorical or otherwise "logocentric" in structure. Nor am I trying to claim that midrash is more valuable than Alexandrian allegoresis; I wish only to clarify the two modes of reading as different in order to understand midrash better.

Let us consider this difference by examining Origen's reflections on his method. In the third book of his great commentary on the Song of Songs, the Alexandrian father has discussed in detail the theory behind his allegoresis. It is explicitly founded on a Platonic-Pauline theory of correspondence between the visible things of this word and the invisible things of God.[9] Origen goes on to say:

> So, as we said at the beginning, all the things in the visible category can be related to the invisible, the corporeal to the incorporeal, and the manifest to

those that are hidden; so that the creation of the world itself, fashioned in this wise as it is, can be understood through the divine wisdom, which from actual things and copies teaches us things unseen by means of those that are seen, and carries us over from earthly things to heavenly.

But this relationship does not obtain only with creatures; the Divine Scripture itself is written with wisdom of a rather similar sort. Because of certain mystical and hidden things the people is visibly led forth from the terrestrial Egypt and journeys through the desert, where there was a biting serpent, and a scorpion,[10] and thirst,[11] and where all the other happenings took place that are recorded. All these events, as we have said, have the aspects and likenesses of certain hidden things. And you will find this correspondence not only in the Old Testament Scriptures, but also in the actions of Our Lord and Saviour that are related in the Gospels.

If, therefore, in accordance with the principles that we have now established all things that are in the open stand in some sort of relations to others that are hidden, it undoubtedly follows that the visible hart and roe mentioned in the Song of Songs are related to some patterns of incorporeal realities, in accordance with the character borne by their bodily nature. And this must be in such wise that we ought to be able to furnish a fitting interpretation of what is said about the Lord perfecting the harts, by reference to those harts that are unseen and hidden.[12]

Origen's text describes a perfect correspondence between the ontology of the world and that of the text. In both there is an outer shell and an inner meaning. We see accordingly the metaphysical grounding of the allegorical method used by Origen, and indeed by Philo[13] as well. In order for the Scripture to have an "inner meaning," there must be an ontological structure that allows for inner meaning. Allegoresis is thus explicitly founded in a Platonic universe. Indeed, it is no accident that for Origen, the Song of Songs has three meanings, a corporeal one, a pneumatic one, and a psychic one, for we have here the "Platonic tripartite man—body-soul-spirit—applied to the Word of God, in which Origen sees an incarnation of the Holy Spirit."[14] Moreover, as Lawson has pointed out, "If the Logos in His Incarnation is God-Man, so, too, in the mind of Origen the incarnation of the Pneuma in Holy Scripture is divine-human."[15]

All this is very far from the description of hermeneutic activity which the midrash offers:

Ben-Azzai was sitting and interpreting [making midrash], and fire was all around him. They went and told Rabbi Akiva, "Rabbi, Ben-Azzai is sitting and interpreting, and fire is burning all around him." He went to him and said to him, "I heard that you were interpreting, and the fire burning all around you." He said, "Indeed." He said, "Perhaps you were engaged in the inner-rooms of the chariot [theosophical speculation]." He said, "No. I was sitting and stringing the words of Torah [to each other], and the Torah to the Prophets and the Prophets to the Writings, and the words were as radiant/joyful as when they were given from Sinai, and they were as sweet as at their original giving. Were they not originally given in fire, as it is written, 'And the mountain was burning with fire' [Deut. 4:11]?"[16]

Ben Azzai does not speak of having achieved the original meaning or inner meaning or hidden meaning of Torah, but only of having read in such a way that he reconstituted the original *experience* of revelation.[17] He did what he did, not by linking texts with their meanings but by linking texts with texts, that is, by revealing the hermeneutic connection between the Prophets and Writings and the Torah. For the midrash the correspondences are not between things seen and their hidden or inner meanings, but between texts and the historical contexts in which they were produced or to which they apply, or texts and other texts, between signifiers and signifiers, not between signifiers and signifieds. In midrash, emotional and axiological content is released in the process of generating new strings of language out of the beads of the old. Indeed, if Origen is correct in his description of his own, and it would seem, *mutatis mutandis*, of Philo's hermeneutics, his type of allegoresis is only possible in a Platonic world of ideal forms, for which there is precious little evidence in early rabbinic thought. In midrash, the Written Text is not read by recovering the Oral Event of its original speaking as in a logos theology, but neither is the process of reading it characterized by absence as in some contemporary theories of meaning; rather it is re-citing the Written Torah, as in Ben-Azzai's wonderful experience, recreating a new event of revelation.

The crucial concept for understanding how the midrash relates the texts of the Writings to the text of the Torah is the concept of *dugma* or *mashal*. *The text of the Writings is itself understood as a mashal*, that is, as a series of readings in figurative language of the text of the Torah, which provides through these figures powerful emotional and axiological realizations of the narrative situations described mimetically in the Torah itself. Moreover, the formal device of mashal is, as we have seen, used self-consciously by the midrash as a tool for "stringing together the verses of the Torah and the Writings." Thus the common prophetically used mashal which compares Israel to a bride and the Covenant to a wedding provided the rabbis with sufficient motivation for reading the Song of Songs as they did, as a figurative poem interpreting the *text* of the love between Israel and God at the moment of their nuptials—the Exodus and its sequels. Jeremiah's, "I have remembered for you the grace of your youth, the love of your honeymoon, your following after Me in the wilderness" [Jer. 2:2] or Isaiah's, "as the groom rejoices over his bride, so shall your God rejoice over you" [Isa. 62:5]—these were the models for application of the mashal, song of Songs, to the love of bride and bridegroom at the Red Sea and at Sinai.[18]

The first text I will analyze here illustrates very nicely the reading of Song of Songs as a mashal which interprets the Torah. The text is found in *Song of Songs*

Rabba on the verse, "My dove in the clefts of the rock, let me hear thy voice"
[Song. 2:14]:

> The one of the house of R. Ishmael teaches: In the hour in which Israel went
> out from Egypt, to what were they similar? To a dove which ran away from a
> hawk, and entered the cleft of a rock and found there a nesting snake. She
> entered within, but could not go in, because of the snake; she could not go
> back, because of the hawk which was waiting outside. What did the dove do?
> She began to cry out and beat her wings, in order that the owner of the
> dovecote would hear and come save her. That is how Israel appeared at the
> sea. They could not go down into the sea, for the sea had not yet been split
> for them. They could not go back, for Pharoah was coming near. What did
> they do? "They were mightily afraid, and the children of Israel cried out unto
> the Lord" [Exod. 14:10], and immediately. "The Lord saved them on that
> day" [Exod. 14:30].[19]

What is going on in this text? First of all, the clearly figurative utterance, "My
dove in the clefts of the rock, let me hear thy voice," is being expanded into a
full narrative, or rather it is being provided with a narrative context in which it
can be read. What is the dove doing in the clefts of the rock? Who is addressing
her? Why does he want to hear her voice, or why is it necessary that she make
a sound? All of these questions are being answered by narrative gap-filling. The
dove is in the rock, because she is afraid. The rock is not a sufficient protection
for her. The speaker is her master, and she must cry out so that he will save
her. However, the claim is being made that this figure refers to a concrete
situation in Israel's history, the crisis situation at the shore of the Red Sea. In
order that we experience fully that situation, that we understand the predica-
ment of the people, why they cried out unto the Lord and why He answered
them, the verse of Song of Songs is associated with it, by means of the mashal
or narrative figure. This is not truly an interpretation of a verse of Song of
Songs, but rather of a verse of Exodus.[20] The assumption having been made
that Solomon wrote his poem as a key to the reading of the Torah, that poem is
then read by reading it into (literally) a narrative context in the Torah. Its
figures are made concrete by being identified with particular situations and
characters from the Torah history. Those situations are rendered axiologically
and emotionally sharper by the figures of the poetic text.

As evidence for this claim, I would like to offer another text, a parallel
version, indeed, of the same text, from the Mekilta, which originates in the
same "school of R. Ishmael":

> *They were mightily afraid, and the children of Israel cried out unto the Lord* [Exod.
> 14:10]. *Stand still and see the salvation of the Lord* [Exod. 14:13]. To what were
> the Israelites at that moment like? To a dove fleeing from a hawk, and about
> to enter a cleft in the rock where there is a hissing serpent. If she enters there
> is the serpent! If she stays out there is the hawk! In such a plight were the

Israelites at that moment, the sea forming a bar and the enemy pursuing. Immediately they set their mind upon prayer. Of them it is *interpreted* in the tradition:[21] "O my dove that art in the clefts of the rock, let me hear thy voice."[22]

Now we can see clearly what I would claim is probably the original context of this mashal. The interpreter, in order to render the situation of the children of Israel with the sea at their front and the enemy at their back sharp and tangible, adopted the figure of a dove fleeing from an eagle and a snake, a figure which brings the pathos of the situation home very poignantly. However, that figure is not drawn from the imagination of the midrashist but taken from the stock of figures given in the tradition, in the sacred writings, i.e., in the mashal which was "formulated" by Solomon to enable us to understand the words of Torah. Note well that in neither case (neither as interpretation of the verse of Song of Songs nor as interpretation of the verse in Exodus), do we have a translation of the verse to another level of signification, a pairing of a signifier with a signified. We have rather the establishment of an intertextual connection between two signifiers which mutually read each other. The narrative-mashal here is not a literary form but a hermeneutic figure (to use Bruns's apt formulation); it is a *dugma*, pattern or figure, which is used by the midrashist to enable the two verses to speak to each other.

Now, admittedly, there is nothing in the verse of Song of Songs here which explicitly directs our attention to the situation and the verse of Exodus, although there is a hint in the verse, "I have compared thee to a horse in the cavalry of Pharoah." Hence, we might feel that the midrashist has gone beyond what we would call reading in "chaining the words of Torah to the Writings." It will be instructive, therefore, to see cases in which precisely the same technique is used, where, I submit, we would freely grant that the Writings are indeed interpreting a verse from the Torah. We do not have far to look. In the previous chapter, I have shown how one of the Psalms has been used by the Mekilta in precisely the same way that we find Song of Songs being used here. That text in Psalms *does* indicate explicitly that it refers to the narrative situation of the Exodus: "When Israel went out of Egypt." In other words, there we have a case where the surface form of the later poetic text is manifestly a reference to the earlier prose narrative—a situation which is, of course, very common in the Bible and particularly in Psalms. In fact, many critics consider the psalm titles which place the poems into specific narrative contexts in the life of David to be a kind of proto-midrash.[23] They perform the same kind of hermeneutic activity which the midrash is doing on the psalm and also on the Song, namely, to place the poetic text into a specific historical narrative context. The hermeneutic move which the midrash makes in order to relate the text of Song of Songs to Exodus is the same as the one used in the mashal analyzed in the previous chapter to relate the psalm to Exodus. In both instances, a figurative dialogue, a poetic personification of somewhat vague reference, is given a historical context which illumines and sharpens the motivations and events of the prose text. The vehicle of the narrative creation in both cases is the mashal, which fulfills a formal function ancillary to the hermeneutic coreading of the two texts.[24] I claim that this method of reading the Song of Songs, placing its dialogues into the historical context of the Exodus (which is the primary approach of *Song of Songs Rabba*), was inspired by such textual situations as the explicit relationship of Psalm 114 and Exodus 14. Essentially, then, the midrashic reading of Song of Songs manifests what Fishbane has called "the widespread tendency in early rabbinic midrash to 'historicize the non-historical,' that is, to correlate the psalms of the MT with events known from the sacred history—in line with the dictum that 'everything which David said in his book was said of himself, of all Israel, and of the past and future of Israel.' "[25] This is what the rabbis meant when they said that Song of Songs is a mashal.

For another example of this hermeneutic principle, we turn to the midrash on the Song of Songs, where again we find the above verse being related to Exodus:

> R. Eliezer decoded [*patar*] the verse in the hour that Israel stood at the sea. *My dove in the cleft of the rock in the hiding place of the steep* [Song 2:14], that they were hidden in the hiding place of the sea—*Show me your visage*; this is what is written. "Stand forth and see the salvation of the Lord" [Exod. 14:13]—*Let me hear your voice*; this is the singing, as it says, "Then Moses sang" [Exod. 15:1]—*For your voice is lovely*; this is the Song—*And your visage is beautiful*; for Israel were pointing with their fingers and saying "This is my God and I will beautify Him" [Exod. 15:2]. [Dunansky, p. 73]

In this text, as in the previous one, the verse is interpreted as referring to the crossing of the Red Sea, albeit to a different moment in that passage. The earlier reading placed it in the moment of desolation before God showed His saving hand, as it were, while here it is read at the very moment of salvation. The verse of Exodus, where it says, "stand forth," is tallied with the verse of Song of Songs where the speaker appealing to his beloved who is hidden calls to her to come out from hiding and show him her face. The rest follows from this. The last clause requires explanation, however. The word which I have translated "visage" is generally glossed "countenance." However, its root is from the verb "to see." Moreover, it can be understood as a participal of the causative form of that verb, thus meaning "showing or pointing out." R. Eliezer, accordingly, takes it as if to mean, "And your pointing is beautiful," that is, when you pointed to Me with your fingers and said (in the song at the sea), "*This* is my God and I will ascribe beauty to Him."[26]

R. Akiva interprets the verse of the Song of Songs using the same hermeneutic principles but applying the text to a different context in Exodus, namely the revelation at Sinai:

R. Akiva decoded the verse in the hour that they stood before Mt. Sinai. *My dove in the cleft of the rock in the hiding place of the steep* [Song 2:14], for they were hidden in the hiding places of Sinai. *Show me your visage*, as it says, "And all of the people saw the voices" [Exod. 20:14]—*Let me hear your voice*, this is the voice from before the commandments, for it says "All that you say we will do and we will hear" [Exod. 24:7]—*For your voice is pleasant*; this is the voice after the commandments, as it says, "God has heard the voice of your speaking; that which you have said is goodly" [Deut. 5:25].

For R. Akiva as for R. Eliezer, the verse from the Song of Songs is a figurative description of the Jewish people, though not at the Red Sea but at Sinai. However, R. Akiva's reading in this version that "Let me see your visage" means the "seeing" of the voices is somewhat difficult, as the speaker of the verse seems to be God all through, and of course it was the people who saw the voices, not God. There is, to be sure, a lovely irony in the idea that both seeing and hearing refer to voice; the people saw God's voice, as it were, and God heard their voice.

These interpretations are to be explained by the tannaitic claim that the Song of Songs was actually said with reference to either the events at Sinai or the crossing of the sea. As my late teacher, the great talmudist Saul Lieberman, has shown, each of the tannaim of the midrash reads the Song of Songs *consistently* as referring to one or the other of these moments in the saving history.[27] The verses of the Song of Songs are accordingly interpreted by identifying not their signifieds but their cotexts, not that to which they refer in the world, but the texts of the Torah which decode them—and which they decode in turn. Once again, we find in the Mekilta a parallel to our passage which neatly reverses the relationship of verse to verse; the interpreter becoming the interpreted:

> *Under the mountain* [Exod. 19:16]. This teaches that the mountain was uprooted from its place and they drew near and stood underneath it, just as it says, "For you drew near and stood under the mountain" [Deut. 4:11]. *Of them it is interpreted in the tradition*: "O my dove who art in the clefts of the rock" [Song 2:14]. "Let me see thy appearance," that is, the twelve pillars for the twelve tribes of Israel. "And let me hear they voice," these are the ten commandments, "For thy voice is lovely," after the ten commandments, "And thy appearance is beautiful—And all of the congregation drew near and stood before God" [Lev. 9:5].

Again we have a text from the Song of Songs which is explicitly marked as interpretation of the Torah's narrative discourse—"Of them it is interpreted in the tradition."[28] This parallel interprets the text of *Song of Songs Rabba*, and in its turn, also is interpreted by it. First of all we learn from here what R. Akiva meant when he said that the Jews were hidden in the clefts of Sinai. In the context of the general disruption of nature which is described at the time of the revelation at Sinai, it is perhaps not too extravagant on the part of the rabbis to interpret the verses of standing under the mountain concretely, i.e., that the mountain was flying in the air and the people quite literally stood under it. Once this move has been made, at any rate, the tally between this verse and the verse from Song of Songs is appropriate. God addresses the people of Israel, the dove, calling out to them from their hiding place under the mountain—in the clefts of the rock—with great poignancy, "Let me see your face." Moreover, we now have a clue to the reading of the difficult passage in the version of the *Song of Songs Rabba*. Notice that the same difficulty occurs in this version as well but displaced slightly. To be sure, the verse "Let me see your face" is no longer read as being in the context of God's showing of His voice to the people, but is now read as the people's showing of themselves to Him by building monuments.[29] But, the verse "Let me hear thy voice" is now Israel's speech, meaning "Let me hear the ten commandments." The key is that the verse is read as dialogue. "Let me hear thy voice" is indeed the people speaking to God, and His response is, "Indeed thy voice is lovely," since you accepted the ten commandments so willingly and "God has heard the voice of your speaking; that which you have said is goodly." Similarly we can understand now the "Let me see your visage" of the version above as part of a dialogue. The people ask to see the voice, and God answers, Indeed since even before the commandments were given you have expressed with your voice trust and faithfulness. Finally, the very mashal of Song of Songs applied to the Sinai hierophany has transformed the midrashic imagery of that moment entirely. Thus we read in the Mekilta:

> *And Moses brought forth the people out of the camp to meet God.* R. Yose said, Yehuda used to interpret "The Lord came from Sinai" [Deut. 33:2]—Do not read it literally, but read: "The Lord came to Sinai," to give the Torah to Israel. I, on the other hand, do not say that, but indeed "God came *from* Sinai," to receive Israel as the bridegroom comes forth (from the bridal canopy) to meet the bride. [Lauterbach, p. 218]

I can now suggest answers to the questions with which I began this chapter. The rabbis of the midrash who understood that the Writings as a whole are a reading of the Torah did not perceive the Song of Songs as being at all like a lock to which the key has been lost. They understood it rather as a hermeneutic key to the interpretation of Torah. The way in which the Writings were comprehended as interpretation was by relating the more or less vague situations of various poetic texts to specific parts of the Torah. The reading method was accordingly not allegorical—relating signifier to signified—but intertextual—relating signifier to signifier. But it is indeed possible for midrashic-intertextual readings to be substantially the same thematically as allegorical readings (e.g., to relate to the love of God for Israel), since the Torah-texts to which the Song of Songs was understood to refer describe the relationship of Israel to God. Thus the very same thematic material could be transposed, as it were, from the midrashic mode of the earlier rabbis to the allegorical mode of the later ones. This should not obscure for us, however, the fundamental differences between the two types of reading. For the rabbis of the midrash, the highest reality, other than God Himself, of course, is the Torah—that is, a text, not an abstract idea. No wonder, then, that reading on the highest level in midrash is intertextual reading, the connecting of texts to the ultimate Text, and not allegoresis, the connecting of texts to abstract ideas. Only in certain rabbinic circles—the Hellenistic Judaism of Philo in the midrashic period, or the later Platonically influenced Judaism which became dominant from the time of R. Saadya Gaon on—could allegorical reading methods replace the earlier midrash of the rabbis.

In the next and final chapter, we will read closely a particular instance of the reading of the Song of Songs as a mashal and examine its consequences in history.

·8·

BETWEEN INTERTEXTUALITY
AND HISTORY:
THE MARTYRDOM OF
RABBI AKIVA

♣

> Indeed the problem becomes one of rethinking the concepts of 'inside'
> and 'outside' in relation to processes of interaction between language
> and the world. Dominick LaCapra[1]

The relation between "textuality" and "history" has often been presented as if they were mutually exclusive ways of understanding the literary text. One extreme model, which has sometimes been called the formalist model, sees literature as occupying an autonomous ontological realm, divorced from and "above" the material and social conditions of its production. The other extreme, the historicist one, understands the text to be wholly determined by and to be a reflection of its historical circumstances.[2] Theorists have been struggling toward a more nuanced view of this relation than either of the above positions would allow.[3]

Reflection on midrash has been divided into virtually the same two schools of thought as above. Traditional scholarship has considered midrash a wholly transparent reflection of the historical conditions obtaining at the time of its creation. This is in spite of the fact that its explicit generic claim is to be interpretation of a text which belongs to another time and place. Indeed, it may be because of this claim. Since midrashic interpretation often seems so far from what we might imagine as paraphrase, it seems inevitably to condemn itself to a reading which takes it as a reflection of something else, almost as a kind of historical allegory, disguised as pseudocommentary. This version of historicism has the virtue of emphasizing the vital, ideological import of midrash, but underestimates the contribution to ideology of reading the Bible. More recently, theorists working in the "deconstructive" mode have read midrash in terms suggesting that it is a kind of protodeconstruction, a hermeneutics of Dionysian free play with the biblical text.[4] This move has had the great virtue of leading to a reconsideration of these texts as a *reading* of the Bible, but

117

seems to undermine the very significance of that reading for social practice, indeed for life and death.

A revised conception of the hermeneutics of midrash ought accordingly to allow us to reunderstand its relation to history and rabbinic culture and account for both its character as interpretation and its relation to life in historical time. My purpose in this chapter will be to draw together many of the themes of the book by studying closely one passage of the Mekilta. In my reading of this text, I will try to reveal a much more complex and exciting relationship between hermeneutic and historical practice than has been imagined by scholars of midrash until now.[5]

> *This is my God, and I will beautify Him* [Exod. 15:2]. Rabbi Akiva says: Before all the nations of the world I shall hold forth on the beauties and splendor of Him-Who-Spake-and-the-World-Came-to-Be! For, lo, the nations of the world keep asking Israel, "What is thy beloved more than another beloved, O most beautiful of women?" [Song. 5:9], that for His sake you die, for His sake you are slain, as it is said, We have loved you unto death [*'ad mwt*] "for thus do the maidens [*'almwt*] love Thee" [Song 1:3]—and it is said, "for Your sake we have been killed all the day" [Ps. 44:23]. You are beautiful, you are heroes, come merge with us!
>
> But Israel replies to the nations of the world: Do you know Him? Let us tell you a little of His glory: "My beloved is white and ruddy, braver than ten thousand. His head is purest gold; His hair is curls as black as a raven. His eyes are like doves by springs of water. . . . His cheeks are like perfumed gardens. . . . His palate is sweetmeats and He is all delight; This is my beloved and this is my friend, O daughters of Jerusalem" [Song 5:10 ff.].
>
> And when the nations of the world hear all of this praise, they say to Israel, Let us go along with you, as it is said, "Whither is thy beloved gone, O thou fairest among women? Whither hath thy beloved turned, that we may seek Him with thee?" [Song 6:1].
>
> But Israel replies to the nations of the world: You have no part of Him; on the contrary, "My beloved is mine, and I am His; I am my beloved's, and He is mine; He feedeth among the lilies" [Song. 2:16 and 6:3].[6]

Let us recapitulate some of the ways in which this text manifests differences from commentary as traditionally understood:

(1). Meaning is produced in the creative interaction between text being read, reader, and other texts, and does not even pretend to be a simple paraphrase of the interpreted text.[7]

(2). There is a certain erasure of difference between the text being interpreted and the interpreting text.[8]

(3). These last two result in an ambiguity of reference in the interpreting text. When and where does the conversation presented in the midrash take place?

(4). A crucial moment in the reading of this midrash is accomplished by linguistic play: the pun on *'almwt* (maidens) as *'al mwt* (until death).

Scholars of the historical school have universally reduced this text to a reflection of events that took place in the time of its speaker, R. Akiva, who died a martyr's death. Thus, the leading scholar of rabbinic thought, E. E. Urbach, argues with regard to our text, "Hadrian's decrees and the *consequent facts* of martyrdom as the supreme expression of the Jew's love for his Creator gave rise to interpretations that discovered in Canticles allusions to Jewish martyrology and to the uniqueness of Israel among the nations of the world. R. Akiva already expounded, 'I shall hold forth . . . ' "[9] Notice that Urbach begins his quotation *after* the verse upon which R. Akiva's midrash is presented as an interpretation, thus showing that he regards the claim of the midrash to be interpretation of that verse as irrelevant. Similarly, the historian Yitzhak Baer argued that "R. Akiva already expounded and said of the verse, 'This is my God': I shall hold forth. . . . The verse 'my beloved is white and ruddy' *alludes to the ecstatic vision* to which the martyrs were privy in the days of their torture and the hour of their death."[10] Again no effort is made to account for how R. Akiva's statement is connected as an interpretation to the Exodus verse. Even more explicitly, Gedaliah Alon remarks that "the passage *reflects* memories from after the war of the destruction, or it *describes* a reality from after the war of Quietus."[11] The reduction of the midrashic text to a reflection of its historical circumstances is thus practically a commonplace of the earlier scholarship in spite of the obvious truth that the passage claims to be doing something radically different. Moreover, it is universally assumed by these scholars that the historical context, so-called reality, is transparent and self-understood and can therefore have explanatory force with regard to the midrashic text.

In a passage quoted above, chapter 1, Joseph Heinemann has argued that it is the strangeness and apparent arbitrariness of the midrash, its distance from the plain meaning of the biblical narrative, which leads scholars to read its discourse as a transparent reflection of the time of the midrashists.[12] Such motivation for historicism depends on assuming that the "plain" sense is obvious (and indeed that there is such an entity); and, moreover, that this plain sense was believed in by the rabbis,[13] who nevertheless ignored it in favor of some other discourse about the meaning of the text (or, even, *ostensibly* about the meaning of the text). I would like to begin, then, by analyzing the interpretive moves of our midrash as they function in this text to produce its meanings. If we can detect here that the midrashic reading is generated by hermeneutic principles, which although different from ours, are not arbitrary or unexpected within their own system, then a major support for the purely historicist interpretation of midrash will have been weakened.

In an interpretive text, even one that locates meaning in the "shuttle space between the interpreter and the text,"[14] it makes sense to begin by looking at the interpreted text: "This is my God, and I will beautify Him" [Exod. 15:2]. This verse presented certain difficulty to its rabbinic readers. "Is it possible for flesh and blood to beautify their Creator!?"[15] R. Akiva's answer to this wonderment is that people beautify God when they sing His beauty. Up till now, then, we have a paraphrase of the verse. We begin to have midrash, however, with the expansion of this paraphrase into a full-fledged narrative with two protagonists, a conversation which is nowhere signified in the original verse, and with the importation of an entire passage from the Song of Songs. These are the sorts of moves which have led previous interpreters to locate the meaning of this text transparently in the time of the interpreter. However, it seems to me that this discourse is considerably more complex than such readings suggest, and much more of the story can be shown to have been generated by a practice of interpreting Scripture. I would like to show through my reading that it thematizes not the facts of martyrdom or some other extratextual reality, but precisely the issue of history itself; that far from being a simple reflection of facts which "gave rise to interpretations," it is a resource for the creation of that interpretation which is not secondary but integral to a life lived in a text.

The crucial word of the verse for my interpretation is the smallest, namely the demonstrative, "this." While there are many verses of the Bible in which the demonstrative can be read (or is even most simply read) as *anaphora* or *kataphora*, for the rabbis, "this" is compellingly deictic,[16] as certified by the following passage:

> *This month shall be for you* [Exod. 12:12]. R. Ishmael says: Moses showed the new moon to Israel and said to them: In this way shall you see and fix the new moon for the generations. R. Akiva says: This is one of the three things which were difficult for Moses to understand and all of which God pointed out to him with His finger. And thus you say: "And *these* are they which are unclean for you" [Lev. 11:29]. And thus: "And *this* is the work of the candelabrum" [Num. 8:4]. . . . R. Shimeon the son of Yohai says: Is it not a fact that all the words which He spoke to Moses He spoke only in the day? The new moon, of course, He showed him at night. How then could He, while speaking with him at day, show him the new moon, at night? R. Eliezer says: He spoke with him at day near nightfall, and then showed him the new moon right after nightfall. [Lauterbach, I, pp. 15-16]

A verse which is talking about a month is interpreted as being about the new moon, because it includes the demonstrative "this," which for the rabbis always signifies seeing and pointing with a finger, even where such an interpretation leads into obvious logical contradictions with other interpretive commonplaces, namely that God only spoke with Moses by day.[17] It is no wonder, therefore, that R. Akiva reads the verse, "*This* is my God," as signifying a theophany, an experience in which the Jews could point with their fingers at the visible God. We have, moreover, explicit evidence that this was the reading of our verse from R. Eliezer's remark in the Mekilta that from this verse we learn that, "a slave saw at the sea what neither Isaiah nor Ezekiel nor all of the other prophets ever saw."[18] That such a view was generally accepted is suggested, moreover, by the line from the daily evening prayer, "Thy children saw Thy power, splitting the sea before Moses; '*This* is my God,' they uttered and sang."

Another important signifier in the verse is the pronoun, "my." On my reading, it is this morpheme which sets up the rhetorical situation which R. Akiva's story expands. If there is a "my," then it seems that there is a "not yours." Indeed, in this verse the first person singular pronoun is repeated no less than four times.[19] As James Clifford, following Emile Benveniste, has acutely remarked, "Every use of 'I' presupposes a 'you,' and every instance of discourse is immediately linked to a specific shared situation."[20] It is hardly surprising, then, that the midrash understands "This is my God" to imply a rhetorical or dramatic situation in which Israel is addressing some other nation, and saying, "This is my God" and not yours.

For the rabbis, the Song of Songs is the record of a historical theophany, and in particular, the description of the lover in 5:9-16 is the description of God, as He was seen on that occasion.[21] Although there is some controversy among the early rabbis as to whether the theophany referred to is the one at Sinai or the one at the Red Sea, our text obviously fits into the view that reads it at the Red Sea. Accordingly, it is entirely plausible that R. Akiva associates the deictic "this" of "This is my God," with the same deictic of "This is my lover and my friend, O daughters of Jerusalem" in the Songs of Songs passage. The dialogue with the "daughters of Jerusalem" (who, if the maiden is Israel, must be the Gentiles) produces virtually the whole narrative. The story that R. Akiva tells is then generated, as it were, of itself by the force of the association of the two texts. The chapter of Song of Songs begins with the maiden (to be sure, after some coyness on her part) pursuing her lover through the streets of Jerusalem and being beaten and wounded by the guards. She adjures the daughters of Jerusalem to find her lover for her, in spite of her wounds, and tell Him that she is lovesick for Him. The daughters wonder at this request, and ask, "What is thy beloved, that you have so adjured us"—even though you are suffering so much for His love? Come join with us, "O most beautiful of women." At this point in Akiva's interpolating narrative, the maiden, Israel, answers: Let me describe His beauty, as I have seen Him, "*This* is my God, and I will sing His beauty. My beloved is white and ruddy. . . . *This* is my lover and this is my friend, O daughters of Jerusalem." The maidens become jealous and want such a lover also, but Israel answers, "My beloved is mine and I am His."

This reading of "my God" as mine and not yours was certainly amplified by the "This is my beloved and this is my friend, O daughters of Jerusalem" in the Song of Songs passage, and most explicitly by "My beloved is mine and I am His." I suggest, then, that the story is simply, for R. Akiva, the unpacking of the meaning and rhetorical force embodied in the verse, "This is my God and I will beautify Him," as it is unpacked by that text which, as I have shown in the previous chapter, was understood as the key to the meaning of this historical moment, the Song of Songs.

However, this reading is paradoxical and problematic, because the dialogue between the Jews and the Gentiles certainly could not have taken place alongside of the Red Sea. The Jews were not being killed for their God then, nor were there any Egyptians left alive with whom to talk. However, locating this story in historical time is also problematic, in spite of the views of the above-mentioned scholars. There simply was no time in which Jews were being killed en masse for the love of God, and there was a simultaneous desire of many Gentiles to convert to Judaism. Accordingly, the arguments of the historians as to whether the text refers to this period in the life of R. Akiva or that one only serve to demonstrate this paradoxicality of reference, this impossibility of interpreting our text as an indirect reference to historical events.[22] Moreover, the deixis of "this" in the Song of Songs verse suggests that an experience of theophany present to those speakers is also being evoked.

Here we have figured perfectly the paradoxical time of midrashic reading. The linguistic transformation of anaphora into deixis thematizes the issue of midrash brilliantly. Anaphora is the very figure of absence. "This which I am telling you about; this which was in the past; this which is history." Deixis is the very figure of presence. "This which I am pointing at; this which you can see." The absent moment of theophany is thus transformed into an evocation of a present moment of vision of God both in the form and in the content (or rather in the indistinguishable form-content) of the midrash. The absent moment of revelation is transformed into a present moment of reading. The text of the Text and the text of history (reality) merge, however tensely. When could this theophany be taking place, since it is not at the crossing of the Red Sea itself? A more detailed reading of the text will be required before we can suggest an answer to this question.

The midrash represents the relationship of God and the Jewish people as an erotic one—through the reading of Song of Songs into Exodus. However, Thanatos also introduces itself into this erotic idyll—formally and thematically. "For, lo, the nations of the world keep asking Israel, 'What is thy beloved more than another beloved, O most beautiful of women' [Song 5:9], that for His sake you die, for His sake you are slain, as it is said, We have loved you unto death [*'ad mwt*], 'for thus do the maidens [*'almwt*] love Thee' [Song 1:3]—and it is said, 'for Your sake we have been killed all the day' [Ps. 44:23]." Note that the theme of death is a simultaneous intrusion into the world of the text and into text of the world. This intrusion is represented in three ways: first, by the insertion of the verse from the beginning of the Song of Songs into a context which interprets the fifth chapter; second, by the violation of the language of that verse, via the transformation of *'almwt* [nubile maidens], the very symbol of Eros (here, however, maidens represented as desiring subjects and not as desired objects)[23] into '*al mwt* [until death], and third, by the insertion into this context of another text entirely, the verse from Psalm 44, "We are killed for You all the day." The violation of textual space which the midrash enacts can be read as a figure for the violation of the erotic relationship between the Jew and God implied by the fact that Jews are being killed in the real world of R. Akiva. Put yet another way, the transformation of '*almwt* into '*al mwt*, of love into death, is itself a representation of the question directed at God in other texts as well: If You love us so much, how come You kill us?

However, the text alludes to an answer as well. As we have seen often in this book, midrash often signifies by allusion to other biblical passages.[24] These allusions are discovered by observing the ungrammaticalities of the midrashic text, that is, linguistic forms which either do not quite fit their context or belong to another linguistic stratum. While the phrase, '*al mwt*, could mean "until death" in rabbinic Hebrew, its grammar is sufficiently unusual to call attention to itself; the normal form would be rather '*ad mwt*, as the midrash indeed glosses it. I would read this nearly ungrammatical form as an intertextual clue. The only place in the Hebrew Bible where '*al mwt* occurs in the sense of "until death" is verse 15 of Psalm 48. Moreover, this verse begins also with a language strongly reminiscent of the very verse that R. Akiva's midrash is reading, "*This* is God, our God, until eternity. He will lead us unto death."

The verse of the psalm overflows with potential meanings. The sober medieval commentator, R. A. Ibn Ezra, glosses it as follows:

> '*almwt* like '*wlmit*, until eternity, [the written consonants are the same; only the pronunciation varies], for He exists until eternity and leads until eternity. The Massorete has read this as two words, and their meaning is "until our death". R Moshe says it is from the root '*lm*, youth; He will lead us always as the fashion of the maidens, as He led us in the days of our youth.

We need not choose between these meanings, but from the perspective of contemporary reading practice can assume that they are all latent in the verse—eternity, death, and eros—a whole world of psychological resonances in a single word.

This verse is also (on rabbinic hermeneutical principles) a record of a theophany, again because of the deictic "*this*." Rabbis of a period only slightly later than R. Akiva animate the rich ambiguity of the Psalms verse by reading "until death" as "maidens," in precisely the reverse move of R. Akiva's reading of "maidens" as "death" in the Song of Songs verse:

> Rabbis Berechia and Helbo and Ula and Rabbi El'azar in the name of Rabbi Hanina have said: In the future God will lead the dance of the righteous . . . and they will point to Him with their fingers, as it says, "*this* is God, our God,

until eternity. He will lead us until death (*'al mwt*)" as maidens (*k'alamwt*), in the dances of the righteous.

It seems to me not too much to suggest, therefore, that R. Akiva's midrashic transformation of "maidens" into "until death" alludes to this very verse, in which death is transformed into maidens by the midrash. It is not only the two signifiers that can substitute for each other, but also their signifieds as well. Death becomes eros and eros death.

Now it is very important to note that Psalm 48 is itself a meditation on history. The psalmist, speaking at some indefinite time, recalls the distant past of the splitting of the sea in a series of blatant allusions to Exodus 15, the same text which R. Akiva is interpreting.[25] Moreover, he claims, "As we have heard, so have we seen," the very transformation of history into present experience which R. Akiva enacts by his transformation of anaphora into deixis. Finally, the psalmist draws past and present together with the future with his "In order that you tell the last generation: *this* is God, our God, until eternity. He will lead us until death." The psalm replicates in its thematics the very interpretation of history that the midrash makes both in its thematics and in its hermeneutic method. For the psalmist, it seems, the promise of God's self-revelation, of seeing Him again as He was seen at the crossing of the sea, redeems the vicissitudes of history. Indeed, the Greek translator of the Bible, Aqilas, a contemporary and colleague of R. Akiva, himself translates the *'al mwt* of the verse as *athanasia*, which the Palestinian Talmud, in its turn, retroverts as "the world in which there is no death." This suggests very strongly to me that R. Akiva's narrative with its paradoxical time-reference is, in truth, an eschatalogical narrative. For the rabbis the crossing of the sea was the type, of which the final redemption will be the antitype.[26]

Strong support for the eschatalogical reading of this story comes from yet another allusion. The phrase which the "daughters of Jerusalem" use to formulate their request to seek God with Israel, "Let us go along with you," is an exact quotation from the eschatalogical prophecy of Zech. 8:20-23, in which the Gentiles seek to join Israel, and it is couched in an archaic grammatical form, which is only found in biblical Hebrew.[27]

> Thus saith the Lord of hosts: The nations and the dwellers of great cities will come. And they will go, the dwellers of each one, saying, "Let us go and seek the face of the Lord, and seek out the Lord of hosts. I will go, even I." And there will come many nations and mighty peoples to seek the Lord of hosts in Jerusalem, and to seek out the face of the Lord.
> Thus saith the Lord of hosts: In those days, ten Gentiles will hold onto the garment of a Jew and say, "*Let us go along with you,* for we have heard that God is with you."

We find the same hermeneutical pattern that we have found above. A linguistic anomaly in the midrashic text—in this case the use of an archaic biblical form—is actually an allusion to another biblical text, which provides an important clue to the interpretation of the midrash. When we combine the midrashic text itself with its biblical subtexts, we can generate a strong reading of it. The interpreter stands in a position of desire. His Torah tells him of a moment of perfection when the people stood in such a marvelous union with God that what a slave saw then, no one has seen since. How can the desire to relive that moment of presence be fulfilled? the distance between the present reader and the absent moment of Presence is the tragedy of history. R. Akiva conquers history by bringing it into the present. For him, as well as for the psalmist, that which we have heard is what we have seen, and if death, time, and history interfere, they can be conquered through a reading strategy which eradicates them by effacing the difference between past, present, and future. Anaphora becomes deixis. This reading strategy is called midrash. Perhaps, then, what this midrash has to teach us about textuality is something about the inadequacy of the very oppositions that we make between textuality and history, or between intertextual reading strategies and those grounded in the outside world.

> In the hour that they took R. Akiva out [to be executed], his disciples said to him, "Our teacher, so far? [i.e., is this necessary]" He said to them, "All of my life I was troubled by this verse, 'And thou shalt love the Lord with all thy soul'—even though He takes your soul, and I said, when will it come to my hand that I may fulfill it? Now that it is come to my hand, shall I not fulfill it?"

R. Akiva's midrash joins Eros and Thanatos, and so do the stories of his death. According to the text just quoted above, R. Akiva died for the love of God; indeed he died because he held that this was the only way to fulfill the commandment "to love the Lord with all your soul." This is the "reality" to which the historians quoted above were appealing when they interpreted the midrash as a reflection of the events of the rabbi's life. However, these "events" are no less artifactual, no more factual, than the very midrash they are purported to be the explanation and referent of. Nevertheless, these texts must be connected. The love joined with death or fulfilled by death seems the same in both the midrash and the historiographical legend. If we do not read the midrash as a reflection of this "historical" event, how can we account for their congruence? I would suggest that we substitute for the language of "reflection" and "referentiality," which explicitly privileges one kind of text over others, a language of intertextuality. Seen in that light, R. Akiva's midrash and the story about his martyrdom belong to the same historical context and complex—neither is the context nor the explanation of the other, but both belong to the same cultural process. I suggest that R. Akiva's reading of the Torah, his midrash, led him to an apocalyptic view of the religious life. The high moment of union with God which the Jews experienced at the crossing of the sea could only be relived in two ways—on the national level at the moment of the *eschaton*, and on the personal level, by dying a martyr's death.

This ideology of death as the necessary fulfillment of the love of God appears often in texts of the time of R. Akiva. Thus we read in a halakic text of his period: "And thou shalt love the Lord with all thy soul: [This means] even when he takes your soul, and so it says, 'For Your sake have we been killed all of the day.' "[28]

Now this text is particularly significant for us, because it brings into the textual complex the exact same verse of Psalms which I considered an intrusion in the midrash of R. Akiva on "This is my God, and I will beautify Him." It seems that while we cannot speak of any precise historical background which determines the midrash, we can grasp hold in it of a very crucial cultural/ideological moment, the moment of the creation of the idea of martyrdom as a positive religious value per se. True, in the past also there was a concept of martyrdom, but it was very different from this one. The former model was that of the Hasmonean period, in which the martyr refuses to violate his or her religious integrity and is executed for this refusal; now we find martyrdom being actively sought as the only possible fulfillment of a spiritual need. To put this in more classical Jewish terminology: in the past martyrs refused to violate a negative commandment (to worship idols); in the present, they are fulfilling through their deaths a positive one (to love God).

The astounding thing is that we can almost actually catch this transition happening in our texts: "When Rabbi Akiva died a martyr's death, a verse from Canticles was also applied to him, 'Joshua b. Jonathan used to say of those executed by the wicked Turnus Rufus, They have loved Thee much more than the former saints, "sincerely have they loved Thee." ' "[29]

There were, indeed, saints in former times, that is, those who were willing to die for the faith; so why have R. Akiva and his fellows "loved Thee much more than the former saints"? I would claim that this is because they died with joy, with a mystic conviction; not only was it that their deaths were necessary, but that they were the highest of spiritual experiences. This transition is already identifiable in the parallel story of R. Akiva's martyrdom in the Palestinian Talmud:

> Rabbi Akiva was being judged before the wicked Tunius Rufus. The time for the reading of the "Shema" ["Hear O Israel", which includes the verse, "Thou shalt love the Lord with all thy soul!"] arrived. He began to recite it and smile. He said to him, "Old man, old man: either you are deaf, or you make light of suffering." He said, "May the soul of that man expire! Neither am I deaf, nor do I make light of suffering, but all of my life I have read the

verse, "And thou shalt love the Lord, thy God with all your heart, and with all your soul, and with all your property." I have loved Him with all my heart, and I have loved Him with all my property, but *until now, I did not know how to love Him with all my soul.* But now that the opportunity of [loving Him] with all my soul has come to me, and it is the time of the recital of the "Shema" [once again, the very moment to fulfill the commandment of loving God with all one's soul], *and I was not deterred from it; therefore, I recite, and therefore I smile.*[30]

In this text, we catch R. Akiva in the act, as it were, of discovering that dying is the way to fulfill the commandment of loving God (and, perhaps, as well, the way to relive the experience of seeing God in all His beauty). I am not claiming, of course, that this is "what actually happened," but rather that the text is the representation of a moment in the history of an ideology. Here R. Akiva did not know until now how to fulfill the commandment; in the (later) Babylonian version quoted earlier he already knew from before what it was he had to do, and was just waiting for the opportunity. These are then not two competing "reflections" of circumambient reality but two diachronically emplaceable stages in cultural history—the history of an idea. Our midrash, with its concatenation of Eros and Thanatos, death and the maiden, also represents the ideological, spiritual base and source for this very idea. It is hardly the case, then, that the midrash reflects some privileged external, unsemioticized reality. Reality exists—R. Akiva is not in a prison-house of language but in a Roman jail. He will undoubtedly be executed, but it is he who transforms this execution into a consummation of erotic love for the beautiful King.

This reverses, as well, the hierarchy which Baer assumed for our midrash and ecstatic vision. He interpreted R. Akiva's midrash of the Song of Songs by claiming, "The verse 'my beloved is white and ruddy' alludes to the ecstatic vision which the martyrs were privy to in the days of their torture and the hour of their death."[31] However, while torture may indeed be an external reality, ecstatic visions of the Godhead are a cultural production—a text. Not only, I would claim, does R. Akiva's midrash not reflect his martyrdom nor allude to his ecstatic visions; I suggest that it was rather the hermeneutic, intertextual connection of the Song of Songs with the Song of the Sea, of "This is my God and I will beautify Him" with "This is my beloved and this is my friend, O daughters of Jerusalem," and indeed, with "This is God, our God, He will lead us unto death," which inspired the idea of erotic, mystic death, led to the creation of the ideology of martyrdom, and indeed may have produced the ecstatic visions awarded to the martyr. R. Akiva may very well have had the ecstatic vision of the beloved at the hour of his death, but his midrash could hardly reflect that experience; if he did have such a wonderful experience, it was the reward his life in midrash gave him.

Scarcely divorced from history, but even more intimately connected with it than the historians imagined, midrash is a way of reading and living in the text of the Bible, which had and has profound implications for the life of the reader. If my reading has any cogency, R. Akiva is represented in the tradition as having died a martyr owing to his way of reading. Moreover, his model had profound implications for the development of martyrology. All through the Middle Ages, Jews went enthusiastically to a martyr's death with R. Akiva's words on their lips.

Epilogue

> . . .midrash gives us an insight into what interpretation always is (whatever the method) when interpretation *matters* to human life. In hermeneutical terms, midrash shows the historicality of understanding.[32]

We have come full circle. As remarked in the citation from Bruns in chapter 1 midrash is best understood as a continuation of the literary activity which engendered the Scriptures themselves. Because of this literary history, the Bible is characterized already by a degree of self-reflexivity, self-citation, and self-interpretation, which is perhaps more evident than in literatures that have had a different type of history.[33] The rabbis, as assiduous readers of the Bible, developed an acute awareness of these intertextual relations within the holy books, and consequently their own hermeneutic work consisted of a creative process of further combining and recombining biblical verses into new texts, exposing the interpretive relations already in the text, as it were, as well as creating new ones by revealing linguistic connections hitherto unrealized. This recreation was experienced as revelation itself, and the biblical past became alive in the midrashic present. The Song of Songs—as the high point of poetry in the Scriptures, understood as the record of a theophany—became the focus of desire for the two greatest theophanic moments in biblical history: the revelation at Mt. Sinai and the crossing of the sea. Midrash, by continuing the process of creation of Scripture, by being Oral Torah and not mere paraphrase of Written Torah, became a spiritual vehicle for the reliving of these great events, for making them present.

Many have sought to characterize midrash as an updating of Scripture, an effort to make it relevant to present day life and problems. James Kugel has well expressed the incompleteness of this view:

> And if we are to designate the Halakic reading of Scripture as a bridge between the Bible and the present-day Jew, out of fairness one must add that the bridge has another (if anything, greater) lane going in the opposite direction. For in midrash the Bible becomes, as stated, a world unto itself.

Midrashic exegesis is the way into that world; it does not seek to view present-day reality through biblical spectacles, neither to find referents of biblical
prophecy in present-day happenings, nor to find referents to the daily life of
the soul in biblical allegory. Instead it simply overwhelms the present; the
Bible's time is important, while the present is not; and so it invites the reader
to cross over into the enterable world of Scripture.[34]

This is a powerful and elegant formulation. My only disagreement is in the
dichotomy it makes between the two directions of the lane. In this essay, I hope
to have contributed something to an understanding of specifically how the
process of crossing over into the world of Scripture takes place in one midrashic
text. However, the reader who crosses over into the enterable world of Scripture remains nonetheless in his/her own, and inevitably his/her crossing into
the world of Scripture has powerful implications for life. We have seen just
what this "crossing over" into the world of Scripture could mean for such a one
as R. Akiva. The halakic bridge for him became a bridge between life and
death, and its meaning was revealed to him through his midrash. Poised thus
between intertextuality and history, midrash reveals the inadequacy of any
model of culture which divorces one way of making meaning from another.
The Torah read and lives lived are equally processes of making reality yield
human meaning, and midrash subsumes them both.

NOTES

Introduction

1. Gary Porton, "Defining Midrash," in *The Study of Ancient Judaism*, ed. J. Neusner (New York, 1981), pp. 59–60.

2. James Kugel, "Two Introductions to Midrash," in *Midrash and Literature*, ed. Geoffrey H. Hartman and Sanford Budick (New Haven, 1986), p. 91.

3. In an article, "The Date of the *Mekilta* de-Rabbi Ishmael," *HUCA* 39 (1968), pp. 117–144, Wacholder claimed that this midrash is a much later pseudepigraphic work. His view has been decisively and definitively disproved by Menahem Kahana in his article, "The Editions of the *Mekilta de-Rabbi Ishmael* on Exodus in the Light of Geniza Fragments" [Hebrew], *Tarbiz* 45 (1986), pp. 515–520. The Mekilta may be in the main, in fact, the earliest of rabbinic midrashic texts, although its final recension seems to have been a little later than some other early midrashim.

4. Whatever midrash is, it certainly is *not* "the process whereby a later writer revises or even reverses details of an earlier tale to make it conform to the growth of ethical doctrine," as Frank McConnell has it in his introduction to *The Bible and the Narrative Tradition*, ed. Frank McConnell (Oxford, 1986), pp. 10–11).

5. "As an anthropologist, I can't help remark that this ["believe in"] seems a somewhat disingenuous phrase for you to use here; it masks more than it asserts, and what it masks is vitally relevant" [Jonathan Boyarin].

6. I am by no means the first to address these questions in these terms. See chapter 1 for some historical discussion of the problem.

7. I place these terms in quotation marks because it is precisely their adequacy which will be at issue here.

8. Hans Frei, " 'Literal Reading' of Biblical Narrative in Christian Tradition," in *The Bible and the Narrative Tradition*, p. 73.

9. I would like to thank J. Derrida for his encouragement of my project and particularly for reading a very early version of some of this work and commenting on it. He is an extraordinarily generous teacher.

10. Wolfgang Iser, *The Act of Reading* (Baltimore, 1978), p. 21.

11. Riffaterre claims that the text controls and dictates its reading, including the filling in of its gaps in effectively only one way, while Iser leaves room for varying actualizations of the text. Cp. Iser's *The Act of Reading*, pp. 24 and 37–38 with, e.g., Riffaterre's "The Intertextual Unconscious," *Critical Inquiry* 13 (1987), p. 372.

12. There is an important analogy, yet to be explored, between the way that Jewish discourse and women's discourse have been marginalized. "Judaeo-Christian" repeats in significant ways the kind of suppression that "man" does. Cf. Julia Kristeva, "Women's Time," *The Kristeva Reader*, ed. Toril Moi (Oxford, 1986), p. 196.

13. Frank Kermode, *The Genesis of Secrecy* (Cambridge, Mass., 1979), p. 126.

14. Susan Handelman, *The Slayers of Moses: The Emergence of Rabbinic Interpretation in Modern Literary Theory* (Albany, 1982).

15. José Faur, *Golden Doves with Silver Dots* (Bloomington, 1986).

1. Toward a New Theory of Midrash

1. Yitzhaq Heinemann, *Darkhe ha'aggadh* [The ways of the aggadah], 3rd ed. (Jerusalem, 1974). I have spelled Heinemann's first name as Isaak throughout in accordance with German usage.

2. Compare the remarks of Susan Handelman, whose only citation of Heinemann's great work in her book, *The Slayers of Moses*, is to suggest that he "does not deal with the *philosophic* issues of meaning," (p. 234, n. 1), whereas, as Stern has pointed out in his review of her book (David Stern, "Moses-cide: Midrash and Contemporary Literary Criticism," *Prooftexts* 4 [1984], p. 197; see also his "Literary Criticism or Literary Homilies," *Prooftexts* 5 [1985], pp. 96–97), this is precisely what Heinemann's work is about, i.e., understanding aggada in terms of an articulated theory of literary meaning. The fact that we might see the philosophical grounding of his view as unsatisfactory from our present perspective is no excuse to ignore its presence. Indeed, the fact that a critic such as Handelman found it so easy to dismiss Heinemann only shows all the more how important it is to assess his work in English.

3. The traditional acronym for Rabbi Moses ben Maimon.

4. *Guide of the Perplexed*, III, 43. I have quoted the text in the translation of Shlomo Pines (Chicago, nd), pp. 572–573.

5. A. Geiger, *Wiss. Zeitschrift* V, p. 81, quoted in Heinemann, p. 198.

6. Of course, this is not meant to be taken literally. Benno Jacob was a Reform rabbi.

7. On this point, see the Section in this chapter entitled, "Toward a New Theory of Midrash."

8. David Stern insightfully defines homily as precisely that kind of interpretation with which it makes no sense to argue, *because it is really not claiming to be interpretation at all*, but a rhetorical device for entertainment and persuasion, without the authority of the text. Therefore, by definition, dialectic on the meaning of the text indicates that the text is not homily, whatever our view of the truth-value of the interpretations offered. See also the important paper of Judah Goldin, "The Freedom and Restraint of Haggadah," in Hartman and Budick, *Midrash and Literature*, pp. 57–77, esp. pp. 67ff.

9. This point has been made elegantly and forcefully with regard to the Bible by Meir Sternberg, *The Poetics of Biblical Narrative: Ideological Literature and the Drama of Reading* (Bloomington, 1985), pp. 24–25.

10. In a recently delivered lecture, Josef Stern has argued that in fact the Rambam is arguing that the midrashim are philosophical allegories and that his meaning here is also allegorically conveyed.

11. Joseph Heinemann, "The Nature of the Aggadah," in Hartman and Budick, p. 49, (emphasis added). This citation does not represent Heinemann's full judgment and

understanding of aggada, which is, in fact, much more nuanced than this single quotation would indicate.

12. Perhaps the classic of this genre of midrash studies is E. E. Urbach's *The Sages: Their Concepts and Beliefs*, trans. Israel Abrahams (Jerusalem, 1975). See also J. Elbaum, "R. Eleazar Hamoda'i and R. Joshua on the Amalek Pericope" [Hebrew], *Studies in Aggadah and Jewish Folklore* (=*Folklore Research Centre Studies* VII (Jerusalem, 1983), pp. 99–116. Compare also Chernus's interpretive methods discussed below, ch. 4.

13. Joseph Heinemann, *Aggadah and Its Development* [Hebrew], (Jerusalem, 1974), p. 75.

14. Ibid., pp. 77–78.

15. In fact, even Heinemann's assumption that this tradition is more ancient and independent of rabbinic midrash is very questionable from a scholarly point of view. The Targum may actually be quoting precisely this very midrash!

16. Ibid., pp. 4–5. On the opposition between history and life, see Hayden White's essay, "The Burden of History," in his *Tropics of Discourse* (Baltimore, 1978), pp. 27–50.

17. Paul de Man, *The Resistance to Theory* (Manchester, 1986), p. 77, has hinted at the power of George's presence in German cultural life. It is worth mentioning, however, that by the time *Darkhe ha'aggadah* was being written, George and his school had quite receded into the background in Germany itself. This would be another example, then, of the anthropological principle of the conservatism or archaism of the periphery.

18. As a curiosity, I would like to mention that none of the books or articles on the George school which I have read mentioned that Gundolf's real name was Gundelfinger or that he was Jewish, a fact that is not without its ironic importance considering the pan-Aryan tendencies of the circle.

19. Much of the information in the following paragraphs in drawn from G. R. Urban, *Kinesis and Stasis: A Study in the Attitude of Stefan George and His Circle to the Musical Arts* ('S-Gravenhage, 1962). As I am not a Germanist, I have had to rely quite heavily here on secondary sources. However, for the purposes of this chapter, I believe that such reliance is not a serious fault, and the alternative would probably have meant that the chapter could not have been written.

20. Ibid., p. 32.

21. Ibid., p. 33. Urban points to the enormous influence that Gundolf had even on such sober thinkers as Lord Alfred North Whitehead. Thus Whitehead asserts: "This notion of historians, of history devoid of aesthetic prejudice, of history devoid of any reliance on metaphysical principles and cosmological generalizations, is a figment of the imagination. The belief in it can only occur to minds steeped in provinciality—the provinciality of an epoch, of a race, of a school of learning" (*Adventures of Ideas* [London, 1933], p. 4).

22. Urban, p. 35.

23. See Hayden White, *Tropics of Discourse*, pp. 53–54, for convenient overview.

24. Urban, p. 35.

25. Ibid., p. 38.

26. Another perspective on Heinemann is that provided by David Stern, who in a recent article says, "A[nother]. . . model for midrashic discourse, framed in Romanti-

cist language and virtually Viconian mythopoeiac terminology was proposed by Isaac Heinemann in his classic *Darkhe ha'aggadah.*" David Stern, "Midrash and Indeterminacy," *Critical Inquiry* 1:1 (1988), p. 146, n. 25. Stern correctly points out the Viconian connections in Heinemann's thought. Heinemann himself cites Croce. A fuller reading of Heinemann than what I am undertaking here would have to take both elements into consideration and attempt to account for them together. I hope to provide such a reading in a version of this text to be published separately. In that text I plan also to deal more fully with the influence of romanticism on the history of research on midrash in the *Wissenschaft des Judentums.* Midrash has been made to play a role in this ideology analogous to that of *Volkspoesie* for the Romantics. Bialik was quite explicit on this point, as are those critical schools dominant in some Israeli universities in which midrash is studied as the ancient folklore of the Jewish people.

27. Wolf Lepenies, "Between Social Science and Poetry in Germany," *Poetics Today* 9:1 (1988), pp. 117–145.

28. Ibid., p. 123.

29. Ibid., p. 140. See also, George Messe, *Nationalism and Sexuality* (Madison, 1985), p. 58: "Stefan George drew into his coterie some of the best minds in Germany. The poet as intuitive seer was not a new concept at the *fin de siècle*; men like Nietzsche, Richard Wagner, and Gabriele D'Annunzio had already looked upon themselves as prophets of a personal renewal that would change the nation as well."

30. He has referred above to the popular identification of Friedrich III and Frierich I in the stories of the German folk.

31. Heinemann is referring to Lévy-Bruhl, and Handelman accuses him of being unaware of theory!

32. Already in 1922, in his essay on Goethe's *Elective Affinities,* Walter Benjamin mounted a scathing attack on Gundolf's book on Goethe. Walter Benjamin, "Goethes Wahlverwandtschaften," *Gesammelte Schriften,* ed. Rolf Tiedemann and Hermann Scweppenhäuser (Frankfurt am Main, 1974), Vol. I part 1, pp. 123–203. The attack on Gundolf is on pp. 155ff.

33. Lepenies, p. 131.

34. It is, moreover, a very questionable claim. There are many scholars who have argued that the distinction between *peshat* as plain meaning and *derash* as application is later than the Talmudic period entirely, while others have located it in the period of the late Babylonian Amoraim. Heinemann makes no chronological distinctions whatever, as has been pointed out in an otherwise laudatory review of his book by Eliezer Margoliot in *Behinot* 2 (1952), pp. 77–78. On this issue in general see the excellent article of Raphael Loewe, "The 'Plain' Meaning of Scripture in Early Jewish Exegesis," *Papers of the Institute of Jewish Studies* I (1964), pp. 140–185, and material cited there. According to Loewe's study, the term *peshat* in tannaitic literature means "authoritative interpretation," no more and no less.

35. See White, *Tropics of Discourse,* pp. 58–60 and passim. Also Dominick LaCapra, *History and Criticism* (Ithaca, 1985), especially the chapter, "Rhetoric and History," pp. 15–45.

36. Frank Kermode, "The Plain Sense of Things," in Hartman and Budick, pp. 179–194.

37. For some clarification of this notion and its place in midrashic studies see my

review essay entitled "Literature and Midrash" in the *Jewish Quarterly Review* (January, 1989).

38. James Kugel, "Two Introductions to Midrash," in Hartman and Budick, pp. 77–105.

39. Jacob Neusner, "The Case of James Kugel's Joking Rabbis and Other Serious Issues," in his *Wrong Ways and Right Ways in the Study of Formative Judaism* (Atlanta, 1988), pp. 59–73.

40. Kugel, p. 93.

41. Neusner, p. 67 (emphasis mine). Neusner repeats the same error in reading Kugel on p. 73. This misreading seriously distorts his entire understanding of what Kugel is about.

42. Ibid., p. 63. Neusner's characterization of all of the participants in this so-called circle, as well as the faculties of Judaic studies of Israeli universities en bloc, Yeshiva University, and Harvard as "possessed . . . by the Orthodox" reveals his own possession more than anything else. (To be sure, Yeshiva and Bar Ilan Universities are in some sense possessed by the Orthodox.)

43. Jacob Neusner, *Canon and Connection* (Lanham, 1987).

44. He admits as much when he cites only one text as being the one from which he has learned everything there is to be known about intertextuality *Wrong Ways and Right Ways* (p. 34). And then, from that one text, he chooses only one acceptation of the term "intertextuality"—arguably the clearest but certainly not the most sophisticated. I suspect that Robert Scholes was pulling a naive colleague's leg when he sent him to one article in a field which has spawned by now almost a small library.

45. This formula is meant to leave room for the many contested areas vis-à-vis "intertextuality" in the literature.

46. Neusner, p. 62. This is doubly ironic in the light of Neusner's almost virulent attack on Baron in the same volume for not being aware of the latest theories in economic history. It may indeed have been the case, but then neither, clearly, is Neusner aware of the latest developments in literary theory and the theory of literary history, so a little more charity toward others would seem to be called for.

47. In this sense, speaking of "inner-biblical midrash," which is practically a commonplace of modern biblical study, seems to me rather putting the cart before the horse. Rather we should understand midrash as post-biblical Scripture—or as the rabbis called it, "Oral Torah."

48. Gerald Bruns, "Midrash and Allegory." in *The Literary Guide to the Bible*, ed. Frank Kermode and Robert Alter, (Cambridge, Mass. 1986), pp. 626–627.

49. *Song of Songs Rabba*, pp. 42. See ch. 7 below for the full context of this citation.

50. See chapter 7 below.

51. White, p. 60.

52. My translation from *Bereshit Rabbah*, ed. Theodor-Albeck, vol. 1, p. 3. I wish to thank Menahem Kahana for calling this very important passage to my attention.

53. The conceptual framework is that of Michael Riffaterre, as cited in the introduction.

2. Reciting the Torah

1. Simon Rawidowicz, "On Interpretation," in *Studies in Jewish Thought*, ed., Nahum Glatzer, (Philadelphia, 1974), p. 52.

2. Julia Kristeva, *Semiotike* (Paris: 1969), p. 146. Implied here is a claim about the notion of intertextuality. It has been claimed that what distinguishes "intertextuality" from the traditional study of "sources and influences" is the anonymity and generality of the former as "discursive space," as opposed to the specificity and identifiability of the latter. Jonathan Culler, *The Pursuit of Signs* (Ithaca, 1981), p. 106, has raised this question. If this be true, then as Culler claims, it becomes quite impossible, by definition, to study the intertexts of a specific text. The solution may be assayed by distinguishing differently between "sources and influences," which is a *diachronic* concept, and "intertexts," which is a *synchronic* concept. This means that the distinction between traditional sources and influences and intertextuality is not located in the anonymity and generality of the latter versus the identifiability of the former, but in their systemic status. Sources and influences are comparable to the historical reconstructions of diachronic linguistics, while intertextuality is a function of the semiotic system of relations and differences present in the literary and linguistic system at a given moment. Intertextuality may therefore comprise a *specific* identifiable discursive space which makes a *specific* text intelligible. Now we may assume that while often the intertexts of a given text will not be remembered consciously, ("anonymous discursive practices, codes whose origins are lost") there is no reason why there should not be other intertexts whose origins are not lost and discursive practices which "make possible the signifying practices of later texts," but are not anonymous. Accordingly, we can then proceed to study allusions and even quotations in literature as a synchronic semantic phenomenon, intertextuality, without thereby confusing it with the diachronic study of sources and influences. This is a different sort of distinction from the one usually made between allusion which is intentional and intertextuality which is not. Cf. James Chandler, "Romantic Allusiveness," *Critical Inquiry* 8 (1982), pp. 464–465. In my matrix, allusion and quotation, as well as the lost codes and anonymous discursive practices, are all species of one genus, as opposed to sources and influences. For a similar perspective see Ziva Ben-Porat, "Intertextuality" [Hebrew], *Hassifrut* 34 (1985), pp. 170–178 (English abstract, p. vi), especially, p. 170.

3. See, for example, even Isaak Heinemann, "For the depictions of the sages are not 'interpretations' in the scientific sense, but even in the places where they gave their words a 'prooftext' [*asmakhta*] from the Bible, in truth they were following the path of artistic creation." *Darkhe ha'aggadah*, p. 23.

4. Galit Hasan-Rokem, *Proverbs in Israeli Folk Narratives: A Structural Semantic Analysis* (Helsinki, 1982), p. 55, has described the semantics of this tension.

5. This does not mean that one can say anything one wants about the text and that all interpretations are equally legitimate. I only make this point because this seems to be a common misconception about midrash (and, for that matter, deconstructionism).

6. By this term I do not mean poetry as opposed to prose but *belle lettres* as opposed to expository or interpretive prose. I do not want to use the term "literature," because it is so contested.

7. Mikhail Bakhtin, quoted in T. Todorov, *Mikhail Bakhtin: The Dialogical Principle* (Minneapolis, 1984) p. 62. Todorov's book is itself an admirable exposition of Bakhtin's thought, composed almost entirely of quotations.

8. For the theory of intertextuality as both violating and preserving a tradition, see the discussion in my "Old Wine in New Bottles," *Poetics Today* 8:4 (1988), pp. 540–542 where some comparison to modern poetics is undertaken as well.

9. Stefan Morawski, "The Basic Functions of Quotation," in *Sign, Language, Culture*, ed. Greimas et al. (The Hague, 1970). p. 694. (emphasis mine).

10. This is a very different position from those interpretations of midrash that see it as belonging to folk literature. For another case in which folk traditions are cited and made part of the intertextual structure of the Mekilta, cf. Lauterbach's edition, p. 176ff.

11. Both the text and its interpretation are somewhat obscure. Some have understood that the snake falls apart from fear of the bird! (The Hebrew allows both readings.) It is the horror of the snake, however, which the text wishes to convey, and that reading renders it incoherent. Moreover, in Stith Thompson's *Motif Index of Folk Literature* (Bloomington, 1955–58), we read of birds that die when their shadows are stepped upon (D 2072.0.4), to which type I believe our tale belongs. B 765.14.1, i.e., "serpent reduces man to a heap of ashes by its gaze" also seems tangentially relevant. Perhaps more to the point, we should notice that this text actualizes a sort of topos (practically a universal at some deep structural level) of narrative structure in which the hero has to pass through a maze, guarded by a monster in order to achieve a desired end. The emphasis on the tracklessness of the waste and the terror of the snakes would be then a vivid realization of what is present within the structure of the biblical account of the passage to the promised land. This explanation accounts for the presence within this text in the immediate sequel of an apparently irrelevant story about snakes which otherwise seems to be merely attached by association. By this means, the intertextual equation, snake=monster, is made explicit and underlined. This interpretation has been suggested by Michael Riffaterre's oral comments regarding the ubiquity of this basic narrative structure in European texts.

12. This is why it is misleading to speak of inner-biblical midrash. There is something else going on when the text being interpreted is canonized, than in the precanonical situation.

13. Other language could be used to describe this basic opposition, to wit, Jakobson's (largely discredited) metonymy and metaphor, or even displacement and saturation (as in Riffaterre's usage, among others). Moreover, these correspond in fiction to what is called narrative and description (cf. Michael Riffaterre, "On the Diegetic Functions of the Descriptive," *Style*, vol. 20 [1986], pp. 281–295). The point is that these refer to obvious and closely related aspects of all language.

14. Aside from changing Judah to Yehuda, I have cited here Judah Goldin's excellent and elegant translation of this passage in *The Song at the Sea* (New Haven, 1971), pp. 124–125.

15. For another, see below.

16. Palestinian Talmud, Rosh Hashana, 3:5=58d.

17. Goldin, p. 124 n.

18. For the cultural significance of such paradigms, see below, chapter 5.

19. Usually translated "parable," but see discussion below and especially chapter 5.

20. It would be tempting to see this double movement as a resolution of the difficulty provided by the fact that the verse doubles itself by continuing, "And the pillar of cloud

moved from in front of them and went behind them." Once again, biblical critics, noticing this superfluity, have hypothesized a juncture between J and E at this point. The objection to such an interpretation is, however, that the second movement in the midrash places the son behind the father again, so it does not seem like an attempt to interpret the second half of the verse.

21. My claim by this interpolation is that the "his" here refers explicitly to God, or at least that the reference is ambiguous—not merely in the connotative manner as in all midrashic king meshalim. The reason for this assertion is the way the verse is quoted, the verse which explicitly refers, of course, only to God.

22. Also drawn from my new translation of the Mekilta, this text has been completely corrupted in current editions, both vulgate and critical, and may only be restored by recourse to the oldest manuscripts.

23. Hasan-Rokem, *Proverbs*, p. 56.

24. This analysis also makes clear the function of those midrashic texts which are *only* quotations strung together, sometimes for pages on end. These would be, on my theory, the very ideal type of midrash.

25. See his "The Reader's Perception of Narrative: Balzac's *Paix du ménage*," in *Interpretation of Narrative*, ed. Mario J. Valdés and Owen J. Miller, (Toronto, 1978), pp. 28–38, especially pp. 35–36. Note that Riffaterre's reading, while it involves reduction, is not ultimately reductive. I emphasize this point because Riffaterre's readings differ from those of many other structuralists, of whom it might accurately be said that they reproduce the form/content dichotomy in such a way that the form of the text comes to be merely one possible way of packaging the content. This charge has been laid against structuralists including Riffaterre by Félix Bonati:

> Jakobson's idea of the poem is precisely that of a discourse that projects over its syntagmatic axis elements of a single linguistic paradigm, i.e., a discourse that essentially repeats (and expands), by successive actualization of different elements of the same paradigm, the meaning that defines that paradigm (a view that recalls some of Riffaterre's analyses). . . . Moreover, the concrete form of the literary work, i.e., the singularity of its shape and determination, appears in it as, if not completely irrelevant, at least not relevant for the production of the meaning of the work. The rhetorical or stylistic differences of different versions of a story must be consequently regarded as merely artistic and not pertinent to their sense. We recognize here the old notion of a deep content that can be expressed by a virtual myriad of more or less pleasant forms. ("Hermeneutic Criticism and the Description of Form," in Valdés and Miller, p. 91.)

I believe that, at least in the case of Riffaterre, what prevents this charge from being accurate is the attention that he pays precisely to the transformations of the matrix paradigm into its successive syntagmatic realizations. While the theory sounds reductive, the practice is anything but. Similarly, the midrashic reduction of the meaning of a complex narrative to an element in a paradigm could be reductive, but somehow is not. The singularity of the narrative always remains with its irreducible residue of meaning. This is not to say, of course, that I accept in every respect Riffaterre's theoretical position. Where I sharply part company with him is in his insistence that the text rigidly controls its own decoding, and even the filling of its gaps, a proposition which is obviously antithetical to my grounding of midrash in a theory of reading.

26. Oral presentation at seminar on "Semiotics of Fiction," at School of Criticism and Theory, 1987.

27. William Sibley Towner, *The Rabbinic "Enumeration of Scriptural Examples": A Study of a Rabbinic Pattern of Discourse with Special Reference to* Mekilta d'R Ishmael, (Leiden, 1973).

28. This text has been analyzed by Towner on pp. 145ff.

29. Ibid., p. 99.

30. Mekilta to Exod. 16:4 and 14. (This is my own translation, based on the best manuscript readings and not on standard editions.) Characteristically, R. Shim'on's very verse is an amalgam of two verses.

31. M. Bakhtin, quoted in pp. 60–61.

32. The phrase "In (or by) your blood you will live," is actually repeated in the verse itself, and it is this repetition on which the midrash hangs its reading.

33. The verb "rebelled" occurs several times in the context of the verse, but the midrashist preferred here the explicit reference to Horev[=Sinai], in order to make his historical point.

34. *Song of Songs Rabba*, ed. Shimon Dunansky (Tel Aviv, 1980), pp. 29–30.

35. I do not wish to take any stand whatever on the historicity of the facts which are related in such stories. Whatever the answer to that question (and I am not sure we will ever have definitive answers to it), the stories nevertheless by definition tell the truth— that is, the truth of the view of the world which we can discern in their form-content.

36. *Babylonian Talmud, Tractate Baba Metsia*, fol. 59a-b.

37. I. Heinemann, *Darkhe ha'aggadah*, p. 11. Susan Handelman, *The Slayers of Moses*, pp. 40–41.

38. In a deeper sense, these two aspects of the content are one, and we have here an explicit reflection of the nexus between political power and "validity in interpretation." See Daniel Cottom, "The Enchantment of Interpretation," *Critical Inquiry* 11 (1985), pp. 573–594, who takes a position very similar to the one in our talmudic story. David Stern has treated the narrative from this point of view in a lecture delivered at Yale University's Faculty Midrash Seminar in Spring, 1985. See his "Midrash and Indeterminacy," *Critical Inquiry* 15 (1988), pp. 132–162. For an excellent general survey of the interpretive tradition regarding this narrative, see Izhak Englard, "The 'Oven of Akhnai': Various Interpretations of an Aggada" [Hebrew], *Annual of the Institute for Research in Jewish Law*, 1 (1974), pp. 45–57.

39. The problem of the historical reference of talmudic stories is an extremely thorny one, particularly stories told in the late Babylonian Talmud about early Palestinian rabbis. Therefore, when I say "R. Yehoshua," it should be understood as shorthand for R. Yehoshua *as represented in this text*.

40. See Handelman, *Moses*, p. 42, who does not italicize the words, "It is not in heaven," although she does italicize, "Incline after a majority," indicating that she has missed the point that the former is a cited verse as well. She thus implicitly accepts the "tame" late reading of R. Yermia [see below] of *what* R. Yehoshua says, and ignores precisely the radical implications of *how* he says what he says.

41. *Babylonian Talmud, loc. cit.*

42. Peter Steiner, "On Semantic Poetics: O. Mandel'stam in the Discussions of the Soviet Structuralists," *Dispositio* I (1976), p. 344. The quotation is from Mandel'stam's "Slovo i kul'tura," Sobranie *socinenij v dvux tomax*, vol. 2 (New York, 1966), p. 266.

43. Hannah Arendt, introduction to Walter Benjamin, *Illuminations* (London: 1970), p. 47 (emphasis mine). It is not unreasonable to suggest that Benjamin, probably more than Freud and Derrida, was influenced in his practice by a knowledge of Jewish textuality. His closeness with Scholem and his kabbalistic research is well known. He may also have very well had some knowledge of midrash, at least through the medium of the German translation of Bialik's famous essay, "Halaka and Aggada." See also George Steiner's introduction to Benjamin's *The Origin of German Tragic Drama* (London, 1977), p. 21, where he explicitly draws the connection between Benjamin's "hermeneutic of and by citation" and Jewish textuality on the one hand, and modernist textuality on the other.

44. Morawski, p. 691.

3. Textual Heterogeneity in the Torah and the Dialectic of the Mekilta

1. Bruns, "Midrash and Allegory," pp. 626–627.

2. The classic statement on this issue is now Meir Sternberg's chapter entitled, "Gaps, Ambiguities, and the Reading Process," in his *Poetics of Biblical Narrative*, pp. 186–229.

3. See the excellent discussion of this issue in Robert Polzin, *Moses and the Deuteronomist*, (New York, 1980), p. 17. See also Sternberg, *Poetics*, p. 227.

4. Among many others, the incisive description in Joel Rosenberg, *King and Kin*, (Bloomington 1986), pp. 4–5 well describes this school of biblical scholarship.

5. Geoffrey H. Hartman, "The Culture of Criticism," *PMLA* 99 (1984), p. 386.

6. At least when backed up by some real documentary evidence (scarce enough in the case of the Bible, as Meir Sternberg emphasizes) and not merely invented in the scholar's own imagination; cf. John Livingston Lowes's classic, *The Road to Xanadu* (London, 1978).

7. For an example of the practice that Hartman's theory engenders see his "The Struggle for the Text," in Hartman and Budick, pp. 3–19.

8. Sternberg, *Poetics*, p. 32.

9. This claim is not, to be sure, entirely original. Indeed, it has been recognized by Sternberg himself, ibid, pp. 188–189. As a matter of fact, the example cited by him there is considered "illegitimate gap filling." While the point *may* be well taken vis-à-vis that particular case, I will try to show in the texts to be discussed here that there are many more cases in which midrash provides exciting and rich interpretive hypotheses to fill the gaps of the biblical narrative. This reading of midrash as an answer to the reductiveness of certain ways of studying the Bible provides us also with a powerful mode of reading midrash itself, a mode which allows it to speak in much richer and more nuanced tones of the heterogeneity and ambiguity of the process of reading, and indeed of life itself.

10. Iser, *The Act of Reading*, is one classic statement. The work of Menahem Perry and Meir Sternberg on the Bible, going back to the 1960s, is another. Much of that work has been embodied in and recast in Sternberg's book.

11. The usual rabbinic term for the Prophets and Writings.

12. Cf. my "Analogy vs. Anomaly in Midrashic Hermeneutic," *Journal of the American Oriental Society*, 106.4 (1986), pp. 659–667.

13. *Merkevet Hamishneh, ad loc.*

14. Horowitz-Rabin, ad loc.

15. As in the interpretation of Meir Friedmann [=Meir Ish Shalom] in his Mekilta commentary, *Meir, Ayin* (Vienna, n.d), ad loc.

16. Cf., however, Rashi in Deuteronomy *ad loc.* who apparently had a different reading in the Mekilta, which could not have contained, at any rate, the words, "to honor Aaron," which are clearly positive in connotation.

17. In spite of various attempts to emend one or another of the attributions the text is certain. Both are cited in the name of R. Eliezer. It may be that there are two traditions of R. Eliezer's statement, as claimed by Ish-Shalom, or it may be, as I have suggested by my paragraphing, that R. Eliezer himself made only the exegetical remark per se that in this case, as in all others, God led the people. His gloss would then be perfectly parallel in form and scope with R. Yehoshua's. Two different commentaries, as it were, on R. Eliezer's exegesis have been appended to two citations of his statement. In any case, it is as we shall see, no accident that these two directly contradictory statements are placed here in juxtaposition.

18. I wish to emphasize the plausibility of this reading of the Nehemiah verse, if only we are prepared to read it strictly, since it says "and made them a chief to return to their work," that is, to return to Egypt and resume their former lives; *then* "they made a golden calf . . . ." The verse from the Torah tells us that this incident came after the golden calf.

19. I realize that I am going out on a logocentric limb here, but I think that the context and the allusion discussed above make this interpretation so persuasive that it can be referred to as "correct."

20. "Stating first one side of a proposition, then the other, with equal vigor." A. Lanham, *Handlist of Rhetorical Terms* (Berkeley, 1968), p. 11.

21. The inspiration for this formulation is M. Bakhtin, "Discourse in the Novel," in *The Dialogic Imagination, Four Essays by M. M. Bakhtin*, ed. Michael Holquist (Austin, Tx., 1981), pp. 259–423. Bakhtin's theories of prose narrative deserve a much more serious consideration in application to the Bible than I can give them here in the scope of this essay. Robert Polzin has done eye-opening work by applying Bakhtin's ideas to biblical studies, as demonstrated by the following quotation, certainly relevant in this context:

> When we reflect upon the disjointed nature of many biblical passages and upon precipitous explanations of widespread editorial activity within it, it is worthwhile to remember that, whatever the historical process that gave rise to the present text, the compositional technique used to analyze these texts should be judged and evaluated primarily by the results it achieves. One can of course assume that wholesale editorial activity is the origin of most of the complicated shifts in perspective so obvious at many points in the biblical

text. If, on the other hand, we assume that many gaps, dislocations, and reversals in the biblical text may profitably be viewed as the result of the use (authorial or editorial) of several different viewpoints within the narrative, then, whether the present text is the product either of a single mind or of a long and complicated editorial process, we are still responsible for making sense of the present text by assuming that the present text . . . does make sense. A particular biblical passage "makes sense," if it repeats compositional patterns already encountered in what precedes it and foreshadows perspectives that lie ahead. (Polzin, pp. 17–18).

22. Note that this tension exists even within Jeremiah, the great prophet of the positive reading of the desert period. See, for instance, 2:17.

23. The rabbinic expression for the paradoxical truth of two contradictory positions. My interpretation of the midrash as representation and thematization of inner-textual tension as hermeneutic dialectic is explicitly marked by the following text from the Babylonian Talmud:

> It is written, "And his concubine betrayed him" [Judg. 19:2]. Rabbi Aviatar said, He found a fly [in the food she prepared him]. Rabbi Yonatan said, He found a hair. Rabbi Aviatar met Elijah and asked him, "What is the Holy One doing?" He answered, "He is studying the text of the concubine of Giv'ah." "And what does He say?" He said to him, "Aviatar, my son, says thus, and Yonatan, my son, says thus." He said, "God forbid, is there doubt before Heaven!?" He said to him, "These and these are the words of the living God."

We have here, in my view, a metamidrashic comment which marks the indeterminacy of the biblical text as inherent in it—even its Author cannot resolve it. To be sure, the story concludes with a weak harmonistic rendering: "Indeed, he found a fly and did not get angry, but when he found a hair, he got angry," but this retreat (which may even be a later gloss on the text) can hardly rescind the radical implications of the whole narrative. I owe the reference to this source to my student, Dalia Hoshen.

24. Cf. Sternberg, *Poetics*, Chapter 11, "The Structure of Repetition: Strategies of Informational Redundancy," pp. 365–440. The repetition which the midrash reads here is, in my opinion, a baroque and sophisticated variant of the forms analyzed by Sternberg. See also above, n. 17.

25. That is the opinion expressed in the Babylonian Talmud, Arakin 15b.

26. Rabbi Moses ben Nahman, *Commentary on the Torah*, ed. C. Chavel (Jerusalem, 1959), p. 366.

27. George Coats, *Rebellion in the Wilderness* (Nashville, 1968), pp. 99–100. Cf. also, Brevard Childs, *Exodus: A Commentary* (Philadelphia, 1974), p. 274: "The relation of the manna to the quail seems strikingly different from Num. 11, but again with evidence of a complex, inner relationship between the stories."

28. Sternberg, *Poetics*, p. 376. A possible objection must be answered here. When critics speak of repetition in the Bible, they are, of course, speaking of obvious repetitions, i.e., situations in which the repetition is unquestionable. Now, many interpreters have managed to explain the two occurrences of the giving of the quail in such a way

that there is no repetition at all, i.e., as referring to two distinct events in the "real world." It is possible to claim, then, that the rabbis here are not "reading" the repetition, but creating it out of whole cloth, as it were. My claim is that the rabbinic reading, which takes these two texts as two versions of the same story, is the most plausible one *on the exegetical level*, that is, at the level of plausible narrative logic, and that the reason that commentators have refused this move is because of the gaps and contradictions that obtain between the two versions.

29. Lauterbach II, p. 107.

30. That is, to be sure, the rabbis of this pericope of the Mekilta. It seems fairly certain that the tanna quoted in TB Arakin 15b saw these as two incidents (contra Meir Ish Shalom in his Mekilta commentary, ad loc.).

31. Using the Peircean taxonomy of signs into "icons," which resemble the signified (as a map does the territory), "indices," which point to its existence by some sort of causal connection (as smoke does fire), and "symbols," which indicate the signified by a conventional assignation of meaning, which has no natural basis.

32. Babylonian Talmud Yoma 75b.

33. I am making the fairly strong assumption that the talmudic text is a rewriting of the midrashic one in this instance, an assumption which has no support except that the talmudic text reads like a simplification of the midrashic one. It makes no difference to the reading, however, if the opposite be true.

34. This type of intertextuality will be discussed at much greater length in chapter 5, where it is applied to the mashal (midrashic parable.) For the nonce, it is interesting to compare Susan Wittig's formulation vis-à-vis the Gospel parable:

> The structure of this duplex semiotic gains its energy and effectiveness from the nature of the semantic relationships which link its components. The first order linguistic sign vehicle is linked *conventionally* and *arbitrarily* to its denotatum, as are nearly all linguistic signs; the second-order material sign vehicle, however, is linked *iconically* to its object in the same way that the structure of a diagram formally exemplifies and exhibits the structure of its object. ("Meaning and Modes of Signification: Toward a Semiotic of the Parable" in *Semiology and Parables*, ed. Daniel Patte [Pittsburgh, 1976], p. 324.)

For further discussion of Wittig's analysis and contrast with the semiotic structure of the midrashic mashal see below chapter 5.

4. Dual Signs, Ambiguity, and the Dialectic of Intertextual Readings

1. Michael Riffaterre, *Semiotics of Poetry* (London, 1978), p. 82. See also John Hollander, *The Figure of Echo* (Berkeley, 1981), p. 92.

2. Michael Riffaterre, *Text Production* (New York, 1983), pp. 64–65.

3. This is bad English, but necessary for understanding the midrash below. What we have here is typical Hebrew construction in which the infinitive is given before the finite verb for various kinds of focusing and emphasizing.

4. As shown in my "Analogy vs. Anomaly in Midrashic Hermeneutic: Tractates Wayyassa and Amaleq of the *Mekilta*," *JAOS* 106.4 (1986), pp. 659–667.

5. R. Eliezer, however, believes that it is always possible to dig for water, so the literal meaning of the text is not sufficient. His interpretation is, however, somewhat cryptic, and must be unpacked as: therefore God must have made it impossible for them to find water in order to exhaust them (and thus to test them, as the *Mekilta of R. Shim'on* reads explicitly). For this motif of exhausting the people to refine and test them, cf. again R. Eliezer in the *Mekilta Wayhi*, par. 1 (Lauterbach I, p. 173): "*But God led the people about, by the way of the wilderness, by the Red Sea. What for?* . . . R. Eliezer says: 'By the way' indicates that it was for the purpose of exhausting them, as it is said: 'He weakened my strength in the way' [Ps. 102:24]; 'of the wilderness' indicates that it was to refine them . . . 'by the Red Sea' indicates that it was to test them". So also here, the same R. Eliezer holds that not finding water was a miracle for the purpose of exhausting them. Moreover, since in the continuation of our story, the Torah says explicitly, "and there He tested them," we can certainly understand R. Eliezer's interpretation here. Finally, it should be pointed out that in Deuteronomy 8, where the story of the manna is rehearsed, we read the following, "And you shall remember the whole way which the Lord your God led you for forty years in the desert, in order to mortify you and to test you to know what is in your hearts, whether you will keep his commandment or not. And He mortified you and starved you and fed you the manna, which you did not know nor your ancestors, in order to make known to you, that not by bread alone does man live, but by that which comes out of the mouth of the Lord will man live" [vv. 2–3]. Now, it can very plausibly be understood that the story of Mara here is a close parallel to that one: God has *prevented* them from finding water [=mortified them], in order to exhaust them, so that He may test them, and they will learn "law and justice" [=by what comes out of the mouth of the Lord].

6. *Wayhi* 5, Lauterbach, I, p. 224. For the whole text of which this is a part, see ch. 2 above.

7. Who are the *dorshe reshumot?* The question is much debated. In a Hebrew paper ("Dorshe Reshumot Have Said," *Moshe Held Memorial Volume* [Beersheva, Israel, 1988], pp. 23–38) I have dealt with this question. To summarize my results there: There is no evidence from rabbinic Hebrew for the term *rashum* meaning allegory, and therefore, no warrant for regarding the *dorshe reshumot* as allegorists, as Lauterbach had claimed. Moreover, this conclusion is consistent with the fact that most of the interpretations cited in the name of this group have no allegorical elements whatsoever. The term apparently means, "the interpreters of sealed texts," i.e., cruces or obscurities. As to the interpretation itself, see above in the body of this chapter.

8. Umberto Cassuto, *A Commentary on the Book of Exodus*, trans. I. Abrahams (Jerusalem, 1967), p. 183.

9. While the text is certain here, the translation and interpretation are highly uncertain. We may read '*leqabbel*' meaning "to receive" or '*liqbol*' meaning "to complain." Moreover, the syntax is not clear. Are the righteous the subject or object of the infinitive, i.e., does it mean that the righteous are not difficult to accept or to be accepted, to complain or to be complained to? All of these options have been maintained by some commentator or another. Now, one relevant textual point must be emphasized. Most readings, including the Oriental texts unanimously and some European texts, take this as a gloss on "And he cried out unto the Lord" alone and not the continuation of the verse. This must mean, at least, that it is Moses's action which is being interpreted here

and not God's response. Moses has no difficulty in complaining or being complained to. Since the first seems incoherent, if only because it seems obvious that everyone has the right to cry out to God, only the latter seems acceptable. Thus: Hence, the righteous are not difficult of receiving. Gloss: Receiving Israel's plea and praying for them immediately [Naftaly Berlin, *Birkat Hanatziv* [Jerusalem, 1970], ad loc.). Or: They readily listen to complaint and seek to help, for Moses did not get angry, but rather listened to their complaint and prayed for them to God (Lauterbach).

10. I am led to some perhaps wild speculation as to whether this privileging of an oral phenomenon in the text is not consistent with R. Yehoshua's formulation of his literalist demands as reading the text, "in accordance with its sound (*kishmu'o*)".

11. Cassuto, *Commentary*, p. 127.

12. *Tanhuma Exodus*, par. 24. I have translated the text from the Yemenite manuscript of the Columbia University Library. I presume that this is the text which Chernus cites as *Exodus Rabba* 23.3, for this language is not found in *Exodus Rabba*. I shall have occasion to cite the *Exodus Rabba* passage immediately see n. 25 below. Such midrashim as *Tanhuma* are very often best read as commentaries on the earlier midrashic texts. As such, while not definitive, they can be taken to represent the understanding of the earlier texts which their earliest extant readings provide.

13. It is worth noting that the term for law, *hoq*, is traditionally understood to mean a law which is counter to reason.

14. See Childs, pp. 269–270 for discussion of such views.

15. The "others" interpret the verse figuratively. It doesn't say, "And [Moses] threw [it] into the water," but "And he threw in the water." The "others" read thus: And [Israel] threw [himself] down in [the matter of] the water. Not a miracle but a prayer sweetened the water.

The distribution of divine attributions is a nice stylistic feature. They pleaded and prostrated themselves like a son pleads with his *father* and a disciple with his *master*, so did they plead and prostrate themselves before their *Father*, saying, *Master*.

16. The motivation for this controversy is not clear to me. R. El'azar is, at any rate, explicit. Since it says, "And he threw it into the water, and the water became sweet," the second, unnecessary use of "water" must somehow imply that the original water was bitter and that water became now sweet, i.e., that it is new water. None of the commentaries gives a satisfactory explanation of R. Yehoshua's view. *Perhaps* R. Yehoshua's interpretation of the whole pericope led him hither. The people have traveled at the behest of Moses, not of God (according to R. Yehoshua); they did not find water (without divine intervention to prevent them from doing so, "according to its sound," i.e., the literal meaning of the words with nothing added). If upon coming to Mara, they found water which had always been bitter, where is God's plan, where is His instruction in all this? But if the water was naturally sweet and God made it bitter for a moment, there is the moment of divine plan and instruction.

An attractive, but by no means probable, interpretation is given by R. Meir Simcha, in his Pentateuch Commentary, *Meshekh Hokhma* (Jerusalem: n.d.). He suggests that the controversy here is directly related to the one above on the nature of the complaint. R. Yehoshua, who holds that this was a temporary and unusual behavior, maintains that the water was only bitter for a moment. R. El'azar, who maintained above that the complaining was habitual, holds also that the water was habitually bitter, as it were.

17. As various commentators have noted, R. Yehoshua's remark is explicable in the light of a tradition cited several times in the Talmud, and in *Seder Olam*, chapter 5 (see also Chaim Milikovsky, "The Red Heifer before Sinai: Ancient Tradition or Scribal Error," in *Studies in Rabbinic Literature, Bible and Jewish History* [Hebrew], ed. Y. Gilat et al. [Ramat Gan, 1982], pp. 268–277), that when it says in the Ten Commandments, "as God hath commanded you" [Deut. 5:12 and 16], with reference to the commandments of the Sabbath and honoring one's parents, it means, "as God hath commanded you—at Mara." It is then entirely appropriate that those two items mentioned here are (cf. TB Sanh. 66b, Shabb. 87b). Moreover, as Ish-Shalom points out, precisely these two items are associated as the bases of the holiness of Israel in Lev. 19:3.

R. El'azar seems to focus rather on the meaning of the words "statute" and "law." The use of "statute" to refer to forbidden sexual relations is supported by him via the quotation of Lev. 18:30 (and see vv. 3 and 5), while his interpretation of "law" as civil law requires no prooftext. This tradition is also partly preserved in the Talmud (Sanh., loc. cit.), where it is asserted that the civil laws were given at Mara, and our very verse is cited as prooftext. Also cf. Mekilta, beginning of *Neziqin*, where a similar tradition is preserved. R. Meir Simcha has noted that for both tannaim, "statute" refers to the conduct of man toward his Maker, while "law" is conduct between man and man.

18. The midrash plays on the feature of the Hebrew language by which a finite verb is emphasized by a preceding infinitive, reading the two verb forms as two clauses. The use of the rubric, "hence they said," indicates that this text was circulated in mishnaic form, and is being *quoted* in our midrash. In the mishnaic form, the abstract principle is stated, and then the prooftext is cited (or not, as the case may be), as opposed to the midrashic form, in which the verse is cited and then its commentary. The quotation of a mishnaic statement in the midrash results in a double citation of the verse as here, both as lemma and as prooftext.

19. R. Yehoshua understands, "Hearing the voice of the Lord" very literally, as opposed to its idiomatic sense, "obey." Since the only place in which Israel heard the actual voice of the Lord was the Ten Commandments, this verse is taken to refer to that occasion. "From the heavens He caused you to hear His voice" [Deut. 4:36].

The next two identifications are more difficult to understand. *Haggadot* usually means legends or stories, so how does one "do" them? The Natziv understands the "doing" here to be the act of telling the legends: "It is taught in *The Fathers of Rabbi Nathan* that "the keys of the fear of the Lord rest in the *haggadot*." And this is the [meaning of], "And you shall do what is straight": You will cause the hearts of Israel to come closer by means of the voice of God which you have heard." The Natziv takes "decrees" to mean the additions which the rabbis make to the Law to guarantee its maintenance. "Hearken" means literally "give ear to," and these decrees are often called "ears of the Torah" (meaning something like handles to the Torah, i.e., that which helps it be "carried." [This use of "ear" is also of course found in English: "Little pitchers have big ears."] Cf. the text cited in this chapter, below, where the same midrashic pun is found.) *Halakot* means the unwritten laws, passed down by oral tradition. R. Meir Simcha has nicely explained R. Yehoshua's identification of "statutes" with these laws. R. Yehoshua above explained "statute" as the laws of the Sabbath. Now the laws of the Sabbath are described in the Mishna as "few Scriptures, many *halakot* [Hagiga 2:6]," ergo "statutes are *halokot*." This last point, which seems very well taken, may afford us a clue to a better appreciation of the others. "Decrees" may also mean the commandments *written* in the Torah; these are "the decrees of the King." Now, if we assume *haggadot* to mean here not legends or stories, but simple interpretations or applications of verses, then we can give a very nice reading. If you will do [follow] the simple applications, which anyone can understand, and moreover hearken unto the decrees written in the Torah, and not only that but also keep all of the oral laws, then. . . . The progression is from that which is rationally understood to that which is at least explicitly written, to that which must be taken on faith. *Haggadot* certainly can mean applications of Scripture. Cf. W. Bacher, "The Origin of the Word Haggada (Aggada)," *JQR OS*, vol. 4 (1892), p. 429, and esp. pp. 410 and 418ff. Bacher could well have cited our passage in support of his thesis.

20. Cf. n. 18 above.

21. R. El'azar begins his exposition of the verse also by explaining the repetition of the verb "hear." He says that since it is a conditional sentence, "If you will hear, I will not inflict," one could have understood that God is giving a choice here, as in "If you don't smoke, you won't get sick. But it's up to you." It therefore says, "you will hear," to emphasize that this is no condition or choice but a command. If you do that which you *must* do, then it will be well with you—"If you don't steal, you won't be imprisoned. But you don't really have the moral or legal choice."

An interpretation of the double verb form from another source is then inserted parenthetically. If you will hear this verse, you will hear everything, for this is a principle which includes the whole Torah.

We return now to R. El'azar, who, unlike R. Yehoshua, does not take this "hearing" the voice as literal and physical, but as obeying. Why then is it expressed as "hearing the voice"? Because one who obeys the word of God is as if standing in God's presence and hearing His living voice. The image is that of a "student, who stands and serves before his teacher," a common expression for disciplehood. Just as one who serves the disciples of the wise hears Torah from their very mouths, in their voices, so one who obeys and serves the Master of the Universe hears the Torah in His voice.

No special argument is required to support the reading of "that which is straight" in the eyes of the Lord as honest dealing. Since this is mentioned here as a sort of synecdoche for the Torah as a whole, "it is accounted. . . . " The next identifications seem clear as well. One "hears" the *halakot*, precisely because they are the unwritten oral component of the law. "Statute" as sexual morality is a repeat of R. El'azar's own identification as given above.

22. Lee Patterson, *Negotiating the Past: The Historical Understanding of Medieval Literature* (Madison, 1987), pp. 150–151.

23. Ibid., p. 151.

24. Saint Augustine, *On Christian Doctrine*, trans. D. W. Robertson, Jr. (Indianapolis, 1958), p. 30. For a reading of Augustine somewhat different from Patterson's, see David Stern, "Midrash and Indeterminacy," *Critical Inquiry* 15:1 (1988), p. 145.

25. Ira Chernus, "History and Paradox in Rabbinic Midrash," in his *Mysticism in Rabbinic Judaism*, Studia Judaica, Band XI (Berlin, 1982). pp. 130–131.

26. An issue with which I am *not* dealing here is the question of the historical accuracy of the attribution of views to particular tannaim (the early rabbis). This is an extremely thorny issue, and not relevant, in any case, to the argument of this chapter. Whether it be the actual views of the actual tannaim or a later redactional construct with which we

are dealing would only be relevant if we were anxious to posit a specific real historical context for these texts, which I am not.

27. R. El'azar breaks up the word "of starvation" into two, "comes starvation". This is a move typical of his approach to language as I have shown in the paper cited in the previous chapter, "Analogy vs. Anomaly in Midrashic Hermeneutic," pp. 659–667.

28. The term "anomalist," taken from Harold Bloom, indicates a linguistic philosophy which does not suppose a stable connection between signifiers and signifieds. See n. 27 above.

29. For "joy" as volition, see Yohanan Muffs, "Joy and Love as Metaphorical Expressions of Willingness and Spontaneity in Cuneiform, Ancient Hebrew, and Related Literatures," in *Christianity, Judaism and Other Greco-Roman Cults*, ed., Jacob Neusner, (Leiden, 1975), part 3, pp. 1–37.

30. Yohanan Muffs, "The Joy of Giving," *JANES 11* (*The Bravmann Memorial Volume*), p. 97 and passim.

31. See n. 27 above.

32. The cited gloss is Rashi's based on midrash.

33. The text here is very difficult in fact. It reads in all manuscripts, "*not* coming to you," which is incoherent, because there seems no way that the words "to you" could have been interpreted by R. Yehoshua to mean their opposite. Hoffman [*Mekilta dR. Shim'on*] deletes the "not," and his emendation is accepted by all modern commentators. It must be admitted that if the text is not emended, it represents a serious difficulty for my reading of the whole passage, for then R. Yehoshua would be saying: even though you are not worthy, I have given you the manna out of My own free will. Ephraim Urbach in his monumental work, *The Sages: Their Concepts and Beliefs*, trans. Israel Abrahams, (Jerusalem, 1975), p. 497, accepts the emendation as necessary, despite the fact that his reading of this text is otherwise diametrically opposed to mine. (He takes it as a battle over the issue of the "merit of the fathers," see below.)

34. See Childs, pp. 287–88.

35. Urbach, p. 497.

36. This is not to deny, of course, that some psychological or other factors have led the two tannaim (if, indeed, it is their real historical views represented here, and not a construct of the midrash itself) to adopt their respective positions. However, if each position can be shown to be well founded in the biblical text, these personal tendencies become no more relevant or determinable, in my opinion, than whatever personal tendencies lead one physicist to see light as particles and another as waves.

37. Cf. also Michael Fishbane, *Biblical Interpretation in Ancient Israel*, (Oxford, 1985) p. 304.

38. Childs, p. 256.

39. See Childs, p. 259.

40. Meir Sternberg comments, "not *necessarily*: equally possible—'synchronically'—is confusion, irresolution, etc. So why deduce the one and not the other." Sternberg is, of course, completely right. The only answer is an appeal to the well-known principle of charity, namely that we choose to read a text in a way that gives it maximum credit for making some kind of sense. Or to put it another way, if we assume "confusion" and

"irresolution," the text will very quickly cease to be interesting enough to bother with. Cp. Polzin, *Moses and the Deuteronomist*. See also Sternberg, who writes, "James's *The Turn of the Screw*, Gogol's "The Overcoat," Agnon's "Another Face": these multiple systems of gap-filling sufficiently differ from one another (and from our paradigmatic case, the David and Bathsheba story) to give an idea of the scope and implications of this principle. One could easily multiply examples from all literary genres—epic, novel, drama, poetry. The endless critical warfare about their interpretation misses (as well as, unwittingly, establishes) the poetic point. *And so do the attempts to resolve the quarrel by blaming the work itself: the incoherencies that derive from its history of transmission—the staple of biblical source criticism—or from its sloppy execution or even from its disregard for clarity. It is not that any of these explanations of incoherence may be ruled out a priori, but that their abuse obscures the scope and working of ambiguity as a constructive force."* Poetics, p. 227 (emphasis mine).

41. Tony Bennet, *Formalism and Marxism* (London, 1979), p. 146.

42. This is *not* to deny, of course, their historicity, nor even the possibility (probability) that the historical tannaim actually held the views ascribed to them, but only to interpret the textualization of these views by the author of the Mekilta.

43. For examples of sharply bifurcated interpretive traditions of such works see Barbara Johnson's by now classic reading of the hermeneutic tradition on *Billy Budd*, in her *The Critical Difference* (Baltimore, 1980), pp. 79–110, and Sternberg's discussion of *The Turn of the Screw* in *Poetics*, pp. 222ff. Both of these critics show that the bifurcation of the interpretive tradition is a function of difference and dialectic within the text itself. this is not to deny the ideological dimension of all reading, of course, but merely to oppose a reduction of interpretation to the subjective ideologies of readers. For a review of traditional Jewish commentary on another of the murmuring stories, see Nehama Leibowitz, *Studies in Exodus*, [Hebrew], (Jerusalem, nd), pp. 200–212. Again the commentators split between those who explain that the request was justified and necessarily reduce the pejorative connotations of the text and those who understand that there was no real need, but an unjustified rebellion, and explain away the thirst as lack of faith.

44. Nonetheless, there is an aspect of these readings that seemingly cannot be suppressed or accounted for from within the text which is being read and its "warring forces of signification." I am referring, of course, to R. El'azar's insistent connection of every verse to the "merit of the ancestors." Admittedly, he is reading the whole story as a case of God's relenting and not punishing an undeserving and ingrate people, and the merit of the ancestors provides as it were an explanation of His motivations, but surely there were other choices of motivation available to R. El'azar (e.g., the intercession of Moses). Why did he choose, therefore, always to emphasize this one motivation, if not to make some point beyond exegesis? This suggests once again that Rabbi El'azar indeed had some ulterior motive, some ideological ax to grind in his insistence on the merit of the ancestors here. It may be so, and we may never be able to prove it one way or the other, but this does not seem to me in any way to undermine my insistence that the primary motivation for the dialogue of these readings arises in the dialogue within the text itself. Cf. Urbach, *The Sages*, pp. 497ff.

45. Geoffrey Hartman, *Criticism in the Wilderness* (New Haven, 1980), p. 32.

46. I am indebted to Prof. Steven Katz for this insight.

47. Sternberg, *Poetics*, p. 228.

48. Harold Bloom, *A Map of Misreading* (Oxford, 1975), p. 76, (emphasis original).

5. Interpreting in Ordinary Language

1. David Flusser, "The Parables of Jesus and the Parables in Rabbinic Literature," in his *Jewish Sources in Early Christianity* [Hebrew] (Tel Aviv, 1979), pp. 150–210.

2. Susan Wittig, "Meaning and Modes of Signification" in Daniel Patte, ed., *Semiology and Parables* (Pittsburgh, 1976), pp. 319–347.

3. Ibid., p. 323.

4. Ibid., p. 324.

5. Ibid., p. 334.

6. Ibid., p. 335.

7. Ibid., p. 336.

8. See the discussion of her paper in *Semiology and Parables*, pp. 348–384.

9. Also drawn from my new translation of the Mekilta, this text has been completely corrupted in current editions, both vulgate and critical, and may only be restored by recourse to the oldest manuscripts.

10. Childs, p. 220.

11. See below and especially, chapter 6.

12. The word for "handles" and the word "proved" come from the same root in Hebrew. "Handles" is being used in a sense very similar to that of the modern English colloquial phrase, "I can't get a handle on that idea," i.e., a place of access. Cf. Bruns "Midrash and Allegory."

13. *Song of Songs Rabba*, p. 5.

14. That is to say, the Bible explicitly or implicitly ascribes these three works to Solomon; it was the rabbis who explained that the first was written in his youth, the second in his maturity, and the third in his old age, thus providing a sort of typology of the three ages of man.

15. Compare the following use of this term from the same midrash: " 'Your eyes are doves,'—like doves, your figure [*dugma*] is similar to a dove" (*Song of Songs Rabba*, p. 100. *Dugma* is accordingly practically an etymological equivalent of *figura*.

16. Compare David Stern, "Rhetoric and Midrash: The Case of the Mashal," *Prooftexts* 1 (1981), pp. 261–291.

17. Frank Kermode, *The Genesis of Secrecy* (Cambridge, Mass., 1979), p. 77. The term "ado" is cited by Kermode from Henry James.

18. Ibid., p. 81. Kermode is obviously *not* using the term "fabula" in the formalist sense of the sequence of events abstracted from the text in opposition to the *sjuzhet*, the discourse, but rather in the original Latin sense. Kermode even calls this process *midrash*, mistakenly in my view. He is closer to midrash when he speaks on p. 82 of collections of "Old Testament" testimonia about the messiah underlying the Gospel stories.

19. Ibid., p. 85.

20. Ibid., p. 339.

21. White, *Tropics of Discourse*, p. 58.

22. The Hebrew term here is *rashum*, which has been itself interpreted to mean mashal, a meaning which would not be altogether unwelcome here. See, however, chapter 4 n. 7 above.

23. White, p. 59.

24. Yet another image for the hermetic Torah, now that which was possessed but is lost.

25. I.e., the Song of Songs

26. Hence, the analogy between Solomon and the rabbis. Solomon is a sort of protorabbi for the midrash.

27. The order deviates from both the chronological and canonical ones because this passage is an introduction to the midrash on Song of Songs and its author wishes therefore to end his discourse mentioning that book.

28. See David Stern, "Rhetoric and Midrash."

29. Kermode, *Genesis of Secrecy*, pp. 98–99.

30. "It is at least convenient to think of the methodologically describable *fabula* as having historical existence" (Ibid., p. 79).

31. Sternberg, p. 31. for Kermode on this question see *Genesis of Secrecy*, pp. 101–125.

32. His most explicit investigation of this issue is the chapter on Droysen in *The Content of the Form: Narrative Discourse and Historical Representation* (Baltimore, 1986).

33. Louis Marin, "On the Interpretation of Ordinary Language: A Parable of Pascal," in *Textual Strategies*, ed. Josue V. Harari (Ithaca, 1979), p. 245, (emphasis mine).

34. The point I am making is not that only the rabbinic or Solomonic interpretation could make the Torah intelligible, but rather that the text, prior to some kind of ideological structuring and reading, is always, as it were, a closed book. The rabbinic statement is to be considered paradigmatic of the condition of reading of all serious fictional (meaning-carrying) texts.

35. Marin, p. 246.

36. D. Stern's paper, "Midrash and Indeterminacy," represents a somewhat different approach to the problem of how midrashic interpretation is constrained. See also Goldin, "The Freedom and Restraint of Haggadah."

37. By the term "rabbinic" here, I mean that which belongs to the period of the rabbis. It is precisely my point that the mashal is not an erudite or elite structure, but one that was available to anyone competent in the culture.

6. The Sea Resists

1. Sigmund Freud, *Moses and Monotheism* (Harmondsworth, 1985), pp. 283–4, quoted in Christopher M. Johnson, "Intertextuality and the Psychical Model," *Paragraph* 11 (1988), pp. 72–73.

2. See, for the nonce, my "Voices in the Text," *Revue Biblique*, October, 1986, pp. 581–598.

3. See the classic discussion of this matter by Saul Lieberman, "Rabbinic Interpretation of Scripture," in his *Hellenism in Jewish Palestine* (New York, 1950), pp. 70–78.

4. See also Geoffrey Hartman, "The Struggle for the Text," in Hartman and Budick, pp. 3–18, and esp. p. 11 for a similar perspective and a very powerful reading of the story of Jacob and the angel.

5. Samuel Loewenstamm, *The Tradition of the Exodus in its Development* [Hebrew] (Jerusalem, 1987), p. 116. Cassuto makes a somewhat similar argument. After arguing that there was an ancient Israelite epic of the battle between God and the sea and that it was lost at the time of Ezra and Nehemiah owing to theological antagonism, he writes:

> It was, in truth, lost, but not entirely. The basic story it related, which was widely known among the people, was not completely forgotten. The poetic version was no longer extant, but the knowledge of its content did not become extinct. This tradition continued to live in the people's memory, and was given renewed literary expression in rabbinic teaching. The fears that aroused the antagonism of the Torah to legends of this nature, no longer existed in the days of the Talmudic Rabbis, since the danger of idolatry had then already passed. Hence the Sages did not refrain from incorporating the accepted folk tradition in their treasury of legend. ("The Israelite Epic," in his *Biblical and Oriental Studies* (Jerusalem, 1975), vol. 2, p. 102.)

Cassuto deserves every credit for having discovered the fragments of the "Israelite Epic" in the biblical text, but his claim that the material was actually preserved in the folk tradition until rabbinic times seems both naive and unnecessary to me. Loewenstamm's advance over Cassuto's original formulation with regard to the midrash is in his perception that the rabbis could have indeed reconstructed and revived the mythical material from their close reading of the Bible itself. What I am trying to do here which goes beyond both of them is inscribe this particular instance in a theory of cultural dynamics in which repression and the return of the repressed manifested in the intertextuality of all literature is emblematic of culture in general enabling a dialectic of cultural history.

6. Lauterbach, I, p. 229.

7. For these two exegetical possibilities see literature cited in Meir Weiss, *The Bible from Within* (Jerusalem, 1984), pp. 369–370.

8. See Childs, pp. 220–221. See also Martin Noth, *Exodus: A Commentary* (Philadelphia, 1962), pp. 114–116.

9. Cf. Loewenstamm, p. 118.

10. Midrashic reading is, in this sense, congruent with contemporary reading practices. The classic statement on this issue is now Meir Sternberg's chapter entitled, "Gaps, Ambiguities, and the Reading Process," in his *Poetics*, pp. 186–229. See also the excellent discussion of this issue in Robert Polzin, p. 17.

11. It is certainly significant that on verse 14:27 cited above, in which there is no narrative gap, the Mekilta explicitly comments: "The sea will not resist you."

12. Murray Krieger, "Poetic Presence and Illusion," *Critical Inquiry* 5 (1979), pp. 601–602. For the sources of Krieger's definition of "prosopopeia," see Jon Whitman, *Allegory: The Dynamics of an Ancient and Medieval Technique* (Cambridge, Mass., 1987), p. 269.

13. Whitman, p. 272.

14. Cf. Weiss, p. 368: "The events that transpired hundreds of years before your psalmist's time have become, through his description, as though they were vivid events occurring before his very eyes. There are no more boundaries either in time or in space. The psalmist stands face to face with the sea and Jordan, the mountains and hills, and he can turn to them and ask them: What ails you. . . . " It is, in fact, precisely this sense of no boundaries of time or space in the lyric voice that enables the rabbis to project this voice onto Moses himself at the actual events.

15. Cf. Weiss, p. 362.

16. This reading is, to be sure, not the only one that could be adopted here. There is always, at least in theory, the possibility that this story is not meant seriously in a referential way but as a sort of parable or allegory for a more abstract issue. That is certainly the way many scholars and traditional commentators on midrash would read it. The sea's speech would be then only a figure of speech. I cannot disprove such an approach—only say that it seems to go against the tenor of the text as I perceive it. I can perhaps strengthen my claim somewhat by the following reasoning. The rabbis generally make a distinction between mashal (parable) and "reality," true stories in the sense of narrative of events that have actually taken place. The following text shows this opposition clearly:

> R. Eliezer says: The dead whom Ezekiel raised stood on their feet, uttered a song and died. What song did they utter? God kills justly and resurrects mercifully. R. Yehoshua says: They uttered this song: God kills and resurrects, takes down to Sheol and will raise up [1 Samuel 2:6]. *R. Yehuda says: In reality it was a mashal. R. Nehemiah said to him: If a mashal then why "in reality," and if "in reality," then why a mashal?! But, indeed, he meant that it was really a mashal.* R. El'azar the son of R. Yosi Hagelili says: The dead whom Ezekiel raised went up to the land of Israel, took wives and begat sons and daughters. R. Yehuda ben Beteira stood on his feet and said: I am one of their grandchildren, and these are the phylacteries which my grandfather left to me from them. [Babylonian Talmud Sanhedrin 92 b]

This text sharply contrasts mashal with "reality," which must mean then that which has taken physical place in the real world, both in R. Nehemiah's astonishment at R. Yehuda's "inconsistency" and in the way that R. Yehuda's statement is contested by strong counter-claims about the literal referentiality of Ezekiel's narrative. Clearly, then, for the rabbis there is a semantic, cultural opposition between the mashal, which is fiction, and historical reality. Now, our text includes a mashal, and the story of the sea and Moses is the *designatum* of that very mashal. If the mashal is interpretive fiction, then presumably (although not ineluctably) its object (the other of the mashal) is making claims to be "in reality." Finally, I would think that if our text were a philosophical or theological allegory, it would thematize its theological issues more explicitly. As we well know, virtually any text *can* be given an allegorical reading. To my taste there is nothing in *this* text that calls for or authorizes such a practice, although other readers, I am sure, will continue to maintain precisely that. What I am certain of is that this is not meant as a mere playful or entertaining tale; its cultural weight is too great for that.

17. See Cassuto, *Studies*, pp. 80–102.

18. For the forms of the repression of mythological reality in the Bible see the excel-

lent discussion in Benjamin Uffenheimer, "Myth and Reality in Ancient Israel," in *The Origins and Diversity of Axial Age Civilizations*, ed. S. N. Eisenstadt, (Albany, 1986), p. 165, who identifies the processes by which it is accomplished as "reduction, depersonification, ironization, allegorization and antiquarization."

19. This point was suggested to me by Prof. Uriel Simon. Even this reading does not exhaust the highly overdetermined figure of the two gardens.

20. *Shir Hashirim Rabba*, ed. S. Dunansky (Tel Aviv, 1980), p. 5.

21. It is often the case that later midrashic texts begin with earlier ones. That is, the midrashic expansion of the earlier text leaves its own gaps, which are then filled by the latter midrashic reader, *using precisely the same methods as the earlier one*. Our text here is an excellent example of this phenomenon.

22. Cf. Weiss, p. 375, who senses this dialectic within the psalm itself: "The description of the natural phenomena as independent, self-willed activity in verses 3–6 is surprising, according to the interpretation that the idea intended to be conveyed by the description is the dominion of God in nature." The midrashic reading is, in my view, precisely an evocation of this dialectic.

23. Weiss could well have referred to the Mekilta to support his contention that "the psalm is not a hymn of praise to God Who revealed Himself in the exodus from Egypt by choosing Israel; it rather expresses the idea that the choice of Israel was a revolution in Creation, or, more exactly, a new Creation" (p. 374).

24. Louis Ginzberg in his *The Legends of the Jews* (New York, 1954), vol. III, p. 19, translates "a semblance." The Hebrew word, which appears here spelled *m'yn* is completely ambiguous between these two readings; however, it seems to me that "a fount of strength" is more idiomatic for Hebrew.

25. The narrative expansion of this midrash is exploiting yet another sense of the root *hll* of the verse, namely "hollowness" and thence "channels." This is the source of the sea's request to the earth to make channels for him.

26. I. Heinemann, *Darke ha'agadda*, p. 19.

27. Emphasis mine.

28. It is striking how often in the first book of "The Prelude" the issue of labor is raised. The poem can be read as a verse version of an apprenticeship novel with all of the social and historical implications of that genre. But that is not my text. Cf. Kristin Ross, "Rimbaud and the Resistance to Work," *Representations*, 19 (1987), pp. 62–87.

29. Gershom G. Scholem, *Major Trends in Jewish Mysticism* (New York, 1961), p. 8.

30. Babylonian Talmud, Yoma, 69b.

31. Lieberman notes that "the Rabbis never directly and explicitly assailed the heathen rites of mysteries. They simply had no reason to engage in such attacks. Unlike the earlier Hellenistic Jews the Rabbis were no longer struggling with gentile paganism. They mostly preached to Jews. To Judaism the mysteries represented no danger. A Jew had to become an idol worshipper before he could be initiated into the mysteries. In the first centuries C.E. the Jews were so far removed from clear-cut idolatry that there was not the slightest need to argue and to preach against it." Saul Lieberman, *Hellenism in Jewish Palestine*, pp. 120–121. See also Ephraim Urbach, "The Laws of Idol Worship and Historical-Archeological Reality," *Israel Exploration Journal* 9 (1959), pp. 149–165 and 229–245.

32. Fredric Jameson, *The Political Unconscious* (Ithaca, 1981), p. 213.

7. The Song of Songs, Lock or Key

1. *The Five Scrolls with Various Commentaries*, ed. and trans. [from Arabic into Hebrew] Joseph Kafah (Jerusalem, 1962), p. 26.

2. Gerald L. Bruns, *Inventions: Writing, Textuality, and Understanding in Literary History* (New Haven, 1982), p. 31.

3. This, of course, does not preclude the mashal's requiring some interpretation or even remaining partially (or wholly) obscure. Other factors than an original generic "darkness" may lead to obscurity, and a text whose "intention" was to be crystal clear may only appear to us through a glass darkly.

4. *Song of Songs Rabba*, p. 6.

5. Bruns, "Midrash and Allegory," p. 637. I wish to thank Prof. Bruns for making this paper available to me before its publication.

6. In spite of the title of Bruns's essay, he does not discuss the relationship of midrash to allegoresis, but rather discusses the midrashic and allegorical methods separately as early hermeneutic techniques. Bruns's discussion of allegoresis is as insightful and sympathetic as his discussion of midrash.

7. See, for example, Marvin Pope, "*Song of Songs*," *Anchor Bible* (Garden City, N.Y., 1977), p. 19: "It is clear that Akiva must have understood the Song allegorically . . . ."

8. See E. E. Urbach, "The Homiletical Interpretations of the Sages and the Expositions of Origen on Canticles, and the Jewish-Christian Disputation," *Scripta Hierosolymitana* XXII (1971), pp. 247–275.

9. I am using the English translation of R. P. Lawson, *Origen, The Song of Songs: Commentary and Homilies* (Westminster, Md., 1957), book 3, section 12, p. 218. The citations below are to this edition Cf. Jon Whitman, *Allegory*, p. 63.

10. A reference to Deut. 8:15. For a midrashic reading of this verse which points up by contrast precisely the difference between the midrashic and allegorical methods, cf. chapter 2 above.

11. For the closest we get in early midrash to an allegorical reading of "thirst," see above, ch. 4.

12. Lawson, p. 223.

13. Whitman writes that it is "Origen, who first conceives of the different kinds of interpretation as a simultaneous tripartite 'depth' within a given passage, rather than simply alternate strategies for various passages" (p. 63). It may be that Origen first articulated such a theory explicitly, but surely Philo denied the literal sense of neither the historical nor legal passages of the Pentateuch, while at the same time giving them an allegorical reading.

14. Lawson, introduction, p. 9. Whitman (p. 63) identifies this tripartite division as Stoic. (But see p. 41, where the Platonic soul itself is identified as tripartite.) See his discussion (pp. 62–63) for a scriptural source for the triple reading as well.

15. Lawson, p. 9.

16. *Song of Songs Rabba* 42.

17. "Revelation is never something over and done with or gone for good or in danger of slipping away into the past; it is ongoing, and its medium is midrash, which makes the words of Torah rejoice 'as when they were delivered from Sinai' and 'as sweet as at their original utterance.' " Bruns, "Midrash and Allegory," p. 637.

18. The last point was already made by the medieval commentator, R. A. Ibn Ezra in the introduction to his commentary on the Song of Songs.

19. *Song of Songs Rabba*, pp. 72–73.

20. The very opening of this midrashic text makes it clear that its hermeneutic focus is the Exodus passage, and indeed, plausibly, its very origin was in the midrash on that book (see below immediately), which strengthens my reading that the Song is the interpreting, the Torah, the interpreted, text.

21. In this sort of context, this term always means the Prophets and Writings. See discussion above, chapter 3.

22. Lauterbach I, p. 211.

23. See Michael Fishbane, *Biblical Interpretation in Ancient Israel*, pp. 403–408 for discussion of this issue as well as literature cited there.

24. Notice that that text very nearly does without the mashal altogether, beginning to quote the verses from the psalm even before the mashal is begun, thus strengthening the argument that the mashal has a secondary function. In my earlier analysis of the text in *Prooftexts* 5, I argued that the mashal is almost completely superfluous here; that it would be almost enough merely to juxtapose the psalm to the verse in order to make the hermeneutic points. However, I believe that claim was exaggerated. First, there is no question that the mashal sets up the *dramatis personae*, the buyer, the king, and the guard, in a way that would not be possible without its narrative. Second, the mashal of the ambiguous sale *does* contribute to the meaning of the text, as I have tried to show in the previous chapter. Nevertheless, the exegetical revelation created by the juxtaposition of the two texts is nearly independent of the mashal. It should be pointed out that in modern editions of this text, the first citation of the verse from Psalm 114 is deleted, obscuring the point I have just made about the relative significance of the psalm and the mashal in doing the hermeneutic work of this text.

25. Midrash on Ps. 17:1, quoted in Fishbane, p. 404. The quoted phrase is from Nahum Glatzer, *Untersuchungen zur Geschichtslehre der Tannaitin* (Berlin, 1933), pp. 45–61.

26. The entire next chapter will be devoted to a Mekilta text which describes this moment.

27. "The Teaching of Song of Songs" [Hebrew], in Gershom Scholem, *Jewish Gnosticism, Merkabah Mysticism, and Talmudic Tradition* (New York, 1965), pp. 118–127, and especially p. 123. Lieberman even claimed that the rabbis held that the Song was actually recited at Sinai or at the crossing of the sea and not by Solomon, but see my "Two Introductions to the Midrash on the Song of Songs" [Hebrew], *Tarbiz* 56 (1987), pp. 479–501, where an alternative reading is developed claiming that they indeed held that Solomon wrote the Song, but as an interpretation of the Exodus events.

28. It is remarkable how unwilling commentators are to take this explicit marking seriously, e.g., Lauterbach, who here and always translates this perfectly clear expression as, "Of them it is declared in the traditional sacred writings."

29. A not unproblematical interpretation in its own right.

8. Between Intertextuality and History

1. Dominick LaCapra, *Rethinking Intellectual History* (Ithaca, 1983), p. 26.

2. See Pierre Bourdieu, "Flaubert's Point of View," *Critical Inquiry* 14:3 (1988), 539–545 for a recent restatement of this dichotomy. However, in truth the differences between the New Criticism and Russian Formalism are greater than their similarities. This is true also of "Deconstruction," which is often dubbed "formalist" by its detractors. See Tony Bennet, *Formalism and Marxism*, for an excellent demonstration of how unformalist "Formalism" is.

3. Dominick LaCapra, *History and Criticism* (Ithaca, 1985), theorizes this issue very clearly.

4. Of the American variety! Susan Handelman, *The Slayers of Moses*, is the most extreme example of this approach to midrash.

5. I will cite the works of some representative midrashic scholars of the "old historicist" school below.

6. I have generally followed here the elegant translation of Goldin, *The Song at the Sea*, pp. 115–117, only modifying it where my manuscripts have a better reading.

7. It is this feature which has led many scholars to define "midrash" as the "other" of the "plain interpretation" of the Bible. See Gary Porton, "Defining Midrash," pp. 59–60. However, as Porton has argued, "The distinction between 'hidden' and 'plain' is often a result of our present view of Scripture." Moreover, in the present state of literary theory, the very concept of 'plain' meaning is often called into question. See Frank Kermode, "The Plain Sense of Things," pp. 179–195.

8. As this text demonstrates, William Scott Green ("Romancing the Tome: Rabbinic Hermeneutics and the Theory of Literature," *Semeia* 1987, p. 160) exaggerates when he claims, "Thus, in rabbinic Judaism the writing and discourse of scripture had to be inherently separable from, and could be neither merged nor confused with, the commentary upon them. To mix the two would have deprived the rabbis of an artifact to control and violated the basic levitical distinction between the sacred and the profane. In rabbinic writing, therefore, passages and words of scripture are almost always identified as such by an introductory formula, such as 'thus scripture says,' 'as it is written,' or 'a scriptural tradition says.' " Thus, while there is much in Green's paper with which I agree, our text shows the error of this claim, as many (if not most) of the scriptural citations are merged with the discourse of the midrash with no mark of their scriptural origin—the references are, of course, not in the text. As Goldin has already remarked, "Note how the Midrash amalgamates the biblical statement with its own" (*The Song at the Sea*, p. 116, n.). Moreover, textual scholarship on midrashic manuscripts has shown that the earlier the manuscript and the more reliable it is, the *less* often it marks the citations with the formulae that Green quotes. The claim for the identification of text and reading made by Handelman and others is, therefore, supported strongly by the philological rigor in the name of which Green is speaking.

9. Urbach, "The Homiletical Interpretation of Canticles," p. 250 (emphasis mine).

10. Isaac Baer, "Israel, the Christian Church, and the Roman Empire" [Hebrew], *Zion* 21 (1956), pp. 2–3 (emphasis mine).

11. Gedaliah Alon, *The History of the Jews in Eretz Israel in the Days of the Mishna and the Talmud* [Hebrew] (Tel Aviv 1956), p. 327, n. 25.

12. Joseph Heinemann, *Aggada and Its Development*, p. 75.

13. Note that even were we to grant the first assumption, that the text does have a univocal, original meaning, the second would still be questionable. See on this R. Loewe's fine study, "The 'Plain' Meaning of Scripture in Early Jewish Exegesis," *Papers of the Institute of Jewish Studies* I (1964), pp. 140–185.

14. Hartman and Budick, introduction, p. xi. I would perhaps rephrase this as "between the text and the interpreter."

15. The words are of R. Ishmael (the contemporary and colleague of R. Akiva), as preserved in the Mekilta. In Goldin's volume, *Song at the Sea* they are on p. 113.

16. For an extensive and deep analysis of the midrashic reading of the deictic, see Betty Roitman, "Sacred Language and Open Text," in Hartman and Budick, pp. 159–179.

17. Porton, p. 83, completely misses the import of this passage. He remarks that "we have several different comments on the verse. . . . all of the comments are not really related to one another." But of course they are, and that is precisely the issue. The questions raised by R. Shimeon and answered by R. Eliezer only arises because R. Akiva reads the "this" as deictic and takes the verse to refer, therefore, to God's pointing out the new moon to Moses.

18. Goldin, *Song at the Sea*, p. 112. Lauterbach, vol II, p. 24.

19. Although this is obviously not the only possible way to read the pronoun, it does seem typical of the midrash; in several other cases in the same midrash, the pronoun read as excluding others (at least partially). Thus, on the previous verse we read: "Another interpretation of *My strength* ['*zy*]: Thou art the Helper ['*wzr*] of all the inhabitants of the world, but mine above all! *And the Lord is my song*: Thou art the theme for song for all the inhabitants of the world, but for me above all!" (Goldin, *Song at the Sea*, pp. 108–109). The very equivocation of the midrash here seems to me to support my reading. The midrashist is uncomfortable with the suggestion that God is the helper of Israel alone and the "theme for song" of Israel alone, but that is what the pragmatics of the pronoun suggest very strongly. In my judgment, this is what generates the formulation, "of all the inhabitants, etc."

20. James Clifford, "On Ethnographic Authority," *Representations* 2 (1983), p. 133.

21. See the classic article of my teacher, Saul Lieberman, "The Teaching of Song of Songs" [Hebrew], in Gershom Scholem, *Jewish Gnosticism, Merkabah Mysticism, and Talmudic Tradition*, pp. 118–127, and especially p. 123. See also my "Two Introductions to the Midrash on the Song of Songs," pp. 479–501, and previous chapter above.

22. See M. D. Herr, "Persecutions and Martyrdom in Hadrian's Days," *Scripta hiersolymitana*, xxiii (1972), p. 13.

23. This was emphasized to me by Jonathan Boyarin. Indeed the very passage of Song of Songs itself here is a very eloquent representation of feminine desire, and the description of the beloved, with its enumeration of his beautiful parts, is nothing if not a blazon, traditionally in Europe a representation of masculine desire and reification of feminine

beauty. (See Nancy Vickers, "The 'blazon of sweet beauty's best': Shakespeare's *Lucrece*," in *Shakespeare and the Question of Theory*, ed. Patricia Parker and Geoffrey Hartman [New York, 1985], pp. 95–116.) Does this render ancient Hebrew society any less patriarchal? I rather doubt it, but it does perhaps further unsettle "literature" as a univocal reflection of other social practices.

24. See E. Slomovic, "Patterns of Midrashic Impact on the Rabbinic Midrashic Tale," *Journal for the Study of Judaism*, XIX (1988), pp. 61–91.

25. See Robert Alter, "The Psalms," in Alter and Kermode, pp. 257–258.

26. This is, in fact, one of the few examples of true typology in midrash.

27. Alon Goshen-Gottstein pointed out to me the importance of this passage for understanding R. Akiva's midrash, although he does not accept my interpretation.

28. *Sifre Deuteronomy* ad Deut. 6:5.

29. Urbach, "Canticles," p. 251.

30. Palestinian Talmud, *Berakot* 9:5.

31. Baer, pp. 2–3.

32. Bruns, "Midrash and Allegory," p. 632.

33. See also Alter introduction, p. 31, who remarks "the strong elements of internal allusion in Hebrew Scripture that at many points make it a set of texts in restless dialogue with one another."

34. Kugel, "Two Introductions to Midrash," p. 90.

INDEX

Aaron, 43, 45, 47
Abraham, 10
Acmeist poetics, 37
Adam, 23, 24
Aesthetics, 9
Akhmatova, Anna, 37
Akiva, Rabbi, 113–14, 117–29
Allegoresis, 20, 108–109, 110
Allegory, 19, 108, 115, 116, 152n
Alon, Gedaliah, 119
Ambiguity, 57–79
Amoraim, aggada of, 19
Anaphora, 122
Anomalist methods, 72
Apocalypse, 13
Archetypes, 85–86
Arendt, Hannah, 37–38
Aristotle, 1, 18
Auerbach, Erich, 41
Augustine, 68–69, 71

Bakhtin, Mikhail, 12, 23, 140n
Bar Kochba rebellion, 5
Ben Azzai, Rabbi, 109, 110
Benjamin, Walter, 37, 139n
Benveniste, Emile, 121
Bible, 1, 2, 4, 15–18; Deuteronomy, 25,
31–32, 35, 44–45, 76; as dialogical in
nature, 12, 33; Ecclesiastes, 83, 107;
Genesis, 16, 17–18; as historiography, 90;
Isaiah, 25–26; Jeremiah, 25–26, 42, 44, 46,
60, 110; Job, 86–87; Kings, 70; nonreductive
way of reading, 40; Numbers, 42–45, 47,
52–56; original sources of, 40; as *parole* and
as *langue*, 29; Pentateuch, 76; Proverbs, 64,
65, 83, 107; Psalms, 76, 96, 98, 112, 123; as
a self-glossing text, 39, 80, 92; Song of
Songs, 20, 32–33, 83, 87, 105–116; verses
of, and syntagmatic relations, 28–29
—Exodus, 22, 31, 71, 86, 95–96, 100, 118,
120–21; and gap-filling, 41–42, 47; and the
manna story, 71, 74–76, 77; and repetition,
49–56; and the Song of Songs, 107, 111–14,
122; the story of the bitter waters of Mara,
43, 58–70; text, indeterminacy of, 86–87;

Wittig on, 80, 82; Yermia on, 36. *See also*
Torah
Bloom, Harold, 79, 147n
Bruns, Gerald, 15–16, 18, 20, 154n, 155n; on
the Bible, as a self-glossing book, 39; on the
Song of Songs, 106, 107, 112

Cassuto, Umberto, 2, 11, 60, 63, 98, 151n
Cause and effect, 8
Charity, 69
Chernus, Ira, 69–70
Childs, Brevard, 75–76, 77
Christ, 108
Citation, 26–38
Clifford, James, 121
Communion, 16
Cotexts, 23, 26
Countenance, 55–56
Creation, 16, 17–18
Croce, B., 18

Death, 123–24, 125–27
Deconstruction, 19
Diachronic methods, 19, 39–40
Dostoevsky, Fyodor, 14
Double reading, 58–71
Dual signs, 57–79

Ef'eh, 25
Egypt, 43, 45, 48
El'azar, Rabbi, 61, 144n, 146n, 147n, 148n
El'azar Hammonda'i, 72, 73, 74
'El'azar of Modi'in, Rabbi, 65, 67–68, 71–79
Eliezer, Rabbi, 36–37, 42, 43, 45–47, 114, 120,
140n, 143n, 152n
Eliot, T. S., 37
Elisha, waters of, 69, 70
Epistemology, 11, 78
Eros, 123, 125–27
Eternal, the, 10, 17, 123–24
Ethics, 45. *See also* Morality
Evil, 36, 103

Faith, 25–26, 33, 61
Fishbane, Michael, 113

159